THE BLUEGRASS MUSIC COOKBOOK

THE BLUEGRASS MUSIC COOKBOOK

BY PENNY PARSONS,
KEN BECK, AND JIM CLARK

*To Joyce
Finger Pickin Good!
Penny Parsons*

JOHN F. BLAIR, PUBLISHER

WINSTON-SALEM, NORTH CAROLINA

DESIGN BY DEBRA LONG HAMPTON

COVER DESIGN BY LIZA LANGRALL

FRONT COVER PHOTOGRAPHS (CLOCKWISE FROM TOP):

THE ORIGINAL BLUE GRASS BOYS, COURTESY OF DAVE FREEMAN; DOC WATSON, COURTESY OF SUGAR HILL RECORDS;

THE SELDOM SCENE, COURTESY OF SUGAR HILL RECORDS; THE STANLEY BROTHERS, COURTESY OF GARY REID;

AND DEL McCOURY, COURTESY OF KEITH CASE & ASSOCIATES.

BACK COVER PHOTOGRAPHS (CLOCKWISE FROM FAR LEFT): LAURIE LEWIS, COURTESY OF UNDER THE HAT

PRODUCTIONS; RICKY SKAGGS, COURTESY OF R.S. ENTERTAINMENT; SAM BUSH, COURTESY OF SUGAR HILL RECORDS;

NASHVILLE BLUEGRASS BAND, COURTESY OF SUGAR HILL RECORDS; AND JIMMY MARTIN, COURTESY OF JIMMY MARTIN.

PHOTOGRAPHS ON PAGES 5, 6, 10, 18, 26, 34, 52,

60, 67, 74, 81, 85, 102, 106, 107, 108, 112, 113, 114, 119, 123,

125, 136, 143, 155, 166, 174, 175, 187, 196, 201, 203, AND 211

BY PENNY PARSONS

LIBRARY OF CONGRESS CATALOGING-IN-PUBLICATION DATA

PARSONS, PENNY.

THE BLUEGRASS MUSIC COOKBOOK / BY PENNY PARSONS, KEN BECK, AND JIM CLARK.

P.   CM.

INCLUDES INDEX.

ISBN 0-89587-162-9 (ALK. PAPER)

1. COOKERY. 2. COUNTRY MUSICIANS—UNITED STATES—MISCELLANEA.

I. BECK, KEN, 1951– . II. CLARK, JIM, 1960– . III. TITLE.

TX714.P3763 1997

641.5—DC21   97-7346

IN MEMORY OF BILL MONROE,

THE FATHER OF BLUEGRASS

1911–1996

CONTENTS

ACKNOWLEDGMENTS

The Bluegrass Music Cookbook would have been an impossible task to complete without the assistance of many fine folks who enjoy bluegrass music and good cooking.

First, we express our gratitude to all our friends at John F. Blair, Publisher. President Carolyn Sakowski believed in this project from the start. And we appreciate the insightful editing of Andrew Waters and Sue Clark and the design and graphics work of Liza Langrall and Debbie Hampton. Everybody on the Blair team has worked hard to make this project a reality.

We thank all of the folks who shared some of their favorite recipes with us. The degree of helpfulness and participation from bluegrass artists and their families was simply phenomenal. Attributions are given with all of the recipes inside the cookbook.

We're indebted to the following folks who joined our culinary jam session and helped us gather the recipes and photographs: Hazel Smith, Brenda McClain, Les Leverett, Tommy Goldsmith, Robert K. Oermann, Walter Carter, Ronnie Pugh, Lance LeRoy, Keith Case & Associates, Dave Freeman, Gary Reid, Alice Gerrard, Tom Robinson, Sharon Watts, Katrina Hurt, Traci Thomas, Will Gailey, Kerry Hay, Nancy Cardwell, Norm Parenteau, Charlie Rainwater, Barry Poss, Leslie Pardue, Ken Irwin, Doug Dillard, Ginger Boatwright, Jim Photoglo, LeRoy McNees, Roland White, Helen Story, Carol Lee Cooper, Carol Rae, Hairl Hensley, Jack Tottle, Tim White, J.T. Gray, Anita Hogan, Cash Edwards, Traci Todd, Benny Smith, Phil Leadbetter, Stacie Vining, Gladys Flatt, Brenda Green, Randall Franks, Sherae Barham, Mary Macon Doubler, Vicki Langdon, Vernell Hackett, Joy McReynolds, Betty McInturff, Hilda Stuart, Shelby Jean Craig, Millie Clements, Sophie Tipton, Frank Sutherland, Louise Scruggs, Jack White, Clark Gallagher, Steve Jarrell, Linda Stewart, Monty Hitchcock Management, Ardena Moncus, Lee Grant, Kathy Helms, Kathy Puckett, Dixie Hall, Jean McCoury, Allison McCoury, Alfred Akemon, Rex Perry, Jerry Carter, Darlene Hamilton, John Campbell, Albert K. Culbreath, Drew White, Kathy Helms, Bob Tedrow, Maria Camillo, Mike Seeger, Jim Mills, and James Alan Shelton.

Unless otherwise noted, the photographs

throughout the book are courtesy of the artists, record labels, or *The Tennessean*; or they are from the personal collections of the authors.

We're especially grateful to Dan Hays and all of the staff and members of the International Bluegrass Music Association for their encourage-ment and assistance with this project, and for giving their blessings to the cookbook's support of the IBMA's Bluegrass Trust Fund.

We thank all of these people for adding essen-tial ingredients to the recipe for this book. We appreciate it!

Bill Monroe, the "Father of Bluegrass," originally described his music as "the high lonesome sound." He made his first record in 1936 and joined the Grand Ole Opry in 1939.

INTRODUCTION

If ever there was a match made in heaven, it has to be bluegrass music and good cooking. Just like good home cooking, bluegrass music comes from scratch. It's pure, straightforward, and magical.

And so it was over lunch one day about two years ago (we get all of our best inspirations when we're around food) that we found ourselves talking about our favorite music, good foods, *The Andy Griffith Show*, and first one thing and then another. Then, between bites, it occurred to us that putting together a collection of favorite recipes from a few of our bluegrass friends would be a flavorsome little project. After all, many bluegrass musicians are known for being good cooks—or at least for knowing where to find great food.

The more we chewed the idea over, the more we thought this cookbook would be a lot of fun to put together. As we began to look into the idea, we quickly realized that we had the potential for creating a truly special tribute to bluegrass . . . expressed through recipes.

The initial idea grew from a little cookbook into one with more than 375 wonderful recipes

from top bluegrass performers. Along the way, we ended up tracing the history of bluegrass music by following a trail of recipes. To spice things up further, we made a special effort to include lots of photographs (we ended up with more than two hundred—many of them quite rare). Throughout the book, we've stirred in biographies of prominent bluegrass musicians and short articles about various aspects of bluegrass music. And for trivia buffs, there are dozens of trivia tidbits and quizzes to challenge your knowledge of bluegrass. In short, we hope you'll find this cookbook as enjoyable to read as it is to use for cooking.

The thing that has really made this cookbook such a joy for us to compile has been the participation of the musicians and their families and friends in helping us gather recipes, photographs, and information. In all, more than 180 bluegrass performers—a real "Who's Who" from every era of bluegrass music—are represented with recipes in this book. There are photographs of each performer, along with information about their careers.

Beyond the enjoyment that *The Bluegrass*

Music Cookbook brings to cooks (and eaters), we're especially pleased that a portion of the proceeds from the sale of every book is benefitting a worthy cause, the International Bluegrass Music Association's Bluegrass Trust Fund, which works to provide assistance to bluegrass professionals and their families when they're experiencing financial emergencies. Good music, good food, and a good cause—that's the combination we've tried to create.

On that note, we'll simply say that we hope you enjoy these finger-lickin' favorites from bluegrass music's finger-pickin' best!

Penny Parsons, Ken Beck, and Jim Clark
January 1997

A FEAST HERE TONIGHT: TASTE THE FLAVOR OF BLUEGRASS

So you've got a bunch of bluegrassers over for dinner. Wade through the sea of pickers in the kitchen and get going early. "Bile 'Em Cabbage Down" and don't forget to turn the hoecakes 'round neither. Start the "Country Ham and Red Gravy." Turn on the skillet for "Short'nin' Bread." Your flour of choice is "Martha White." Jaw a while with "Angeline the Baker" to make sure your biscuits have that "Southern Flavor." Get someone "Shucking the Corn." "Hot Corn," "Cold Corn"? You decide. Get big ideas when the fiddles play "Chicken Reel" and "Dill Pickle Rag." Remember that it's "Peach Pickin' Time in Georgia." And fix it all with "Sugar Coated Love."

Now go out to the patch and pick you a "Watermelon Hanging on the Vine," while keeping an eye out for "Blackberry Blossom." Then set up the picnic table; you've been "Singing All Day," and it's time for "Dinner on the Ground." Somebody wake up Paw; we can't start without "Father's Table Grace."

Wind up your feast with ice cream, but don't eat too much and get the "Rocky Road Blues." Here's the hard part: keep those musicians away from the "Good Old Mountain Dew." A "Little Glass of Wine" might do the trick instead.

Thomas Goldsmith

APPETIZERS

RECIPE FOR A HAPPY DAY

1 cup friendly words
2 heaping cups understanding
4 heaping teaspoons time and patience
Dash of humor
Pinch of warm personality
Small group of bluegrass pickers, all instruments in tune

Measure words carefully and add heaping cups of understanding. Use generous amounts of time and patience. Cook with gas on front burner. Keep temperature low. Do not boil. Add the dash of humor and pinch of warm personality. Season to taste with the spice of life. Serve in individual molds.

Delbert White
WhiteHouse Harmony

A GARDEN WE MIGHT ALL PLANT

First, plant four rows of peas: presence, promptness, preparation, and perseverance.

Next, plant three rows of squash: squash gossip, squash indifference, and squash criticism.

Then, plant four rows of lettuce: let us obey rules and regulations, let us be faithful to duty, let us be loyal and unselfish, and let us love one another.

No garden is complete without turnips: turn up at meetings, turn up with a smile, turn up with new ideas, and turn up with determination to make everything count for something good.

Jim Parker
WhiteHouse Harmony

HERALD ANGEL WINGS

3 to 5 pounds chicken wings (or any other part of the chicken that you like)

Sauce:
These are very approximate ingredients; you can add or subtract depending on your tastes.

1 cup soy sauce (preferably tamari)
1 cup rice wine, white wine, or sherry
$^1/_3$ cup water
2 tablespoons grated or chopped ginger root
2 to 6 cloves garlic (depending on how much you like garlic), finely chopped
1 tablespoon sugar
1 tablespoon cornstarch
Something hot like sesame oil, chili powder, etc., if you like your wings spicy

The recordings made by Hazel Dickens and Alice Gerrard during the 1970s virtually paved the way for all of the women who are performing bluegrass today. Prior to that time, what few women there were in bluegrass were limited to playing supporting roles; they served as backup singers, occasionally as bass players, or as managers of their husbands' careers, as in the case of Louise Scruggs. Hazel and Alice stepped forward and took the spotlight, and they were a powerful duo. They sang with raw emotion and their songs, many of which were self-penned, presented women as strong role models. Many successful musicians, including Bob Dylan, Naomi Judd, and Tim O'Brien, have acknowledged the tremendous influence of Hazel and Alice on their musical development. Several of Hazel and Alice's groundbreaking recordings have recently been reissued on compact disc, and they still perform together occasionally.

Photograph courtesy of Alice Gerrard

Mix all of the sauce ingredients together and pour over the chicken. Mix well and marinate in a refrigerator for at least 1 hour, or overnight. Broil or grill until done. The wings may get black on the outside, but that's OK.

Makes 8 to 12 servings.

Alice Gerrard

WINDJAMMER BUFFALO WINGS

Served with bleu cheese dressing and celery sticks.

Bleu cheese dressing:

8 ounces sour cream
4 ounces bleu cheese, crumbled
¼ cup parsley, chopped
¼ cup mayonnaise
I tablespoon milk
I tablespoon lemon juice

Mix well, cover, and refrigerate.

I medium bunch celery, cut into strips and set aside

Wings:

6 tablespoons butter or ¾ stick margarine
2 tablespoons hot pepper sauce

3 pounds chicken wings, split with joints discarded (about 27 or 28 wings)

Heat the butter and hot sauce, stirring occasionally. In a broiling pan, arrange the chicken wings and brush with the butter mixture. Broil for 10 minutes. Turn the wings and brush with more sauce. Broil for 10 to 15 minutes longer, or until the wings are golden and done. Serve with the bleu cheese dressing and celery sticks.

Makes 8 servings.

Millie and
Vassar Clements

CITY TIES

¹/₃ cup self-rising cornmeal
²/₃ cup self-rising flour
2 eggs
Milk (to form medium batter)
Salt to taste
4 medium onions
4 cups shortening

Mix the cornmeal and flour together. Add the eggs and milk and mix well. Slice the onions into rings and dip into the batter, coating each ring thoroughly. Melt the shortening (or use vegetable oil) in a medium-sized boiler. When a drop of batter cooks without separating, put the battered rings, one at a time, into the hot oil. When the onion rings are crispy brown on bottom, turn and brown the flip side. Drain on paper towels and place in a 200° oven to keep warm.

Makes about 6 servings.

Ginger Boatwright

STUFFED MUSHROOM DELIGHT

24 large fresh mushrooms
1 pound bulk pork sausage
1/2 cup chopped onion
2 tablespoons minced parsley
1/8 teaspoon salt
1/2 teaspoon pepper
8 ounces cream cheese, softened

Clean the mushrooms with damp paper towels. Remove the mushroom stems and set the caps aside. Chop the stems. Combine the chopped stems and sausage in a large skillet; cook over medium heat until browned, stirring to crumble. Drain the meat mixture into a colander, pat dry with a paper towel, and return the mixture to the skillet. Add the onion, parsley, salt, and pepper. Cook over low heat until the mixture is thoroughly heated. Add the cream cheese, stirring until blended. Remove the mixture from heat. Place the mushroom caps on an ungreased baking sheet. Spoon the sausage mixture into the mushroom caps. Broil the caps 6 inches from heat for 5 minutes, or until browned.

Makes 2 dozen.

Ric-O-Chet

Ms. Tambourine Woman of the '70s: Ginger Boatwright, during her time with Red, White, and Blue(grass).

Western North Carolina band Ric-O-Chet was formed in 1987. The band gained national exposure after signing with Rebel Records in 1994. Since then, they have released two albums on Rebel—*Ric-O-Chet* and *Carolina Memories*. Pictured are (l-r) Steve Lewis, David Pendley, Les Deaton, and Randy Greer.

SAN DIEGO SPICY PRETZELS

¾ cup oil
1 package Hidden Valley Ranch dressing
   (original)
½ teaspoon garlic powder
1 teaspoon cayenne pepper
20 ounces pretzels

Put the ingredients (except pretzels) into a bowl. Cover the bowl tightly and shake well. Put the pretzels into a large zip-top plastic food bag. Pour the dressing over the pretzels, zip the bag, and shake 4 times over the course of 1 hour. Makes about 6 servings.

Wayne Rice
Host of "The Bluegrass
Special"
KSON Radio

TALK OF THE TOWN PECAN CHEESE WAFERS

These invoke a holiday mood to me. My early Christmases in my family's antebellum South Carolina farmhouse were warm and memorable—and of course, very traditional. I remember Christmas Eve with carols around the old piano, fireworks (instead of on July Fourth!), and pecan wafers and Russian tea on Grandma's flowered china. My grandmother's pecan wafers, which included new-season pecans from our trees, were wonderful. And nothing went better with them than Mother's Russian tea. These good things are still a tradition with me.

—Martha Adcock

1 stick butter, softened
2 cups grated sharp or extra-sharp cheddar
   cheese
1 cup plain flour
⅛ teaspoon cayenne pepper
½ teaspoon salt
½ cup chopped pecans

Cream the butter and cheese together. Sift the flour, cayenne pepper, and salt together. Add the dry ingredients and pecans to the butter mixture and mix. Form the mixture into 1½-inch rolls, wrap in waxed paper, and chill. Cut thin slices from the rolls and bake on greased cookie sheets at 375° for about 12 minutes. Cool on brown paper bags.
   Makes 3 to 4 dozen.

Martha and
Eddie Adcock

Eddie Adcock began performing on the banjo when he was fourteen. In his early days, he played in the bands of legends such as Mac Wiseman and Bill Monroe, before becoming a legend himself during a dozen years with the Country Gentlemen. He formed IInd Generation with Jimmy Gaudreau in 1971. Then, after a year of playing in David Allan Coe's band in the mid-1980s, Eddie and his wife, Martha, returned to their bluegrass roots—forming Talk of the Town. That band eventually became the award-winning Eddie Adcock Band.

James Alan Shelton played in various bands in eastern Tennessee and southwestern Virginia before joining Ralph Stanley's Clinch Mountain Boys as lead guitarist in 1994. James is also a talented leathercrafter; many bluegrass pickers sport his handmade instrument straps.

CHURCH HILL FRUIT DIP

Delicious with Granny Smith apples or any type of fruit.

8 ounces cream cheese
7 ounces marshmallow cream

Soften the cream cheese to room temperature. Stir the cream cheese and marshmallow cream together until smooth and creamy. Chill and serve.

Makes about 2 cups.

Greta and James Alan Shelton
Ralph Stanley and the Clinch
Mountain Boys

BUELL'S CHEESE WAFERS

From my grandmother, Mrs. Ralph Buell (Mary Eva Crump). These were a favorite at the Crump home in Memphis around 1840.

1 pound sharp cheddar cheese, grated
¼ pound butter, softened
1 teaspoon salt
3 teaspoons Worcestershire sauce
¹/₃ teaspoon red pepper
1 cup flour

Knead all the ingredients together with fingers until well blended. Form the dough into rolls that are 2 inches in diameter. Wrap in waxed paper and keep in the icebox for 24 hours. Slice the dough very thinly and bake on a cookie sheet at 450° for about 7 minutes.

This dough can be kept in the icebox for up to 3 weeks and used when needed.

Makes about 4 dozen.

Buell Neidlinger
The Grass Is Greener

WILD SIDE SHRIMP DIP

1 10¾-ounce can tomato soup
8 ounces cream cheese
1½ cups or 2 pounds shrimp, chopped
¾ cup celery, chopped
¾ cup green onion, chopped
1 cup mayonnaise

Heat the soup, then add the cream cheese and dissolve. Remove from heat. Add the remaining ingredients and mix well. Serve with vegetables or crackers.

Makes about 6 cups.

Jan Harvey, David Harvey,
and Jill Snider
Wild and Blue

Three-time IBMA Vocal Group of the Year, IIIrd Tyme Out was formed in 1991 by Russell Moore, Ray Deaton, and Mike Hartgrove. Their trademarks are those smooth, soaring, precise trio harmonies and gospel quartets. Today the band includes (l-r) Mike Hartgrove on fiddle, Steve Dilling on banjo, Russell Moore on guitar, Wayne Benson on mandolin, and Ray Deaton on bass.

RUSSELL'S FAMOUS DIP

2 9-ounce cans jalapeno bean dip
3 avocados, mashed
1 cup sour cream
½ cup mayonnaise
1 1¼-ounce package taco seasoning
2 tomatoes, chopped
6 scallions, chopped
1 4-ounce can pitted ripe olives, sliced
¼ pound cheddar cheese, grated

In a 3-inch-deep serving dish, arrange a layer of the jalapeno bean dip, followed by a layer of mashed avocados. Blend together the sour cream, mayonnaise, and taco seasoning. Spread the mixture as the third layer over the avocados. Next, arrange a layer of tomatoes, then a layer of scallions, and then a layer of olives. Sprinkle cheese over all. Chill in the refrigerator until serving time and serve with tortilla chips.
Makes about 8 servings.

Russell Moore
IIIrd Tyme Out

TEXAS CRAPSHOOTER CHILI AND CREAM CHEESE DIP

I got this recipe from a guitar player that I used to work with. It's so simple, but it's so good. This dip is best when served warm. I like it with Fritos.

1 10½-ounce can Hormel chili without beans
8 ounces cream cheese, softened

In a microwavable bowl, mix together both ingredients. Microwave the mixture on HIGH for 30 seconds, then stir well. Repeat until the cream cheese is completely mixed into the chili. Serve while it's still warm.
Makes about 2½ cups.

Bobby Hicks

Over his long career, fiddler Bobby Hicks has played everything from bluegrass to country to swing. He is skilled at both lead and harmony fiddling, and he recorded on some of Bill Monroe's most exciting twin- and triple-fiddle instrumentals from the 1950s— including "Cheyenne," "Scotland," and "Brown County Breakdown." Bobby spent a number of years in Las Vegas, performing with Judy Lynn, before returning to his native North Carolina in the 1970s. When Ricky Skaggs burst upon the country scene in 1980, he asked Bobby to be his fiddle player. Bobby continues to tour with Skaggs today as his only remaining original band member.

KUHN CREEK DIP

1 32-ounce package Velveeta
1 10-ounce can diced Ro-tel tomatoes
½ cup pecans, finely chopped
1 pound ground beef, browned and drained
Chopped Jalapeno peppers (optional)

Melt the Velveeta in a saucepan. Mix in the remaining ingredients and serve with your favorite dipping vegetables or chips.
Makes about 10 cups.

Kathy Kuhn
The New Coon Creek Girls

SALLY MOUNTAIN SPINACH DIP

10 ounces frozen spinach, thawed and
   squeezed dry
1 cup sour cream
1 cup mayonnaise
1 bunch green onions, chopped
¼ teaspoon black pepper

Mix together all the ingredients in a bowl. Serve chilled.
Makes about 4 cups.

Rhonda Vincent

DREAM COME TRUE APPLE DIP

8 ounces cream cheese, softened
1 cup brown sugar
¼ cup white sugar
1 teaspoon vanilla extract
1 cup mixed nuts

Mix well the first 4 ingredients, and then mix in the nuts. Keep refrigerated, but remove from the refrigerator 15 minutes before serving. Serve with apple wedges.
Makes about 2 cups.

Rhonda Vincent

NASH RAMBLER AVOCADO/ BLACK OLIVE DIP

Great on chips or crackers, or as a dip for just about anything.

1 large ripe avocado
1 tablespoon lemon juice
2 tablespoons mayonnaise
1 2¼-ounce can chopped ripe black olives
1 tablespoon minced fresh onion
8 ounces cream cheese, softened
½ teaspoon garlic salt (more to taste)
Pepper to taste
Tabasco sauce to taste

Mash the avocado and add the lemon juice and mayonnaise. Add the ripe olives and onion. Mix with the cream cheese. Add the seasonings. This is better if it sets up for a while.
Makes about 2 cups.

Jon Randall

Former Nash Rambler Jon Randall (Stewart) performs with Emmylou Harris during a segment for a "Pathway to Stardom" special on TNN.
Photograph by Jim Hagans

Members of New Grass Revival of the late '70s and early '80s were (l-r) John Cowan, Sam Bush, Courtney Johnson, and Curtis Burch.

This 1988 shot of New Grass Revival shows members (l-r) John Cowan, Bela Fleck, Pat Flynn, and Sam Bush.

New Grass Revival

Bill Monroe had his Blue Grass Boys, and their sound was so influential that a whole type of music became known as "bluegrass." About thirty years later, another band from Kentucky arrived on the scene, calling themselves New Grass Revival. This group's energetic sound was so persuasive that their brand of bluegrass music earned its own name—"newgrass."

Some music critics have called New Grass Revival, in its various forms, the best acoustic band of its time. The original members of New Grass Revival were Sam Bush on mandolin, Courtney Johnson on banjo, Curtis Burch on guitar and resonator guitar, and Ebo Walker on bass (Ebo Walker's a mighty fine fiddle player, too). In 1974, Ebo Walker left and John Cowan took over on bass and lead and tenor vocals. Curtis and Courtney left in 1981 and were replaced by Pat Flynn on guitar and Bela Fleck on banjo.

The one constant in all of the group's configu-

rations, of course, is Sam Bush. If any one person embodies what is meant by "newgrass," it would have to be Sam. And part of the reason that it may be hard to describe newgrass succinctly is that Sam seems to be always in motion. It is that very motion that perhaps best illustrates what the newgrass branch of bluegrass music is all about—that is, high energy, or "Great Balls of Fire."

New Grass Revival broke up in 1990, and the newgrass movement itself has yielded much of its spotlight to the rising tide of "new traditionalists." But for the better part of two decades, newgrass was the energizing force of bluegrass music, attracting new, enthusiastic listeners to the music.

There's no need to fret over the fate of newgrass. The sound is still alive and well with pickers such as Jerry Douglas, Scott Vestal, Russ Barenberg, and Sam Bush himself. And just as with other innovators before them, such as Earl Scruggs, Clarence White, Bill Keith, and the Dillards, New Grass Revival's influence on the music world will be felt for decades to come.

MAJOR LEAGUE ARTICHOKE SPREAD

2 8-ounce cans artichoke hearts, drained and mashed
1 cup mayonnaise
¾ cup Parmesan cheese, grated

Mix all the ingredients in a small casserole dish. Bake at 400° for 30 minutes, or until bubbly brown. Serve with Triscuit crackers.
Makes about 2½ cups.

Lynn and Sam Bush

HARMONY HUMMUS

H'mm, h'mm good!

1 16-ounce can garbanzo beans, drained
Juice of 1 lemon
1 tablespoon sesame oil
Salt to taste
Pepper to taste
Garlic powder to taste
1 tablespoon sesame seeds (optional)

In a food processor, purée the garbanzo beans until they form a paste. Add the lemon juice and sesame oil. Add the spices. If using sesame seeds, you may toast the seeds at 350° for about 10 minutes before stirring them in last. (Do not put sesame seeds in the food processor, as they too will purée.)
Serve as a dip with vegetables or pita bread. Or try my favorite: Make a hummus-and-sliced-tomato sandwich on whole wheat toast.
Makes about 2 cups.

Andrea Zonn

QUICK(SBURG) HUMMUS DIP

Pita perfect!

2 cups cooked chickpeas (garbanzo beans)
¼ cup tahini
4 cloves garlic, chopped
Juice of 1 lemon
¼ cup vegetable broth (optional)

Combine the chickpeas, tahini, and garlic in a food processor and purée until smooth and thick. Add the juice from the lemon and vegetable broth and process until creamy.
Makes about 2½ cups.

Ronnie McCoury
The Del McCoury Band

DONNA'S CHEESE BALL

Cheese wiz!

8 ounces sharp cheddar cheese, grated
8 ounces medium cheddar cheese, grated
1 small onion, grated
1 tablespoon lemon juice
½ cup mayonnaise
½ teaspoon garlic powder
1 teaspoon prepared horseradish
½ cup pecans, finely chopped

Mix all the ingredients together except the pecans. Form the mixture into 2 balls. Roll the balls in the pecans until thoroughly covered. Wrap in plastic wrap and refrigerate until ½ hour before serving. The flavor is enhanced when prepared 12 to 24 hours in advance and served at room temperature.
Makes about 3 cups.

Glenn Tolbert

Glenn Tolbert is regarded as one of the nation's premiere flat-pick guitarists. He and his band, Glenn Tolbert and Company, have a loyal following, particularly around their home base of Birmingham, Alabama. Glenn teaches banjo, guitar, mandolin, and resonator guitar at home and at the University of Alabama-Birmingham. One of his best pupils is his eleven-year-old son, Allen, who is already proficient on the mandolin. Someone once said, "If you look up 'genuine, nice person' in any good dictionary, Glenn's picture is there."

It's hard to imagine a greater friend of bluegrass music than Peter V. "Pete" Kuykendall. Through the years, he has been a performer, songwriter, record producer, festival promoter, music publisher, historian, and IBMA board member. However, he is best known as the longtime editor and cofounder of *Bluegrass Unlimited* magazine. Started in 1966 as a small newsletter, "BU" has evolved into a major national publication and is considered to be the "bible of bluegrass music." In 1996, Pete was inducted into the IBMA Hall of Honor. Pete's wife, Kitsy, is also an enthusiastic and outspoken fan of bluegrass. She has served for several years as the talent coordinator for the annual IBMA Fan Fest. Pete and Kitsy love their watermelon almost as much as their bluegrass!

KITSY'S FAMOUS IBMA HOSPITALITY SUITE CHEESE SPREAD

8 ounces sharp cheddar cheese
6 sweet gherkin pickles
1 green bell pepper, or ½ green and ½ red bell pepper
1 small hot pepper, or dashes of hot sauce such as Tabasco (as desired, but not too spicy)
Enough pickle juice and mayonnaise to bind the ingredients together

Use the shredder blade of a food processor or a meat grinder (I prefer the food processor) to shred the cheese. Transfer the cheese to a mixing bowl. Then use the food processor's steel chopper blade to chop the pickles. Transfer the pickles to the bowl with the cheese. Remove the

The International Bluegrass Music Association

The International Bluegrass Music Association (IBMA) was formed in 1985 as a trade organization devoted to promoting bluegrass music and providing a forum for its members. In 1986, through the efforts of the Daviess County Tourist Commission, the IBMA established its headquarters in Owensboro, Kentucky, not far from the birthplace of Bill Monroe. In August of that year, the first IBMA trade show was held in conjunction with the "Bluegrass With Class" Festival at English Park on the banks of the Ohio River.

The organization grew rapidly, and in 1990, Dan Hays was hired as executive director. Soon plans were announced for the building of a permanent home for IBMA in the new RiverPark Center in Owensboro. This multipurpose arts center, which was completed in 1992, contains three state-of-the-art performance venues, radio and television production facilities, a cafe, and offices. It also houses the International Bluegrass Music Museum, where visitors may tour the IBMA Hall of Honor along with many educational and historic exhibits.

As IBMA has grown, the annual trade show and festival have snowballed. Now called the "World of Bluegrass," the event is a weeklong celebration that is the focal point of the bluegrass calendar. The five-day trade show is attended by hundreds of bluegrass professionals from around the world and features scores of exhibits, seminars, and artist showcases. It culminates on Thursday evening with the International Bluegrass Music Awards Show, broadcast on radio stations around the world. *Billboard* magazine has called this extravaganza "the best awards show of the year." It includes performances by many of the nominees in addition to the presentation of the annual IBMA awards and the induction of the Hall of Honor recipients. The Bluegrass Fan Fest begins on Friday afternoon and features a lineup of more than thirty of the top names in bluegrass, all donating their time to raise funds for IBMA and the Bluegrass Trust Fund.

The many services IBMA offers to its members include extensive computer databases of information, market research, educational and leadership development programs, event liability insurance plans, a bluegrass news service, a group of regular publications which serve to transmit information for professionals within the industry, and a trust fund established to assist bluegrass professionals in times of emergency need. (A portion of the proceeds from sales of this book will be donated to the IBMA's Bluegrass Trust Fund).

The IBMA has over twenty-five hundred members from forty-nine states and twenty-nine foreign countries. For information or a membership application, contact: IBMA, 207 E. Second Street, Owensboro, Kentucky 42303.

seeds from the peppers. With the same blade used to chop the pickles, mince the peppers. Transfer the peppers to the bowl. Sprinkle 1 to 2 teaspoons of the pickle juice over the mixture and toss, then add enough mayonnaise to bind the mixture together. Do not use too much mayonnaise because it will overwhelm the cheese spread and make it too loose. Refrigerate for at least 2 hours. Serve with slices of small rye bread or crackers. You may also serve cut pieces of ham to go over the cheese and rye bread. This is also good as a sandwich.

Makes about 2 cups.

Kitsy and Pete Kuykendall
Bluegrass Unlimited

CROSS-PICKIN' HOT CHEESE DIP

2 pounds Velveeta
1 cup mayonnaise
1 small onion, finely chopped
6 tablespoons jalapeno peppers, chopped

Melt the Velveeta in a double boiler. Add the mayonnaise, onion, and peppers. Pour quickly into a serving container.

If you want really hot dip, you may add more peppers and pour some of the jalapeno juice into the cheese mixture.

Makes about 5 cups.

Greta and James Alan Shelton
Ralph Stanley and the Clinch
Mountain Boys

SELDOM SCENE SPINACH BALLS

Over the years at the Gettysburg Bluegrass Festival, one of our favorite pastimes has been joining with family and friends for dinner smorgasbords. Many wonderful dishes have been created for these events. Here is one of my favorites.

4 10-ounce packages frozen chopped
    spinach, thawed and drained
2 cups chopped onion
2 cloves garlic, finely chopped
8 eggs

Though Fred Travers works hard to douse flames at his day job as a fireman, you'd never know it when he steps on stage and sets the strings ablazing on his resonator guitar. He has a beautiful singing voice as well, and can sing just about any part that is required. Fred has toured with several bands based in the mid-Atlantic area, including the Gary Ferguson Band and the Seldom Scene. His many recording credits include two solo releases, *RadioTone* and *TimeAfterTime*, on Pinecastle Records. Fred also appears on the last recording made by the Seldom Scene.

1 cup melted butter
8 ounces Parmesan cheese, grated
4 cups herb-seasoned stuffing mix (small pieces)

Mix all the ingredients thoroughly. Form the mixture into 1-inch balls. Bake at 350° for 15 minutes. Serve hot. The spinach balls can be frozen and baked later if you don't need the entire batch at one sitting.
Makes about 6 dozen.

Fred Travers
The Seldom Scene

WABASH SAUSAGE BALLS

3 cups biscuit mix
½ cup American cheese, shredded
½ cup cheddar cheese, shredded
½ cup mozzarella cheese, shredded
1 teaspoon sage
½ teaspoon cayenne pepper

1 pound sausage (room temperature)
½ cup buttermilk

Combine the biscuit mix with the cheeses, sage, and pepper. Mix in the sausage and milk with your hands. Form the mixture into 1½-inch balls. On a cookie sheet that has been sprayed with non-stick coating, bake the balls at 350° for about 10 minutes, or until they begin to brown.
Makes about 3 dozen.

Charlie Collins

WALTER'S PRIZE-WINNING CRAB DIP DIVINE

8 ounces mild cheddar cheese
8 ounces Swiss cheese
8 ounces cream cheese
8 ounces lump or shredded crab meat
1 tablespoon brown mustard
1 tablespoon Worcestershire sauce
1 tablespoon lemon juice

Grate or cut the cheese into small pieces. Combine all the ingredients in a bowl. Heat in a low oven or microwave, removing frequently to stir, until the ingredients are thoroughly mixed and of spreadable consistency. Serve with Stone Wheat Thins.
Makes about 4 cups.

Tips:
Crab lovers should use more crab—up to 12 ounces.
Make a few hours ahead of time so the crab flavor can permeate better.
Refrigerate leftovers and use the next morning in an omelette.

Walter Carter
Nashville Mandolin Ensemble

BEVERAGES

BANJO BANANA PUNCH

3 cups sugar
6 cups water
1 46-ounce can pineapple juice
1 12-ounce can frozen orange juice
   concentrate
3 bananas, peeled
Juice of 2 lemons
½ gallon ginger ale

In a large pot, boil the sugar and water, then allow the mixture to cool. Add the pineapple juice and orange juice. Put the bananas in a blender with the lemon juice and mash. Add the mashed bananas to the mixture. Pour the mixture into a freezable container and freeze. When ready to serve, let the frozen mixture sit out until it is slushy, then pour into a punch bowl and add ginger ale.

Makes about 2 gallons.

Sophie (Mrs. Carl) Tipton
and Louise Tomberlain

BLUE RIDGE BREAKFAST SMOOTHIE

2 oranges, peeled
2 bananas, peeled
2 apples (small), cored and quartered
Fresh or frozen strawberries
Fresh pineapple
Any other fruit
Ice, optional

Blend all the ingredients in a blender. Now that's livin'!

Makes about 3 servings.

Ronnie McCoury
The Del McCoury Band

Carl and Sophie Tipton and family made bluegrass out of Rutherford County, Tennessee, for about forty years. For twenty-five years, they produced *The Carl Tipton Show*, a weekday-morning staple on Nashville television stations. Since Carl's death, Sophie continues to carry on the family tradition with her sister Louise Tomberlain. Pictured are (*l-r, in back*) Earl White, Carl Tipton, Sophie Tipton, Al Holderfield, and Bruce Weathers. Clowning around in the foreground is comic Red Murphy.

Jim Vipperman is as at home playing fiddle on the front porch in his hometown of Mount Airy, North Carolina, as he is sitting in with a classical music ensemble for a performance at the North Carolina School of the Arts. When Jim's not playing to entertain audiences, you can usually find him passing along his knowledge of music to Mount Airy's next generation of young music students.

GRANITE CITY GRAPE JUICE

1 cup firm, ripe grapes
½ cup sugar
Boiling water

Wash the grapes and place them in a hot, sterilized quart jar. Add the sugar and fill the jar with boiling water. Seal the jar with a hot lid and ring. Turn upside down on a towel for just a few minutes, then turn right side up to seal the jar.
Makes 1 quart.

Cindy and Jim Vipperman

OTHER'S ORANGE JUICE REFRESHER

⅓ cup frozen orange juice concentrate
½ cup milk
½ cup water
¼ cup sugar or sweetener equivalent
½ teaspoon vanilla extract
5 ice cubes

In an electric blender, whirl together all the ingredients until smooth. Serve at once.
Makes 2 servings.

Sandy and Dean Webb
The Dillards

SIMPLY HIGHSTRUNG FROSTED ORANGE CREAM

¼ cup orange-flavored Tang
2 tablespoons sugar
1 cup milk
½ cup water
½ teaspoon vanilla extract
2 cups crushed or cracked ice

Combine all the ingredients in a blender. Blend well and serve at once. Garnish with mandarin oranges if desired.
Makes 2 servings.

Steve Pye
Highstrung

Florida-based Highstrung signed with Pinecastle Records after winning the International Pizza Hut Bluegrass Showdown Southeastern Championship in 1993 (that's a mouthful!). Pictured here are (l-r) Terry Campbell (bass), Jerry Nettuno (mandolin and guitar), Keith Tew (guitar and mandolin), and Steve Pye (banjo).

HEAD CLEANER RUSSIAN TEA

3 quarts water
2 sticks cinnamon
2 teaspoons (scant) whole cloves
6 tea bags

1 to 1½ cups sugar, to taste
Juice of 3 oranges
Juice of 2 lemons

Boil the cinnamon and cloves in the water for 5 to 10 minutes, then take the water off the heat. Steep the tea bags for about 10 minutes, then take out the bags. Add the sugar and juice. Serve hot. (It's best after 24 hours.)
Makes about 3 quarts.

Martha and Eddie Adcock

IIND GENERATION INSTANT SPICED TEA

2 cups orange-flavored Tang
1½ cups sugar
½ cup instant tea
1 3-ounce envelope unsweetened
    lemonade mix
1 teaspoon ground cinnamon
1 teaspoon (scant) ground cloves

Combine the ingredients and store in an airtight container. Use 1 to 3 teaspoons per cup of water.
Makes about 30 to 40 servings.

Martha and Eddie Adcock

PERFECT ICED TEA

(That is, if you like it sweeeet!)

5 cups boiling water
2 family-sized tea bags
¾ cup sugar
3 cups water

Pour the boiling water over the tea bags and allow tea to steep for at least 30 minutes, or as long as overnight. Remove the tea bags. Add the sugar, stirring until it dissolves, then add 3 cups fresh water.
Serve over lots of ice with lemon in a tall glass. Refreshing and sweet. Perfect.
Makes about 8 servings.

Jill and Jerry Douglas

DANCIN' WITH THE APPLES

6 cups apple juice or cider
1 46-ounce can unsweetened pineapple juice
¼ teaspoon nutmeg
¼ cup honey
3 tablespoons lemon juice
1 teaspoon ground lemon rind
1½ cinnamon sticks

Combine all the ingredients except cinnamon sticks and heat until almost boiling. Use the cinnamon sticks as stirrers or put them into the combined mixture.
Makes 12 cups.

Curtis Burch

JOHN DUFFEY'S ATTITUDE-ADJUSTING WHISKEY SOUR MIX

¹/₃ cup bartender's sugar (quick-dissolving),
    or to taste
4 ounces Tropicana orange juice
12 ounces freshly squeezed lemon juice
6 ounces good Canadian blended whiskey
    (I use Canadian Club)

Mix the ingredients in the order given. Shake well and pour over ice into tall glasses or cups. "Knock yourself out!"
Makes 4 to 6 servings.

John Duffey
The Seldom Scene

SCENE GOLDEN DREAMS

8 ounces cream
8 ounces orange juice
8 ounces triple sec or Cointreau
8 ounces Galiano

Mix all the ingredients together. Refrigerate for 1 hour. Shake well and serve over one ice cube in a medium glass.
Makes 1 quart (6 to 8 servings).

John Duffey
The Seldom Scene

The Seldom Scene in the early '90s were (l-r) John Duffey, Ben Eldridge, John Starling, T. Michael Coleman, and Mike Auldridge.

The Seldom Scene

The Seldom Scene was formed with the avowed purpose of playing for fun. The original members, John Duffey, John Starling, Mike Auldridge, Ben Eldridge, and Tom Gray, first got together in 1971 at a picking party in Washington, D.C. They liked what they heard and decided to play together regularly, but not to tour full time (hence the group's name). Yet, with this band's tremendous aggregation of talent, it's hardly surprising that what started as their "weekly card game" soon became a sustaining career. Now, over twenty-five years later, the Seldom Scene's founding members are regarded as legends in the acoustic music world.

Though the band weathered several personnel changes over the years, John Duffey and Ben Eldridge continued to lead the "Scene" until John's sudden death in December of 1996. By the time of his death, John Duffey had reached legendary status in the bluegrass world and was often referred to as "the father of modern bluegrass music." He was a member of the groundbreaking Country Gentlemen for nearly a decade before helping to found the Seldom Scene. John's phenomenal voice, irreverent wit, and outrageous mandolin solos kept the Seldom Scene on the cutting edge from the beginning.

Some of the most enjoyable moments in a Seldom Scene concert were likely to occur when banjo player Ben Eldridge got a gleam in his eye and eagerly set forth to see if his brand new idea for the song at hand would actually work. Longtime member Mike Auldridge, who left the band in 1995 to perform with Chesapeake, is considered to be one of the best resonator guitar players in the world. He was also a key ingredient in the Scene's beautiful trio harmonies. John Starling, who left the band in 1977 but returned for two years in the early '90s, was a compelling singer and a master of bringing songs from other genres into the Scene's repertoire. Other band members through the years included lead singers Phil Rosenthal, Lou Reid, and Moondi Klein, and bass player T. Michael Coleman.

In 1996, three new members joined the Seldom Scene. Lead singer/guitarist Dudley Connell was a founding member of the Johnson Mountain Boys, the hottest new traditional band of the 1980s. Dudley's tremendous vocal talents were a perfect complement to John's, and his enthusiasm for the music brought a fresh excitement to shows. Resonator guitar player Fred Travers is an excellent singer as well and brought many new possibilities to the band's vocal arrangements. Bass player Ronnie Simpkins, a veteran of the Tony Rice Unit, anchored the rhythm section. This last group made one recording, *Dream Scene*, released in the fall of 1996 on Sugar Hill Records.

The Seldom Scene received countless awards and performed for several presidents. The band's *15th Anniversary Celebration* recording was a Grammy finalist in 1988. Recorded live at the Kennedy Center, the project included guests Linda Ronstadt, Emmylou Harris, Ricky Skaggs, Sharon White, Jonathan Edwards, Tony Rice, and others. The Seldom Scene's many hit recordings include "Wait a Minute," "Rider," "Old Train," and "Muddy Waters."

SOUPS

READY FOR LOVE SPICY VEGETARIAN CHILI

1 onion, chopped
2 cloves garlic, minced
2 tablespoons olive oil
4 15-ounce cans red beans
8 ounces tomato sauce
1 cup water
1/3 cup chili powder
2 teaspoons paprika powder
2 teaspoons ground cumin
2 teaspoons oregano
Salt to taste
Cayenne pepper to taste

In a large skillet, fry the onion and garlic in olive oil over medium heat until golden brown. Add the remaining ingredients. Bring to a boil, stirring often, and then simmer for 40 minutes on low heat, stirring occasionally. Serve with rice, good crusty bread, and salad.

Makes 6 to 8 servings.

Holly Tashian

SHELBY JEAN'S CHILI

2 pounds hamburger meat
1 green bell pepper, chopped
1 onion, chopped
2 cloves garlic, minced
3 tablespoons chili powder
1 15-ounce can tomatoes, chopped
1 20-ounce can tomato sauce
2 15-ounce cans kidney beans
1/2 package onion soup mix

In a large skillet, brown the meat, onion, and bell pepper, then drain. Mix in the other ingredients and simmer for 1 to 2 hours over low heat.

Makes about 8 servings.

Hubert Davis

ONE ATE HUNDRED "FLAT PIK" BLACK BEAN CHILI

1 package Chili-o mix
1 15-ounce can black beans, rinsed and drained
1 15-ounce can chili beans or red beans, rinsed and drained
1 14½-ounce can stewed tomatoes (2 cups fresh tomatoes may be substituted)
Cumin powder (optional)
Cooked rice
Grated cheddar cheese

Mix the beans and tomatoes with chili mix and heat as directed on the package, adding water as needed. Add the cumin powder, if desired. Serve over rice and garnish with grated cheddar cheese.

Makes 4 servings.

Steve Kaufman

Steve Kaufman, pictured here with his wife Donna, is a three-time winner of the National Flatpick Guitar Championship, which is held annually in Winfield, Kansas. Currently living in Maryville, Tennessee, Steve is a nationally respected guitar instructor; he has created several instructional books and tapes, and he regularly conducts workshops.

NIGHT DRIVER GREEN CHILE STEW

This is my improvised version of a popular New Mexico dish. New Mexico is the state where I started playing bluegrass when I was around fourteen. It is one of my four or five home states.

4 or 5 green chilies, roasted (see below)
2 or 2½ pounds stew beef, cut in bite-sized pieces
Vegetable oil
2 ribs celery, chopped
3 cloves garlic, crushed
2 medium onions, chopped
12 ounces stewed tomatoes
1 teaspoon ground cumin
Salt to taste
3 potatoes, chopped

You can purchase the green chilies in a can, but you'll have a better stew if you roast the fresh chilies in your oven at around 400°. When the skins are starting to brown and look as though they're separating from the pepper (this won't take long), take them out, splash some water on them to get some steam going, and cover with a dish towel for 10 minutes. Then peel the skins off and remove most of the seeds. (You can leave some in to add heat to the stew).

The rest is easy. Just brown the meat in a skillet with a little oil. Place the browned meat in a soup pot. Pour some water into the hot skillet to deglaze it and pour the water over the meat in the pot. Add all the other ingredients, except the potatoes. Then add enough water to cover the ingredients by an inch, cover the soup pot, and simmer for 1 hour. When the hour is up, add salt, if necessary. Then add the potatoes and simmer for 15 more minutes.

Makes enough for a 4- or 5-piece bluegrass band.

Chris Jones

Chris Jones arrived on the bluegrass scene in the 1980s via the Weary Hearts, a hot traditional bluegrass band that included Butch Baldassari, Mike Bub, and Ron Block. He has also played with the Lynn Morris Band and Special Consensus. In 1995, Chris formed Chris Jones and the Night Drivers and released his first album, *Blinded By the Rose*.

Singer/songwriter/storyteller Tom T. Hall began his professional career when he joined the bluegrass band the Kentucky Travelers as a teenager. Tom is seen here in the middle of an attempt to enter the *Guinness Book of World Records* with the "World's Largest Bluegrass Band" during Tom T. Hall Day at South Plains College in Levelland, Texas.

TOM T.'S (I LOVE) SKINNY CHILI

2 pounds ground beef
2 14½-ounce cans tomatoes
1 6-ounce can tomato paste
1 4-ounce jar pimientos
3 15-ounce cans red kidney beans
Chili powder to taste
Salt and pepper to taste
3 medium onions, chopped
3 ribs celery, chopped
3 green bell peppers, chopped

Brown the ground beef in a skillet, stirring until crumbly; drain. Combine the tomatoes, tomato paste, pimientos, beans, and ground beef in a stockpot; mix well. Simmer for 2 to 3 hours. Add the chili powder, salt, and pepper; mix well. Add the onions, celery, and green peppers. Cook for 20 minutes longer, or just until the vegetables are tender-crisp for a crunchy texture. Serve with corn bread or crackers.

Makes 8 servings.

Tom T. Hall

SWEET SUNNY SOUTH CHILI

1 tablespoon oil
½ pound ground beef
1 small onion, chopped
1 15-ounce can chili beans (hot)
¹/₃ cup ketchup
1 cup water
1 teaspoon salt
¹/₄ teaspoon pepper
¹/₄ teaspoon sugar
¹/₂ teaspoon chili powder (or to taste)
¹/₄ teaspoon cayenne pepper

Heat the oil in a frying pan. Cook the beef in the pan until lightly browned, then push to one side. Add the onion to the pan and cook until soft. Drain the excess fat. Add the remaining ingredients and mix well. Simmer 30 to 45 minutes. Eat on hot dogs or in a bowl with low-fat cheese and low-fat sour cream. This is very good reheated.

Makes 2 servings, or enough fixings for 6 hot dogs.

Larry Stephenson

Tenor Larry Stephenson began picking at age five and formed his first band in high school. Before starting the Larry Stephenson Band in 1989, he played mandolin with Bill Harrell and the Virginians, as well as the Bluegrass Cardinals.

HOT DOG CHILI

1 tablespoon cooking oil
1 small onion, chopped
1 pound ground beef
6 ounces tomato paste
6 ounces tomato juice
1 teaspoon vinegar
1 tablespoon chili powder
1 teaspoon sugar
Salt and pepper to taste

In a skillet, sauté the onion in oil until tender. Add the ground beef; brown it and drain. Add the remaining ingredients. Cook over low heat for 30 minutes. Serve on hot dogs or in brown beans, or eat by itself.

Makes 3 to 4 servings, or enough sauce for 8 hot dogs.

Wayne Taylor
Blue Highway

Molly O'Day and husband Lynn Davis married in 1941 while playing with the Forty-Niners. In 1945, they landed on **WNOX** Radio in Knoxville, where O'Day became a huge sensation. They toured the South and Northeast, playing the Grand Ole Opry and the **WLS National Barn Dance.** However, in 1952, they decided to leave country music for evangelistic work in West Virginia.

LOW-DOWN CHILI

¹/₃ cup lard
4 pounds beef chuck, cut into ½-inch cubes
1 large onion, chopped
3 cloves garlic, finely chopped
1 cup drained canned nopalitos (cactus pieces)
12 fresh (or canned) serrano peppers, seeded and chopped
3 cups (about 10) fresh tomatillos (Mexican green tomatoes), chopped
6 ounces tomato paste
3 cups beef stock or canned beef broth
¹/₃ cup chopped fresh coriander (cilantro)
5 teaspoons crushed cumin seeds
1¹/₂ teaspoons salt
¹/₂ teaspoon ground black pepper

Heat the lard in a kettle over medium heat. Add the meat, about 1 pound at a time, and remove each pound as it becomes browned. After all 4 pounds are browned, put the onion and garlic in the kettle and cook over low heat until soft. Return all of the beef to the kettle.

Rinse the cactus pieces in cold water, then drain and add to the beef. Also add the peppers, tomatillos, tomato paste, beef stock, coriander, cumin, salt, and pepper. Cover and simmer over low heat for about 2½ hours.

Makes about 12 servings.

Debbie and Lanny Cram
Born Again Bluegrass Band

LYNN'S FAMOUS HOT DOG SAUCE

3 pounds ground beef
¹/₂ cup water
1 large onion, chopped
1 green bell pepper, chopped
3 tablespoons chili powder
1 tablespoon garlic powder
2 teaspoons cumin powder
¹/₂ teaspoon ground red pepper
Salt to taste

Put the ground beef in a pot with the water. Mash with a potato masher until fine. Add the rest of the ingredients and cook for 1½ to 2 hours.

Makes enough sauce for about 20 hot dogs.

Lynn Davis

Renowned guitar player David Grier grew up around music in Laurel, Maryland, and Nashville, Tennessee, where father Lamar played banjo with Bill Monroe. During the 1980s, David demonstrated his virtuosity on lead guitar with the highly regarded Doug Dillard Band. Since then, he has had stints with the Big Dogs, the Country Gazette, the Grass is Greener, and Psychograss. In high demand as a session player, David also has released acclaimed solo albums, such as 1995's *Lone Soldier.* Along the way, he has won multiple IBMA awards for Guitar Player of the Year.

CLIMBING THE WALLS CHILI

1 pound hot sausage
2 pounds ground beef
1 8-ounce jar whole mushrooms, drained and rinsed
3 15-ounce cans light red kidney beans, drained and rinsed
1 10-ounce can Ro-tel tomatoes
4 cloves garlic, minced
2 large onions, diced
3 15-ounce cans Mexican-style stewed tomatoes
3 bay leaves
2 tablespoons chili powder
1/8 cup sugar
1 tablespoon ground cinnamon
Chopped hot peppers to taste

Brown the ground beef and sausage over medium-high heat in a large skillet. Pour off all the grease. Pour all the ingredients, except the sugar, cinnamon, and hot peppers, into a big chili pot. Cook over medium-low heat for 1 hour, stirring often. Add the sugar and cinnamon, plus all the hot peppers. Continue cooking and stirring for

½ hour. The chili is now ready to eat.

Eat this chili over rice or noodles, with sour cream, grated sharp cheddar cheese, or any way you like it.

Makes about 10 servings.

David Grier

JACK SLADE'S 1862 GREEN RATTLESNAKE CHILI

2 pounds pork, cut into 1-inch cubes
16 ounces tomato sauce
12 ounces water (approximate)
6 ounces diced green chilies
2 cloves garlic, chopped
1 small onion, diced
¼ teaspoon ground cloves
¼ teaspoon ground allspice
¼ teaspoon ground cumin
¼ teaspoon oregano
Pinch salt
Pinch pepper
Rattlesnake buttons

Brown the pork in a skillet and drain. Place the meat in a chili pot and add the other ingredients. Simmer over low heat until the chili reaches a consistency and flavor you like. Garnish with rattlesnake buttons.

Makes 6 servings.

Danny Rogers
The Bluegrass Patriots

Based in Fort Collins, Colorado, the Bluegrass Patriots are led by banjo player Ken Seaman, who formed the group in 1980. The group's original members, who probably hold the longevity record for a bluegrass group with no change in personnel, are (*l-r*) Ken Seaman, Glenn Zankey, Rick Bradstreet, Danny Rogers, and Willie McDonald.

RUSTY'S RED (LOW-FAT VENISON) CHILI

- 2 to 3 tablespoons virgin olive oil
- 3 pounds venison, elk, or moose, cut into thumb-size pieces
- Course black pepper to taste
- 2 cups water
- 6 large dried chile peppers, stemmed and seeded
- 6 medium cloves garlic, minced or finely chopped
- 3 medium onions, chopped extra fine
- ½ cup chili powder
- 3 tablespoons cumin powder
- 1 tablespoon leaf oregano
- 1 can or bottle of good beer (lighter than Heineken, heavier than Bud)
- 1 teaspoon paprika
- 2 tablespoons red wine vinegar
- 1 cup stewed and puréed tomatoes
- 2 16-ounce cans beef broth
- 2 tablespoons masa de harina (coarse cornmeal)

Place the olive oil in a large skillet and brown the meat, adding the black pepper to taste. While the meat is browning, boil the chile peppers in 2 cups water for 30 minutes. Remove the peppers from the water and set them aside (save the water). After the meat is browned, transfer it to a large pot and add the garlic, onion, chili powder, and cumin. Add just enough water from the boiled peppers to cover the meat and cook for 1 hour, stirring often and adding water as needed.

While the mixture is cooking, brew the oregano in the beer (like tea, bring the beer to a boil, stir in the oregano leaves, cover, and remove from heat). Taste a piece of meat. When you can taste the seasoning all the way through the meat, add the boiled peppers, the oregano tea, paprika, red wine vinegar, puréed tomatoes, and 1 can of the beef broth. Simmer for 1 hour. Dissolve the cornmeal in the remaining can of beef broth and add to the mixture. Simmer for 1 hour. Remember: The longer the chili cooks, the better it tastes and the more tender the venison becomes. Serve with tortillas, pinto beans and/or rice, and ice cold beer.

Makes about 10 servings.

Russell Smith
Run C&W

CANYON CHILI

This is one of our favorites here in the Southwest. It's a summertime favorite with barbecue, etc. It's also good in the winter for keeping out the chill.

- 2 tablespoons olive oil
- 2 medium onions, chopped
- 1 red bell pepper, chopped
- 1 pound Italian turkey sausage
- 2 pounds ground turkey
- 10 cloves garlic, minced
- 8 ounces green chilies, diced
- ½ teaspoon pepper
- 1 teaspoon salt
- 5 tablespoons chili powder
- 1 tablespoon ground cumin
- 1 tablespoon dried oregano
- 1 tablespoon dried basil
- 1 12-ounce can tomato paste
- 1 28-ounce can Italian plum tomatoes
- 1 cup beer
- 1 32-ounce can black beans, rinsed and drained
- Sour cream
- Cheddar cheese

In a large skillet or Dutch oven, heat the oil over low heat. Sauté the onions and red pepper for about 10 minutes or until tender, but not browned. Add the sausage and turkey and brown over medium heat. Drain any excess fat from the pan. Add the garlic, chilies, pepper, salt, chili powder, cumin, oregano, basil, and tomato paste. Stir in the tomatoes, beer, and beans. Simmer over low heat for 20 to 30 minutes. Taste to adjust the seasonings. Garnish with sour cream and/or cheese. This may be made in advance and reheated.

Makes 10 servings.

Libby and Herb Pedersen
Laurel Canyon Ramblers

EASY MOONLIGHTER TACO SOUP

This one will warm your "innards." It's so easy to make that you'll be surprised when you taste how good it is.

At one time in the early 1960s, Herb Pedersen filled in for Earl Scruggs with the Foggy Mountain Boys while Earl recovered from hip surgery. In the late 1960s, Herb took over on the banjo when Doug Dillard left the Dillards. Since that time, Herb has been based mostly in Los Angeles, where he has always been in demand as both a session musician and singer. (He also has produced several albums, including the Grammy-winning *Trio* album by Emmylou Harris, Dolly Parton, and Linda Ronstadt.) In the mid–1980s, Herb formed the Desert Rose Band with Chris Hillman. In 1993, he formed the popular Laurel Canyon Ramblers, pictured here (*l-r*) Gabe Witcher, Bruce Johnson, Bill Bryson, Kenny Blackwell, Herb Pedersen, and Roger Reed.

1 15-ounce can pinto beans
1 16-ounce jar salsa
1 15-ounce can Mexicorn
1 15-ounce can Mexican-style tomatoes
1 pound (or less) hamburger meat, browned and drained
1 10¾-ounce can tomato soup
1 soup can water

Mix all the ingredients in a pot. Heat and serve. It's even better the second day.

Makes 6 servings.

Claire Lynch

BUBBY'S CHICKEN SOUP

1 whole chicken, cut up
Salt and pepper to taste
4 cloves garlic, peeled
1 whole onion, peeled, with a knife cut at the top and bottom
Fresh dill, or dill weed in a jar
6 ribs celery
6 carrots, broken in half

Boil a tea kettle full of water. Wash the chicken and then pour boiling water over the pieces. (I'm not sure why this is done—only that my grandmother did this, her mother did, and so on.) Place the chicken in a large soup pot. Fill the pot with water until the water level is about 2 to 3 inches from the top. Add salt, pepper, and 2 cloves of the garlic. Bring to a boil. Skim off the white film and oil (you'll have to skim the soup several times while it cooks). Turn heat to simmer. Add the onion, the remaining garlic, dill, celery, and carrots. Salt and pepper again to taste. Cover and cook slowly for 2 to 3 hours. Serve with rice or tiny, thin noodles. (The smell in the house really has a way of making you feel great.)

Makes about 8 servings.

Robin and T. Michael Coleman
Chesapeake

HILLBILLY VEG-HERB SOUP

½ pound bacon
¼ cup diced carrot

"Doc" Tommy Scott hosts his own old-time touring medicine show. Scott has been making music and comedy for over sixty years. He was one of Charlie Monroe's Original Kentucky Partners with Fiddlin' Dale Cole and Curly Seckler, and once teamed with Dave Akeman as Stringbean and Peanut.

¼ cup diced celery
¼ cup chopped green bell pepper
¼ cup chopped onion (optional)
I cup diced potatoes
2 cups water
¼ cup shredded cabbage
2 sprigs parsley
½ cup peas
¼ pound spinach
I cup chopped tomatoes
I teaspoon fresh lemon balm
½ teaspoon chopped basil
I bay leaf
Salt to taste

In a large skillet, cook the bacon until crisp and drain the excess grease. Chop the bacon into small pieces. Sauté the carrot, celery, pepper, and onion in the remaining bacon drippings. Add the potatoes and the 2 cups of water. Simmer until tender and add the rest of the ingredients. Simmer a few more minutes. Serve with crackers or corn bread.

Makes 4 servings.

"Doc" Ramblin' Tommy Scott

AUTUMN VEGETABLE BEEF SOUP

I to 2 pounds stew meat
Flour
Vegetable oil
I onion, quartered (or smaller, if desired)
2 zucchini, sliced
2 yellow squash, sliced
I stalk broccoli (florets only), chopped
4 carrots, sliced
Water
I 16-ounce can whole tomatoes, cut into chunks (do not drain)
2 beef bouillon cubes
I teaspoon oregano
½ teaspoon garlic powder
Salt and pepper to taste

Cut the stew meat into bite-sized pieces. Dredge in the flour and brown in oil in a 6-quart pot. About 2 tablespoons oil may be needed, depending on how lean the meat is. While the meat is browning, prepare the vegetables. Combine the vegetables with the meat in the pot. Cover generously with water (this will be the soup stock). Add the tomatoes (juice and all), bouillon cubes, and spices. Bring to a boil. Cover the pot, reduce the heat, and simmer until the vegetables are really tender (2 hours or more). Serve with hearty rolls.

Makes about 6 servings.

Pattie and Jerry Kinkade
Born Again Bluegrass Band

BARREN COUNTY BROCCOLI-CHEESE SOUP

I stick butter or margarine
I cup onion, diced
I cup carrots, diced
I cup potatoes, diced

1 cup celery, diced
2 cups fresh broccoli, diced
¼ cup green bell pepper, diced
49 ounces chicken broth
½ cup all-purpose flour
2 cups milk
16 ounces Cheez Whiz
Salt and pepper

Melt the butter in a large pot. Sauté the onion, carrots, potatoes, celery, broccoli, and green pepper until tender. Add the chicken broth. Mix the milk and flour, then add to the soup. Bring to a boil and let thicken for 5 to 10 minutes. Add the Cheez Whiz and the salt and pepper to taste. Reduce heat and simmer for 10 minutes.

Makes about 8 servings.

Curtis Burch

James King is one of the best new traditional bluegrass singers of the 1990s. His singing is heavily influenced by the Stanley Brothers, but he has created a powerful high lonesome sound of his own. On stage or off, James loves to sing the old songs that come from the heart.

LONESOME AND THEN SOME VEGETABLE SOUP

6 medium #1 potatoes, peeled and cut into cubes
2 carrots, chopped
1½ pounds ground beef
28 ounces canned whole tomatoes in juice
3 tablespoons sugar
½ cup ketchup
1 tablespoon onion salt
Dash seasoned salt
1 small onion, chopped
15 ounces canned corn
15 ounces canned green beans
Black pepper to taste

Place the potatoes and carrots in a large pot or soup kettle and add water to cover the vegetables. Bring to a boil and cook until tender (10 to 15 minutes). Drain all but 1 cup of the water and set the vegetables aside. Brown the ground beef in a skillet over medium-high heat, stirring occasionally. Drain the fat and set aside. Remove the cores from the tomatoes, then mash the tomatoes in a large bowl. Add the sugar, ketchup, onion salt, and seasoned salt to the tomatoes, and mix well. Add the beef, onion, corn, green beans, and tomato mixture to the potatoes and carrots in the pot. Bring to a boil, then reduce heat to medium and cook for about 10 minutes. Add black pepper to taste. Serve hot with crackers.

Makes 6 to 8 servings.

James King

BLUE GRASS VEGETABLE SOUP

This is good served with Benny Martin Country Corn Bread and Beans.

8 ounces elbow macaroni, uncooked
1 large potato, diced
1 small onion, diced
Salt pork for seasoning
1 carrot, diced
8 ounces white or yellow hominy
Water
1 14½-ounce can whole tomatoes

Combine all the ingredients except the

For nearly half a century, the Sullivan Family has been making great, authentic bluegrass gospel music. No less an authority than Carl Story once stated that the Sullivans are to bluegrass gospel music what Babe Ruth is to baseball (which, of course, would make Carl Story the Lou Gehrig of bluegrass gospel music). More than 200 performers (including Carl Jackson and Marty Stuart) have been members of the Sullivan Family. The group's current members are (l-r) Enoch Sullivan, Margie Sullivan, Joy DeVille, Steve Carpenter, and Earl Sneed.

tomatoes in a large pan. Add enough water to cover the macaroni and vegetables. Let cook slowly over low heat until the vegetables and macaroni can be cut by a fork. Then add the tomatoes and cook for about 10 more minutes.

Makes 4 servings.

Benny Martin

MARGIE'S CORN CHOWDER

2½ cups diced potatoes
1 medium onion, diced
1 cup water
1 16-ounce can whole kernel corn
1 16-ounce can cream-style corn
1 12-ounce can evaporated milk
Salt and pepper to taste
Ham or crisply cooked bacon

Bring the potatoes, onion, and water to a boil in a large saucepan over medium heat. Reduce heat and cover. Simmer for 8 to 10 minutes, until potatoes are tender. Add the corns, evaporated milk, salt, and pepper. Simmer for 3 to 5 minutes. Crumble or chip the ham or bacon over the chowder for flavor.

Makes 4 to 6 servings.

Margie Sullivan
The Sullivan Family

Rob Ickes was named IBMA Dobro Player of the Year in 1996. He has toured and recorded with many of the top names in bluegrass and is currently a member of Blue Highway. Along with several other bluegrassers, Rob appeared in Steven Seagal's latest movie, *The Fire Down Below*.

FLANNERY'S DREAM POTATO SOUP

6 slices bacon, cut up
1 large onion, chopped
3 medium ribs celery, chopped
4 to 5 medium-sized potatoes, coarsely
    chopped and cooked
1 14½-ounce can condensed chicken broth
½ cup water
½ teaspoon dried thyme leaves
1 teaspoon pepper

½ teaspoon garlic powder
2 tablespoons all-purpose flour
1 cup evaporated milk

Fry the bacon in a 3-quart saucepan until crisp. Remove the bacon with a slotted spoon and drain on paper towels. Drain the fat from the pan, leaving 2 tablespoons in the pan. Cook and stir the onion and celery in the pan until the celery is tender (about 6 minutes). Stir in the potatoes, broth, water, thyme, pepper, and garlic powder. Heat to boiling, then reduce the heat. Cover and simmer for 10 minutes. Remove 1 cup of soup broth. Stir 2 tablespoons of flour into 1 cup broth to thicken. Pour this mixture back into the soup, along with the milk and the bacon. Stir and heat for 10 minutes. Enjoy!

Makes about 4 servings.

Rob Ickes
Blue Highway

WASH MY BLUES AWAY POTATO SOUP

6 large potatoes
1 5-ounce can evaporated milk
1 cup regular milk
½ stick butter or margarine
Salt and pepper

Peel and chop the potatoes and cook them in a pot of salt water. When the potatoes are done, drain off the water and mash potatoes by hand. Add the evaporated milk, regular milk, and butter. Heat over low heat but do not boil. Season to taste. If you want thinner soup, add more milk.

Makes 3 to 4 servings.

Larry Stephenson

MAMA'S HAND POTATO AND LEEK SOUP

6 medium to large potatoes (new potatoes
    are best)
4 leeks
2 celery ribs
1 small clove garlic
5 cups water
2 chicken bouillon cubes
1 tablespoon fresh parsley, chopped (or a

small amount of dried parsley)
Salt and pepper to taste
Cream or half-and-half to taste
Cheddar cheese, shredded

Peel the potatoes and cut into small cubes. Wash and trim the leeks and cut into small pieces. Chop the celery into small pieces. Chop the garlic into thin slices. Bring the water to a boil and add the bouillon cubes. When the bouillon dissolves, add the potatoes and celery, and cook for about 10 minutes. Then add the leeks and cook for another 10 minutes. Add the garlic, parsley, and salt and pepper. Cook until the soup starts to thicken (it shouldn't be watery). Remove the soup from heat and add the cream—as much or as little to suit your own personal taste (I like a lot). Dish into medium-sized bowls. Sprinkle a fair amount of cheddar cheese on top (I like a lot). Serve with crackers or bread and butter.

Makes 6 servings.

Hazel Dickens

Appalachian singer and songwriter Hazel Dickens hails from West Virginia and is renowned for her tunes about blue-collar folks, coal miners, and women's rights. Among her most popular and acclaimed songs are "Mama's Hand," "West Virginia," and "Won't You Come and Sing for Me." In 1976, two of her songs, "Black Lung" and "They'll Never Keep Us Down," were prominently featured in the Oscar-winning documentary *Harlan County U.S.A.* Hazel also appeared as a singing evangelist in *Matewan*, John Sayles's acclaimed 1987 film about striking coal miners in West Virginia.

IMPECCABLY TASTY
FRENCH ONION SOUP

This is cheap and easy and so good—especially on cold winter days. It helped get us through the "Blizzard of '96."

Herb Package:

1 bay leaf
4 large sprigs fresh parsley
1 4-inch-long piece celery rib (with leaves)
3 sprigs fresh thyme
2 garlic cloves
2 4-inch pieces leek greens

Place the herbs and celery between the leek greens and tie together with a white cotton thread. This is your herb package.

3 tablespoons unsalted butter
1¼ pounds onions (I prefer yellow ones), sliced thin
3 tablespoons all-purpose flour
1 cup dry white wine
6 cups water
1 herb package (see above)
Salt and fresh ground pepper
12 slices french baguette
3 ounces or more Gruyère cheese, grated (the more the better)

Heat the butter in a large saucepan over medium heat. Add the onions and cook until golden brown and tender (about 20 to 30 minutes), stirring constantly. Add the flour and cook 2 minutes, stirring frequently. Add the wine. Bring the mixture to a boil, then reduce heat and simmer for 2 minutes. Gradually whisk in the water. Add the herb package and season with salt and pepper. Bring to a boil, stirring constantly. Reduce heat and simmer for 30 minutes.

Preheat oven to 400°. Put the bread slices in a single layer on a baking sheet and toast in the oven until golden brown. Turn oven to broil. To serve, put the soup in ovenproof bowls and float the little pieces of toasted bread on top. Sprinkle with lots of cheese and place bowls under the broiler. Broil until the cheese melts. Serve immediately.

Makes about 6 servings.

Robin and T. Michael Coleman
Chesapeake

CLINCH IN A PINCH
LEEK SOUP

The strategy described here can be used for making creamed soups from any vegetables—singly or in combinations. The object is not to overwhelm the flavor of the vegetables themselves with invasive seasonings. Ralph had a lactose enzyme deficiency, so we used soy milk instead of dairy products. However, you can substitute anything from non-fat milk to half-and-half, depending on the richness desired.

Leeks (about 2 bunches)
Water
Soy milk
Salt to taste
Cheddar cheese (optional)
Parsley for garnish

Remove the roots and slit the leeks lengthwise on the flat side. Open and separate the halved leaves. Wash thoroughly under running water. Investigate for any clinging sand or dirt and wash again. Cut off as little as possible of the dark green outer leaves. Cook the leeks in just enough water to cover them until they are somewhat tender. A pressure cooker is especially effective both for speed and the use of little water. Place the leeks, their water, and a portion of the soy milk or milk in a food blender. Blend thoroughly, adding cheddar cheese (in small chunks) to taste. Return the puréed vegetable/cheese mixture to the pot and stir in the rest of the milk. Heat and salt to taste. Serve with parsley garnish.

As with all of my recipes, I leave it up to the cook to decide the proportions to conform to his or her own taste. Here, you might desire more milk or less water. You might add a hint of cheddar cheese, or make cheddar a predominating flavor. Cauliflower and cheddar also make a nice combination.

Servings depend on your technique.

Kate (Mrs. Ralph) Rinzler

PANAMA RED'S ROASTED
RED PEPPER SOUP

3 tablespoons olive oil
1½ cups onion, chopped to a medium dice
1 cup chicken stock

2 cups water
1 teaspoon salt
6 to 7 red bell peppers, roasted, seeded,
    peeled, and chopped
¼ teaspoon cayenne pepper
1 tablespoon lemon juice
Salt and pepper to taste
½ cup heavy cream

Heat the olive oil in a sauté pan. Add the chopped onion to the pan and cook over medium-low heat until onion is translucent. Next, add in the chicken stock, water, and salt. Cook for 15 minutes, then add the roasted red peppers and cayenne pepper. Cook for 3 to 4 minutes, then adjust the seasonings and add the lemon juice. Slowly add in the ½ cup heavy cream. This soup is best served piping hot. Garnish the soup with chopped roasted red peppers, shredded basil, or a dollop of sour cream.

Makes 4 to 6 servings.

Candace and Peter Rowan

Tom Adams, a two-time IBMA Banjo Player of the Year, is really cooking. Before joining the Lynn Morris Band, Tom was a member of the Johnson Mountain Boys. Once you see this picture, you can see why Tom is such a red-hot picker!

TOM'S TOMATO SOUP

A favorite since childhood, this quick and easy recipe provides 121 percent of the U.S. Recommended Daily Allowance of sodium.

1 10¾-ounce can Campbell's condensed
    tomato soup
1 sleeve (¼ pound) original Premium
    Saltines, finely hand-crushed

Empty the soup can into a microwavable bowl. Do not dilute. Microwave on HIGH for 3 minutes and 20 seconds. Stir in 40 crushed crackers (the entire sleeve). Serve immediately and eat quickly. Do not sit down.

Makes 1 serving.

Tom Adams
The Lynn Morris Band

Laurie Lewis loves to fiddle around in the kitchen, but hearing her perform on stage or in recordings will really satisfy your appetite for great bluegrass music. Growing up in California, where she won state fiddling championships, she fell in love with the sounds of Doc Watson, Bill Monroe, and the Stanley Brothers. Since that time, Laurie and her band, Grant Street, have been nominated for numerous Grammy Awards and have developed an enthusiastic national following of their own.

GRANT STREET CURRIED SQUASH SOUP

This is a simple and salubrious soup that I learned from my brother, Jeremy Renton.

2 butternut squash
Garlic (I use 2 or 3 cloves), chopped
1 onion, chopped
4 or 5 celery ribs, chopped
3 to 5 carrots, chopped

Olive oil
3 to 4 tablespoons curry powder
Soup stock

Slice the squash lengthwise, clean out the seeds, and place face down on a greased cookie sheet. Bake in a 350° oven until tender (the skin is usually browned and a fork pierces it easily). Baking time depends on the size of the squash, but it usually takes about 45 minutes.

In a soup pan, sauté the garlic, onion, celery, and carrot in the olive oil. When these ingredients are soft, add the curry powder and continue to cook until brown and reduced. Scoop the squash out of the skin and add to the vegetables. Add the stock of your choice. (I use water and vegetable bouillon with no salt added—preferably Morga or Hugli brands, both of which are very good. They're Swiss companies, but are available in many health food stores or your better markets.) Use enough stock to obtain the desired thickness.

Blend the soup, or use a potato masher to thoroughly mix everything. Heat soup and season to taste. Depending on the condition of the squash skins after your baking and scooping, you can use them as all-natural serving bowls. *Buon appetito!*

Makes about 6 servings.

Laurie Lewis

PEA-CES OF MY HEART SOUP

This can be stored in the freezer in containers and is a great winter soup.

1 hambone (optional)
2 bay leaves
1 or 2 quarts water
1 or 2 16-ounce bags dried split peas

If you eat meat, boil up the hambone with the 2 bay leaves in 1 or 2 quarts water (depending on how much soup you want to make) for a couple of hours. Add the bags of dried split peas. Boil until the peas are fairly soft (45 minutes to 1 hour). Remove the bone and leave the meat. If you don't eat meat, just boil up the peas. If you find that the peas are using up all of the water as they cook, just add more water.

Alice Gerrard has been performing traditional music since her college days. She released her first solo recording, *Pieces of My Heart*, in 1994. She is a fine songwriter and instrumentalist, and frequently teaches in various workshop programs around the country. Today, Alice's primary focus is on publishing *The Old-Time Herald* magazine, a quarterly publication dedicated to old-time and traditional music.

While all of the above is happening, quickly sauté the following ingredients very lightly in olive oil and then set aside:

1 or 2 medium onions, chopped
5 to 10 cloves garlic, chopped or minced
5 to 10 carrots, chopped
4 to 6 ribs celery, chopped

When the hambone and peas are done, add the above vegetable mixture along with:

1 tablespoon dry mustard
1 tablespoon mashed thyme leaves (or dried thyme)
1 teaspoon sesame oil
Something hot, if you like hot
A little marjoram
1 to 2 tablespoons soy sauce
Pepper to taste

This is a very flexible soup. You can add or subtract spices and herbs and amounts of dried split peas and vegetables according to your tastes. If you use salt, take it easy on the soy sauce, or vice versa. Taste before adding in too much of either.

Makes about 6 to 10 servings.

Alice Gerrard

The Nashville Jug Band has been a fixture of the Nashville club scene since the early 1980s. Bluegrassers, blues musicians, jazz singers, songwriters, and rockers mix in the freewheeling act, which has a Rounder LP and an independent cassette to its credit. Pictured in a nightclub performance are (l-r) Steve Runkle, Sam Bush, Ronnie McCoury, John Hedgecoth, Tommy Goldsmith, Roy Huskey, Jr., Jill Klein, David Olney, Dean Crum, Pat McLaughlin, Ed Dye, and Mike Henderson.

JUG BAND SEAFOOD GUMBO

1/4 cup vegetable oil
1/2 cup all-purpose flour
1 tablespoon vegetable oil
2 cups onion, diced
1/2 cup fresh parsley, minced
1 1/2 cups green bell pepper, diced
1/2 cup celery, sliced
3 cups okra, sliced
6 cups canned whole tomatoes, chopped; or
    peeled and chopped fresh tomatoes
5 cups water
1/4 teaspoon dried summer savory
1/8 teaspoon ground rosemary
3 tablespoons lemon juice
2 to 2 1/2 pounds seafood of your choice
Salt and pepper to taste
Hot sauce to taste
Cooked rice

In a saucepan, heat the 1/4 cup of vegetable oil and stir in the flour to make a roux. Cook over medium heat and stir continuously for 20 minutes or until the roux turns dark brown.

Place 1 tablespoon vegetable oil in a large pot. Add the onion, parsley, green pepper, celery, and okra and cook for 10 minutes over medium heat. Add the tomatoes, water, summer savory, rosemary, and lemon juice. Mix in the roux. Simmer 30 minutes.

Add any combination of 2 to 2 1/2 pounds of seafood (peeled and deveined shrimp; raw fresh crab meat; firm cubed white fish, etc.). Cook an additional 5 minutes. Add salt, pepper, and hot sauce. Serve over hot rice.

Makes 10 servings.

Jill Klein
The Nashville Jug Band

The Sidemen are among the regulars at the Station Inn. Pictured here in 1994 are (l-r) Jimmy Campbell on fiddle, Larry Perkins on banjo, Mike Bub on bass, Ronnie McCoury on mandolin, Terry Eldredge on guitar, and Gene Wooten on resonator guitar. Photograph by Peyton Hoge.

The Center of the Bluegrass Universe
By Thomas Goldsmith

It really is "World Famous."

Just as the swinging sign out front tells it, Nashville's Station Inn club draws folks from all over the earth with its nourishing diet of bluegrass and acoustic music. Since 1974, at two different locations, and through a succession of owners, the Station has endured as a musical and spiritual home for pickers great and small. Inside the modest cinder-block building, there's a down-home atmosphere, complete with red-and-white-checked tablecloths, historic posters from dozens of bluegrass happenings, and lots of high lonesome music. The crowds in the often packed club include Vanderbilt University students, professional people, tourists, and other fans of all ages. In a town where country music can get too slick for its own good, the Station often draws Music Row folks in search of a transfusion of hillbilly integrity.

"I can remember seeing Ralph Stanley there and people would come like (producer) Emory Gordy or (songwriter) Guy Clark," journalist-songwriter Hazel Smith says of the Station. "And it'd be dark. And you'd see the tears glisten on their faces when Ralph'd sing songs like 'White Dove,' the mournful sounds right out of the heart of the Primitive Baptist church."

The Station thrives on big turnouts of fans for the likes of the Nashville Bluegrass Band, John Hartford, and the trio of Jerry Douglas, Edgar Meyer, and Russ Barenberg. Other longtime favorites include Ralph Stanley, Claire Lynch, Continental Divide, Del McCoury, and hometown heroes the Sidemen. Sometimes the people-watching is as interesting as the music on stage: you might run into producer-picker-author Jim Rooney, or hit songwriter Pat Alger, or the great Roland White, or British rocker Mark Knopfler, or Vince Gill. For years, Bill Monroe was a regular drop-in guest who would delight crowds by getting up on stage for spur-of-the-moment guest appearances.

On a given night, you're likely to run into people

who do not speak at all Southern, and some who don't even speak English. "They've been here from South America, Australia, New Zealand, Czechoslovakia . . . and a lot from Japan," says J.T Gray, owner of the club since 1978.

From its earliest days and its first location near Nashville's Centennial Park, the Station Inn has served as a place for pickers to meet. In many cases, informal picking led to more permanent bands.

"It used to be there never was a band, as such, at the Station—it was just whoever showed up to play," recalled Nashville Bluegrass Band guitarist Pat Enright. "That's where I met Alan (O'Bryant) and that's where I first played with Roland (White)."

The Station was started, on an initial investment totaling hundreds of dollars, by four couples: Red and Birdie Smith, Marty and Charmaine Lanham, Bob and Ingrid Fowler, and Jim and Wilma Bornstein. Enright recalls regular drop-ins by West End bikers and Metro patrolmen, as well as the long parade of musicians working for peanuts.

After more ownership changes and the move to Twelfth Avenue South, Gray bought the club in 1978 and embarked on a series of renovations and a new strategy of booking "name" acts. As country music and bluegrass gained fans during the '80s, the club became a Music Row favorite for gold record celebrations, parties, and showcase performances. Rising acts like Alison Krauss and the Nashville Bluegrass Band had the help of steady, pre-stardom bookings at the Station. Also, so-called "new acoustic" stars like Jerry Douglas and Mark O'Connor became part of the music mix along with hard-core bluegrass favorites.

Throughout, Gray has retained the freewheeling practice of Sunday night jam sessions, where pickers light on wooden chairs near the club's stage for impromptu music making. "We usually wind up with a big circle up here in the front," Gray said. "Sometimes there's a group in the back, too."

On a recent Sunday, a coterie of pickers held forth in the Station's back room, playing swing, jazz, and bluegrass with considerable expertise. Meanwhile, near the Station's capacious stage, Gray himself joined in as four guitarists, a banjo player, two fiddlers, and an upright bassist played hard-core bluegrass. The music of Monroe, the club's patron saint, was much in evidence—vocal tunes like "Traveling Down This Lonesome Road" and instrumental showcases like "Jerusalem Ridge" and "The Gold Rush." The impromptu sessions unite Station regulars with Music City newcomers. "It seems like there's new people coming in every week," Gray said.

In addition to hosting the top acts in the field, the Station also serves as a sort of one-stop source for bluegrass players and fans. Near the bar where Gray might personally pull you a cold one, a table offers a welter of bluegrass stuff. Not only can you buy the expected bluegrass CDs and periodicals, but you can also choose from bluegrass caps, bumper stickers, cup holders, "Bluegrass Police" T-shirts, Station Inn T-shirts, a flag that reads "Goin' Pickin'" and a print that shows Bill Monroe taking his rightful place among the other immortals on Mount Rushmore.

Near the front door of the club, a cluttered bulletin board offers notices of vintage instruments, opportunities for pro and amateur pickers, and cards from business people who just happen to like the club. "You'd be real surprised—there's doctors, there's lawyers, there's bankers—the people that go there love the music," Smith said. Station regulars so love the music, that on a dark day in bluegrass history, they came to the club for comfort and consolation: when Bill Monroe died, people just naturally showed up at the Station Inn. Doc Watson dropped by. Roland White came and picked and sang for hours. Jim Rooney offered the "True Life Blues" that every bluegrass fan felt that night.

"It went on until about one o'clock," recalls Gray, who was also on stage picking and singing Monroe tunes that night. "It was just a spur-of-the-minute thing. How could we pay tribute to him any better?"

Station Basics

The Station Inn is located at 401 Twelfth Avenue South in Nashville, four blocks off Broadway. Doors open at 7 P.M. and music starts at about 9 P.M., Monday through Sunday. There's no admission charge for the Sunday night jam session; call (615) 255-3307 for information on cover charges and schedules. Food includes pizza, hot dogs, and nacho chips with cheese dip.

CRAZY IN THE NIGHT CATFISH STEW

2 to 4 catfish, dressed
3 cups water
1 slice bacon, chopped
1 6-ounce can tomato sauce
2 medium potatoes, chopped
1 medium onion, chopped
Salt and pepper to taste
1 tablespoon Worcestershire sauce
1 tablespoon light brown sugar
Dash hot pepper sauce
¼ teaspoon thyme

Cook the fish in the water until tender. Remove the fish from the water to cool and retain the water. Fry the bacon. Add the bacon and 1 tablespoon of bacon fat to the water. Add the other ingredients to the water and cook until tender. Remove the bones from the fish and add the fish meat to the stew. Simmer for 30 minutes. Add seasoning to taste.

Makes 4 servings.

Curtis Burch

UNCLE JOSH'S BLUEGRASS STEW

4 or 5 medium potatoes, cubed
4 carrots, sliced
2 green bell peppers, chopped
8 to 10 small green onions, chopped
2 ribs celery, chopped
1 cup plain chicken broth
2 cups cooked, boned, and shredded chicken breasts
1 pound link smoked sausage
2 cups Mexicorn
1 10-ounce can Ro-tel tomatoes
1 or 2 jalapeno peppers, chopped
4 cups water
Salt and pepper to taste

Mix all the ingredients together in a large stew pot. Cook on medium heat for approximately 20 minutes. Then cover, reduce to low heat, and simmer for 1 hour. Add more water if necessary. You may add a little rice to it if you like. This will feed more people than you expect.

Makes 10 to 12 servings.

Josh Graves

Buck "Uncle Josh" Graves (*right*) is known as the "King of the Dobro" and is the man most responsible for bringing the resonator guitar into acceptance as a bluegrass instrument. His credentials are impeccable: He played with Flatt and Scruggs from the mid–1950s until their breakup in 1969. After that, he played with Lester Flatt and the Nashville Grass for a couple of years, and then with the Earl Scruggs Revue for a dozen more years. Today, Josh often performs with master fiddler Kenny Baker (*left*). One constant has been his Dobro named Julie, which he has played for more than fifty years.

Since their early days back home in West Virginia, brother-and-sister duo Tim and Mollie O'Brien have been singing together. They eventually moved to Colorado, where Tim became lead singer/mandolinist/fiddler for Hot Rize, while Mollie took to singing jazz with her husband, Rich Moore. Tim and Mollie teamed up again in the 1980s and began recording a series of albums for Sugar Hill, starting with the classic *Take Me Back*. Tim now lives in Nashville and tours with his group the O'Boys (Scott Nygaard and Mark Schatz). Mollie often joins the group for appearances. Once you've heard this duo, you'll be wanting seconds of those sweet sibling harmonies!

TELL IT TRUE BEEF STEW

2 to 3 tablespoons bacon grease
1 clove garlic
1½ pounds beef round steak, cubed
Seasoned flour
Thyme
Salt and pepper
2 cups beef stock
2 onions, quartered
6 potatoes, quartered
6 carrots, scraped and halved
4 ribs celery, halved
1 bay leaf

Melt the bacon grease in a large pot. Add the whole garlic clove and let sizzle for 1 to 2 minutes. Meanwhile, coat the beef in the seasoned flour and add to the pot. Sprinkle the beef with thyme, salt, and pepper as it is browning. After all the meat is browned, add enough beef stock to cover. Add the onions, potatoes, carrots, celery, and bay leaf. Add more stock if needed. Cook for 1 hour or until the potatoes are done. Adjust the seasoning.

Note: The bacon grease is what makes this delicious. Also, it's better to make this one day ahead in order to let the flavors really sink in. Singing along to any kind of music while cooking helps, too.

Makes about 6 servings.

Mollie O'Brien

When a bluegrass band travels with a six-foot-tall mascot named Seemore Possum, you can be pretty sure they're fun. And when you find out that among the songs the group has recorded are such choice cuts as "5 lbs. of Possum," "Boil Them Possums," and "Possum Party," you can be certain of it. But what you also discover with the band Troublesome Hollow is some of the finest bluegrass music to come out of the hills of east Tennessee. Guitar player Don Ollis and brother Gary Ollis on bass provide the tight harmonies, and Tim White gets in his licks on banjo and vocals. When you see the group coming down the road at night in their Possum Van, you can be sure they've got good music and good fun lined up in their headlights.

5 LBS. OF POSSUM STEW

½ pound thickly sliced warthog meat
    (bacon) (mainly for flavor)
A big bag of pasta noodles (any ol' kind)
2 cans tomato sauce
3 cans cooked tomatoes
Salt and pepper
½ possum (the other half can be used for
    breakfast possum omelettes), dressed

Fry the bacon in a big gramma kettle over a mid-sized fire. Next, fry the possum in the grease till it's golden brown. Take the meat out, add enough water to the kettle to fill it ⅔ of the way, and then boil the noodles. Once the noodles are cooked, add the tomatoes and the possum to the kettle, plus add enough salt and pepper to old granny's taste. Dig in.

Makes 6 to 8 servings.

Possum Nutrition Facts

Serving size: Depends on the possum
Servings per container: Depends on the possum
Amounts per serving: Depends on the possum
Calories: Depends on the possum
Total fat: Depends on the possum
Sodium: Depends on the possum
Total Carbohydrates: Depends on the possum
Protein: Depends on the possum

Tim White
Troublesome Hollow

HUNGRY PICKERS BEEF STEW

2 pounds lean beef, cubed
2 tablespoons shortening
I large white onion, sliced
I clove garlic
I quart hot water
I tablespoon salt
I tablespoon lemon juice
I teaspoon sugar
I teaspoon Worcestershire sauce
½ teaspoon pepper
½ teaspoon paprika
2 bay leaves, whole
Dash of ground allspice
6 small potatoes, peeled
9 small onions, peeled
4 carrots, cut into I-inch pieces
¼ cup all-purpose flour
½ cup cold water

In a large Dutch oven or cast-iron stew pot, brown the cubed beef in the shortening. Add the next 11 ingredients and bring to a boil. Re-duce heat, cover, and let simmer 2 hours. Add the potatoes, onions, and carrots. Cover and simmer for an hour or so until the vegetables are just tender. Remove and discard the bay leaves. Combine the flour and water, stirring until mixture forms a smooth paste. Gradually stir the flour mixture into the stew to form a rich gravy, then heat on medium until gravy is hot and bubbly. Serve with black-iron-skillet corn bread.

Makes 6 servings.

Gary Francis
Flat Creek Skillet Lickers

RICKY'S CHICKEN PICKIN' CORN SOUP

3 or 4 boneless, skinless chicken breast halves
Salt
Pepper
McCormick chicken seasoning
5 tablespoons Wesson oil
I 10¾-ounce can cream of chicken soup
I 10¾-ounce can cream of mushroom soup
I soup can water
4 medium potatoes, cubed
2 medium onions, chopped
I 8-ounce can whole kernel corn
I 15-ounce can cream-style corn
I½ tablespoons cornstarch
I cup water

Cut the chicken into bite-sized pieces. Season with salt, pepper, and chicken seasoning. In a large pot, brown the chicken in oil over medium heat. Remove the chicken from the pot and set aside. In the pot, mix together the cream of chicken soup, cream of mushroom soup, and 1 soup can water. Bring to a boil. Add potatoes and onions, then add whole kernel and cream-style corns. Bring back to a boil and add chicken. Mix the cornstarch with 1 cup water and stir into soup, mixing well. Cover and simmer on medium-low heat for 45 minutes to 1 hour. Stir occasionally to prevent sticking.

Makes about 6 to 8 servings.

Ricky Skaggs

Ricky Skaggs made his television debut at age seven, playing mandolin as a guest on the *Flatt and Scruggs* television show in Nashville. As a teenager, he and his close buddy Keith Whitley were discovered picking in a small Kentucky club by Ralph Stanley. Ralph was so impressed by the similarity of their sound to the Stanley Brothers that he asked them to join his band and tour with him during their school vacations in the early '70s. Ricky later became an integral part of many groundbreaking '70s bluegrass bands, including J.D. Crowe and the New South, the Country Gentlemen, and Boone Creek. He joined Emmylou Harris's Hot Band in the late '70s, released his highly acclaimed *Sweet Temptation* album on Sugar Hill in 1979, and was soon signed by CBS/Epic Records as a rising star. With the debut of his uptown version of Flatt and Scruggs's "Don't Get Above Your Raisin'," he took the country music world by storm and began the "New Traditionalist" movement. But Ricky has never forgotten his bluegrass roots, and today, he often plays at bluegrass festivals with his all-acoustic Kentucky Thunder band.

Important Dates To Remember Matching Quiz

Match the bluegrass artist to his/her birthday.

1. Alison Krauss	A.	September 25, 1947
2. Del McCoury	B.	March 16, 1954
3. Ricky Skaggs	C.	December 30, 1938
4. J.D. Crowe	D.	March 23, 1945
5. Peter Rowan	E.	July 10, 1958
6. Laurie Lewis	F.	April 13, 1952
7. Tim O'Brien	G.	August 27, 1937
8. Tony Rice	H.	July 23, 1971
9. David Grisman	I.	September 28, 1950
10. Doyle Lawson	J.	June 8, 1951
11. Jerry Douglas	K.	February 1, 1939
12. Larry Sparks	L.	April 20, 1944
13. Bela Fleck	M.	July 4, 1942
14. Mike Auldridge	N.	May 28, 1956
15. Sam Bush	O.	July 18, 1954

Answers: 1. H; 2. K; 3. O; 4. G; 5. M; 6. I; 7. B; 8. J; 9. D; 10. L; 11. N; 12. A; 13. E; 14. C; 15. F

Name That Tunesmith Quiz

Match the song titles with their songwriters.

1. "My Little Georgia Rose"
2. "Lonesome Fiddle Blues"
3. "The Old Home Place"
4. "Hard Hearted"
5. "You Are My Flower"
6. "Close the Door Lightly When You Go"
7. "If I Could Only Have Your Love"
8. "Flint Hill Special"
9. "There Is a Time"
10. "Log Cabin in the Lane"
11. "Pickaway"
12. "Is the Blue Moon Still Shining"

A. Dean Webb and Mitch Jayne
B. Millie Clements
C. Melissa Monroe
D. Rodney Dillard and Mitch Jayne
E. Jim Eanes
F. Lester Flatt and Vic Jordan
G. Ginger Hammond Boatwright
H. Jim and Jesse McReynolds
I. A.P. Carter
J. Earl Scruggs
K. Eric Anderson
L. Bill Monroe

ANSWERS: 1. L; 2. B; 3. A; 4. H; 5. I; 6. K; 7. G; 8. J; 9. D; 10. E; 11. F; 12. C

SALADS

BLEU HEARTACHE SALAD

Fresh spinach leaves
Toasted pecans
Raw mushrooms, sliced
Calamata olives, sliced
Citrus fruit, sliced
Bleu cheese, crumbled

For the dressing, mix the following:

1 cup olive oil
$^2/_3$ cup balsamic vinegar
$^1/_3$ cup orange and lemon juice (equal parts)
Basil, parsley, and dill
Salt and pepper to taste

Wash the spinach leaves and break them up into the size you prefer. Toasting the pecans makes the salad a lot better. Any olives would work, but calamata olives seem to taste the best. Orange and grapefruit slices work well depending on what you want—sometimes both. You can make the dressing more or less oily by simply adjusting the amount of oil. I've never seen anybody leave any of this salad on his or her plate.

Makes 8 servings.

Paul Craft

Tennessee native Paul Craft spent much of his childhood in Arkansas and fell in love with bluegrass music while in college at the University of Virginia. During the late '50s, he played banjo with Jimmy Martin and the Sunny Mountain Boys. However, Paul is perhaps best known for his enormous catalog of hit songs, including such memorable tunes as "Drop-kick Me Jesus Through the Goalposts of Life," "Brother Jukebox," "Keep Me From Blowing Away," and "Midnight Flyer." His songs have been recorded by everyone from the Eagles and the Lewis Family to Linda Ronstadt and The Seldom Scene. Paul says, "The first good song I remember writing was 'Raised by Railroad Line,' later recorded by The Seldom Scene." He's been writing hits right on down the line ever since.

Paul Craft is pictured above (*far left with the banjo*) in a 1961 photo of the Bent Mountain Boys, with Mel Hughes on guitar (*middle of the back row*) and Craig Wingfield on resonator guitar (*far right on the back row*). The boys backed up the Brennan Twins on the Old Dominion Barn Dance. The twins are Joan (*seated*) and Judy Blatt (*standing behind Joan*). Their sister, Joyce, is standing next to Judy.

Photographs courtesy of Paul Craft

THROWIN' GOOD TABOULI

1 cup dry bulgur wheat
1½ cups boiling water
1½ teaspoons salt
¼ cup lime (or lemon) juice (fresh is best)
1 heaping teaspoon fresh garlic, crushed
¼ cup olive oil
½ teaspoon mint (dried)
1 packed cup freshly chopped parsley
1 cucumber, chopped
2 or 3 tomatoes, diced
¼ cup red onion, finely chopped
Salt and black pepper to taste

Combine the bulgur, boiling water, and salt. Cover and let stand for 15 to 20 minutes, until the bulgur is chewable. Add the lime juice, garlic, olive oil, and mint. Mix thoroughly and refrigerate for 2 to 3 hours. Add the parsley, cucumber, tomatoes, and onion, and mix gently. Add the pepper and adjust seasoning to taste.
Makes about 4 servings.

Kris Ballinger
The Cluster Pluckers

WIND IN THE WILLOWS WILTED LETTUCE

Salt pork, sliced and fried until crisp,
  then set aside
Garden leaf lettuce
½ cup vinegar
½ cup water

In a skillet, heat the grease from the salt pork. Being careful not to get burned (use a lid for the skillet as a shield), pour the vinegar and water in one side of the skillet. When the liquid is hot, pour it over the lettuce. Carl liked this with the salt pork, corn bread, and new potatoes boiled whole and then browned.
Makes 2 to 4 servings.

Sophie (Mrs. Carl) Tipton

FOLK SINGER'S PEA SALAD

This is a wonderful, cool, and fairly low-cal taste of summer that you can have all year long. I learned this recipe from a great friend of mine,

The Cluster Pluckers of middle Tennessee were featured on Ken Burns's *Songs of the Civil War.* They are composed of (*clockwise from lower left*) **Kris Ballinger, Dale Ballinger, Mark Howard, and Margaret Bailey.** Other Pluckers not pictured include **Blaine Sprouse, Brent Truitt, and Richard Bailey.**

Tammy Farley, from Lexington, Kentucky. She's a big music fan, a great cook, and a CPA by trade (I think she actually counts all the peas first).
Just layer the following in a big salad bowl (keep the stuff in order!):

½ head lettuce, torn into bite-sized pieces
¼ cup onion, chopped
¼ cup celery, chopped
¼ cup green bell pepper, chopped
5 ounces sweet peas (boil these suckers
  about 5 minutes first)
¼ cup cheddar cheese, shredded
¼ cup bacon bits or soy bits, crumbled

Use the following as the topping:

½ pint Miracle Whip
½ tablespoon brown or white sugar

Spread the Miracle Whip over the top of the salad—"sealing" the edges against the bowl.

Sprinkle brown or white sugar over the top, then put the salad in the fridge for about 6 hours. When you're ready to serve this addictive mass to your guests, get a big wooden spoon and mix it all up first. The first time I experienced my "peas salad high," I was hooked for life. If I could stuff it into an IV tube and mainline a serving, I would. Like most tongue teasers, this one will still be great the next day.

Serves 6 normal people, or one pea-lovin' singer like me!

Michael Johnathon

CELLAR DOOR LAYERED CAULIFLOWER SALAD

In a large bowl, layer a head of lettuce (torn into manageable pieces), sliced red onions, and small cauliflower pieces.

Top with the following dressing:

1 cup mayonnaise
½ cup sour cream
A little milk
1 tablespoon sugar
1 teaspoon thyme

Top all with freshly grated Parmesan cheese and ½ pound of cooked, crumbled, crisp bacon.
Makes 6 to 8 servings.

Ben Eldridge
The Seldom Scene

CALIFORNIA BROCCOLI-CAULIFLOWER SALAD

Broccoli florets
Cauliflower pieces
½ cup oily, salted sunflower seeds
½ cup raisins
½ pound bacon, cooked and broken into bits
½ or less red onion, chopped

Mix the salad ingredients together by tossing.

Dressing:

1 cup mayonnaise

2 tablespoons red wine vinegar
½ cup sugar

Mix the dressing ingredients together and pour over the salad, then toss some more.
Makes 6 to 8 servings.

Janice and LeRoy Mack McNees
Born Again Bluegrass Band

CUMBERLAND GAP BROCCOLI SALAD

1 pound broccoli florets
1 medium onion, diced
¼ cup bacon bits

Dressing:

¼ cup sugar
3 tablespoons balsamic vinegar
⅓ cup mayonnaise

Mix the dressing until creamy smooth. Then combine all the ingredients and mix thoroughly. For the best results, allow the salad to refrigerate for 1 to 2 hours before serving.
Makes 4 servings.

Glenn Laney
Knoxville Grass

QUEEN ANNE'S LACE CHEESY BROCCOLI SALAD

1 small onion, chopped
½ cup mayonnaise
¼ to ⅓ cup sugar
2 tablespoons vinegar
Salt to taste
1 large bowl of broccoli, chopped
1 cup mozzarella cheese, grated

Mix the first 5 ingredients and pour over the broccoli. Let stand overnight in the refrigerator. Top with the mozzarella and serve chilled.
Makes 6 servings.

Jean and Del McCoury

High energy bluegrass gospel group 5 For The Gospel was formed in 1989. The Kentucky-based quintet, which writes much of its own material, records for Hay Holler Records and released its first video, *Live in Concert*, in 1996. Pictured here in the front row are: Bill Hamm (*mandolin*) and Rick May (*guitar/mandolin*). In the rear are: Johnny Branham (*banjo*), Pat Holbrook (*bass*), and Gary Waugh (*guitar/harmonica*).

FAVORITE CHICKEN AND BROCCOLI SALAD

1 pound boneless chicken breasts
1 bunch broccoli, chopped
8 ounces fresh mushrooms, sliced
1 6-ounce can black olives, pitted
½ bottle Italian dressing

Roast the chicken breasts in a 350° oven until cooked. Dice the chicken into bite-sized pieces. Add the chopped broccoli, sliced mushrooms, olives, and salad dressing. Mix. Chill for 1 hour.

Makes 4 to 6 servings.

Karen and Gary Waugh
5 for the Gospel

COLONEL'S COLD ARTICHOKE SALAD

1 package MJB chicken-flavored rice
2 green onions, chopped

½ green bell pepper, chopped
¼ teaspoon curry powder
½ cup mayonnaise
2 6-ounce jars marinated artichoke hearts

Cook the rice as directed on the package, but omitting the butter. Allow to cool. Place in a large bowl and add all the other ingredients except the artichokes. Drain the liquid from the artichokes into the salad and stir well. Add the artichokes last to keep them from breaking apart. Chill overnight.

Makes 4 to 6 servings.

Janice and LeRoy Mack McNees
Born Again Bluegrass Band

NELLIE SIMPKINS' POTATO SALAD

3 eggs, hard-boiled
8 potatoes, cooked in salt water then diced
2 medium onions, diced

Brothers Ronnie Simpkins (*with the bowl of potato salad*) and Rickie Simpkins are two of the finest bluegrass musicians produced by the state of Virginia. During the 1980s, they were members of the Virginia Squires—with Rickie on fiddle and mandolin, Ronnie on bass, Sammy Shelor on banjo, and Mark Newton on guitar and lead vocals. The twins went on to be members of the Tony Rice Unit. Rickie is now a sought-after session player in Nashville, while Ronnie most recently played with The Seldom Scene.

In a medium bowl, make layers of potatoes and onions, starting with potatoes. Set aside the hard-boiled eggs.

Dressing:

Pinch of salt
3 eggs (beaten)
¾ cup sugar
1 tablespoon prepared mustard
¼ cup vinegar
¾ stick butter

Beat together all the dressing ingredients except the butter. Melt the butter in a pan, then pour the other dressing ingredients into the pan. Bring the mixture to a boil while stirring constantly. Continue to boil and stir the mixture for a few minutes until the dressing thickens a bit. Pour the dressing over the potatoes and onions, then mix. Slice the hard-boiled eggs and spread over the top of the salad. Keep covered and refrigerated until ready to serve.

Makes 6 to 8 servings.

Rickie and
Ronnie Simpkins

FRET 'N' FIDDLE POTATO AND CARROT SALAD

5 large carrots, cut in chunks
5 medium boiling potatoes
6 tablespoons olive oil
1 clove garlic, pressed
¾ teaspoon salt
1 tablespoon wine vinegar
3 or 4 tablespoons fresh dill, chopped

Boil or pressure-cook the potatoes in their skins and cut into bite-sized chunks while still warm. Steam the carrots. Mix the carrots and potatoes with the olive oil. In a small bowl, mash together the garlic and salt, then add the vinegar and stir until the salt is dissolved. Strain the mix into the vegetables (still warm), allowing the salt to carry the garlic flavor with it but leaving the garlic in the strainer. When the salad is cool, add the dill. This salad's best if it can sit around a while to allow the flavors to mix. It's good served chilled or at room temperature.

Makes 6 servings.

Mike Seeger and
Alexia Smith

Bostonian Bill Keith, who grew up during the folk revival in the Northeast, developed a unique banjo style he based on learning to play fiddle tunes note-for-note. Bill's approach, which became known as "chromatic style," incorporated more scales and was more syncopated than the style created by Earl Scruggs, which until then was the standard for bluegrass banjo players. Bill's distinctive playing caught the attention of Bill Monroe, and in 1963 he became a Blue Grass Boy. Soon after that, Monroe hired singer Peter Rowan and fiddler Richard Greene, forming one of his most exciting bands of that decade. Bill Keith went on to perform and record with a number of other groups over the years. Though he no longer tours regularly, he frequently conducts workshops and makes occasional festival appearances, when he's not busy working with Beacon Banjo Company, makers of the famous Keith Banjo Tuners.

BEACON BANJO POTATO AND GREEN BEAN SALAD

1 pound potatoes
2 pounds green beans
Salt and pepper to taste
3 strips thick bacon
2 shallots, finely chopped
3 tablespoons vinegar
Sour cream
Herbs

Cut the potatoes into bite-sized chunks and boil them in salted water for about 30 minutes, or until they're done but not falling apart. Drain the potatoes and put them into a salad bowl. Cut the ends off the green beans and then cut the beans in half. Cook beans covered in salted water until they're tender. Drain the beans, mix them with the potatoes, and add a little salt and pepper.

Cut the bacon slices into 1-inch-long pieces. Fry the bacon pieces in a pan until they just begin to brown. Remove ½ the bacon fat, leaving the bacon pieces in the pan. Brown the shallots in the remaining bacon fat. Mix in the vinegar, then pour the mixture onto the potatoes and beans. Mix well. Try adding sour cream, chives, marjoram, or tarragon (or your favorite herb) to taste. Serve warm. Goes well with cutlets or sausages. Enjoy!

Makes 8 servings.

Bill Keith

SUNNY ON THE MOUNTAINTOP SAUERKRAUT SALAD

1 15-ounce can sauerkraut, drained
1 large onion, thinly sliced
1 large green bell pepper, thinly sliced
1½ cups celery, thinly sliced
½ cup vegetable oil
½ cup cider vinegar
1¼ cups sugar
½ teaspoon salt
1 2-ounce jar chopped pimientos

Mix all the ingredients well. Refrigerate and serve chilled. It keeps extremely well in the refrigerator.

Makes 6 servings.

*Emma and
Jody Rainwater*

SMOKY MOUNTAIN SAUERKRAUT SALAD

30 ounces sauerkraut
1 cup celery, diced
1 cup green bell pepper, diced
½ cup onion, chopped
1 2-ounce jar pimientos, drained and diced
1½ cups granulated sugar

Jody Rainwater (a.k.a. Charles Johnson) was a member of Flatt and Scruggs's Foggy Mountain Boys from 1949 through 1952. He auditioned for the band as a tenor-singing mandolinist but was hired as a bass-singing bass player! After leaving Flatt and Scruggs, Jody went to work in radio, spending twenty years on the air at WSVS in Crewe, Virginia. He still lives in Crewe, and though semiretired, he works in sales at the local Nissan dealership. His daughter, Charlie, reports that he still plays guitar and mandolin at church and family get-togethers, and that he and his wife, Emma, can often be seen in the audience at area bluegrass festivals.

Fluff the first 5 ingredients in a bowl. Put the granulated sugar on top. Let sit overnight in the refrigerator and do not stir until the next day.

Makes about 8 to 10 servings.

Molly O'Day

KENTUCKY CORN BREAD SALAD

This is really country, and for a quasi-semi-nearly vegetarian like me, this makes my meal-times religious experiences. This mountain dish came from a very good friend of mine by the name of Jeanne Stewart. She, her daughter Jennifer, and another delightful lady, Eileen Hassler, help put together the Troubadour Concert Series, held at the Paramount Arts Center in Ashland, Kentucky. They've booked, hosted . . .

and fed everyone from Bill Monroe and Alison Krauss to Nanci Griffith and Waylon Jennings. And me. They stuffed this dish down my hungry throat one winter afternoon, and I've threatened my wife with drastic artist mood swings if she didn't make this for me. Now, I have yet another reason to look forward to coming home.

With a spoon, mix one package of Hidden Valley Ranch dressing in a bowl with:

1 cup milk
1 cup sour cream
1 cup mayonnaise

Sit this mixture in the fridge for about 30 minutes. Meanwhile, bake yourself a normal pan of the best corn bread you can muster. Any type will do just fine. Then, gather these ingredients:

1 15-ounce can corn (or 1 10-ounce package of frozen corn, boiled), drained
2 16-ounce cans pinto beans, drained
½ cup fresh green bell peppers, chopped
3 fresh tomatoes, diced
½ cup green onions or scallions, chopped
2 cups cheddar cheese, shredded
1 pound crisply cooked bacon, crumbled (optional)

Now, grab your corn bread and crumble it up in your fingers as you layer the bottom of a 9- by 13-inch pan. Layer the corn, beans, and peppers on top of the corn bread. Pour the dressing over the top. Add the tomatoes, onions, cheese, and bacon. Stick the pan in the fridge for about an hour. Give me this and my sweet baby, and there's absolutely no reason ever to leave home again!

Makes 10 servings.

Michael Johnathon

UNION GROVE CORN SALAD

2 cups corn
¾ cup water
1 14½-ounce can black beans, drained
½ cup green onion, chopped
¼ cup green bell pepper, chopped
½ cup red bell pepper, chopped

1 small cucumber, peeled and chopped
2 cloves garlic, chopped
¼ cup cilantro, chopped
1 teaspoon sweet red pepper or chile
    pepper flakes
¼ teaspoon ground ginger
¼ teaspoon salt
2 tablespoons rice vinegar
1 tablespoon sesame oil
1 tablespoon lime juice

In a small saucepan, place the corn in the water and bring to a boil. Take the corn off the burner and let sit for 7 to 8 minutes, then drain. Combine the corn with the next 7 ingredients until all are well blended. In a separate bowl, whisk together the pepper flakes and the rest of the ingredients until blended. Pour the pepper mixture over the corn and mix together. Cover and chill for at least 2 hours.

Makes 6 servings.

Taffy and Gary Ferguson

RIO BOYS
CREAMY ITALIAN TOSS

A nice change of pace for chilled salad lovers.

7 ounces spaghetti noodles
1¼ cups mayonnaise
3 tablespoons vinegar
1 tablespoon prepared mustard
1 tablespoon parsley flakes
1 tablespoon garlic, minced
1 cup tomatoes, chopped
1 cup mushrooms, sliced
1 cup zucchini, sliced thin
1 cup pepperoni, sliced thin
½ cup green bell pepper, chopped
¼ cup onion, chopped

Break the spaghetti into thirds and then cook according to the package directions. Drain the spaghetti. Mix the next 5 ingredients together and toss into the pasta. In a large bowl, combine the chopped items and thoroughly toss with the pasta mixture. Chill for several hours. Enjoy.

Makes 6 servings.

*Jimmy Olander
Diamond Rio*

RED, WHITE, AND BLUE
FRUIT SOUP

(But it's really a salad.)

2 16-ounce cans pineapple chunks, with
    juice
½ honeydew melon, cubed
3 to 4 fresh peaches, peeled and sliced
½ ripe cantaloupe, cubed
½ pint strawberries, halved
Sweet watermelon, cubed

Place all the ingredients in a large, clear salad bowl. Toss very gently and allow to stand long enough for all the flavors to mingle with the pineapple juice. This is a very refreshing dish. Other fruits may be added for more color, such as red seedless grapes (peeled is nice), but blueberries will make it an unpleasant color. Serve blueberries on the side and sprinkle on top of individual bowls.

Makes about 8 servings.

Ginger Boatwright

When you talk about putting your heart into music, nobody does it better than Ginger Hammond Boatwright. Ginger has been around bluegrass since growing up in Pickens County, Alabama, and first rose to national prominence with the innovative Red, White, and Blue(grass) band of the late '60s. Pictured with Ginger are (l-r) bass player Dave Sebolt; guitar player Grant Boatwright, her husband at the time; and fiddle and banjo player Dale Whitcomb.
Photograph courtesy of Ginger Boatwright

ORANGE BLOSSOM CONGEALED SALAD

2 3-ounce packages orange gelatin
3 cups hot water
2 tablespoons sugar
3 tablespoons white vinegar
4 grated carrots
1 20-ounce can crushed pineapple, undrained

Stir and dissolve the first 4 ingredients. Add the carrots and pineapple, then pour the mixture into a 2-quart mold. Refrigerate until set.
Makes 6 to 8 servings.

Hilda Stuart, mom of Marty Stuart

SATURDAY NIGHT STRAWBERRY SALAD

1 3-ounce package strawberry gelatin
1 cup hot water
1 8-ounce can crushed pineapple
8 ounces cottage cheese
8 ounces non-dairy whipped topping

Dissolve the gelatin in hot water, then let cool for 10 minutes. Stir in the other ingredients, pour into a 2-quart mold, and chill until firm.
Makes 4 to 6 servings.

Hubert Davis

TWISTER SALAD

2 cups pretzels, crushed but not fine
3 tablespoons sugar
¾ cup melted butter
8 ounces cream cheese
1 cup sugar
9 ounces non-dairy whipped topping
1 6-ounce package strawberry gelatin
2 cups boiling water
2 10-ounce packages frozen strawberries

Mix the crushed pretzels, 3 tablespoons sugar, and melted butter. Press into a 9- by 13-inch baking dish and bake at 400° for 8 minutes (no longer). Let cool. In a separate bowl, blend together the cream cheese, 1 cup sugar, and

whipped topping. Pour the cream cheese mixture over the pretzel layer. Mix the gelatin with the boiling water and stir until dissolved. Add the frozen strawberries. Let stand for 10 minutes. Pour over the whipped topping layer and then refrigerate. This salad may be made ahead and put into the freezer.
Makes 10 to 12 servings.

*Bobbie Ison for
5 for the Gospel*

RAVISHING LOW-FAT FRUIT SALAD

1 cup cantaloupe, cubed
1 cup pineapple, cubed
2 bananas, sliced
1 11-ounce can mandarin oranges, drained

Combine with a dressing of:
2 tablespoons low-fat mayonnaise
½ cup plain yogurt
2 tablespoons lemon juice
1 tablespoon vanilla flavoring
½ teaspoon (1 packet) Equal artificial sweetener

Makes 4 servings.

Ric-O-Chet

JIFFY APPLESAUCE SALAD

2 cups applesauce
1 6-ounce package orange gelatin
1 15-ounce can crushed pineapple, drained
2 cups ginger ale

Bring the applesauce to a boil. Remove from heat and stir in the gelatin. Stir in the pineapple and ginger ale. Pour into a mold and refrigerate for at least 2 hours before serving. Very refreshing.
Makes 6 servings

Willia and Melvin Goins

GREEN STUFF

This is a refreshing, easy-to-make little diddy. Orange gelatin can be used also—in which case you'd have Orange Stuff. Take your pick.

The Reno Brothers, (l-r) Ronnie, Dale, and Don Wayne, are musical offspring of the late, great banjo player Don Reno. In 1993, they became the hosts of *Reno's Old Time Music Festival* on television.

1 pint large curd cottage cheese
12 ounces non-dairy whipped topping
1 6-ounce package lime gelatin
1 2- to 3-ounce bag crushed walnuts
1 20-ounce can crushed pineapple

In a large bowl, dump the cottage cheese, whipped topping, gelatin, and nuts. Drain the juice from the pineapple and add the pineapple to the other ingredients. Mix by hand with a large spoon until all ingredients are completely green. Chill and serve.

Makes 8 servings.

Dale Reno
The Reno Brothers

NEVER WALK AWAY SALAD

Doyle likes this for an accompaniment with turkey, or any other time, and he wishes no one else in our family liked it.

1 8-ounce can crushed pineapple
Water
1 3-ounce package lime gelatin
½ cup nuts, chopped
½ cup celery, chopped

6 ounces cream cheese, cut into small
   pieces
1 cup heavy cream
Sugar to taste

Drain the juice from the pineapple into a measuring cup and add enough water to make 1 cup. Boil the juice/water and dissolve the gelatin according to the package instructions. Let cool. Add the crushed pineapple, nuts, celery, and cream cheese. Whip the cream and sweeten it to taste with sugar. Fold the whipped cream into the mixture and pour into an 8-inch square pan or a pretty mold. Chill for several hours. Remove the salad from the mold to serve.

Makes 4 servings.

Suzanne and Doyle Lawson

STRAW INTO GOLD SALAD

¾ cup boiling water
½ envelope plain gelatin
1 3-ounce package lime gelatin
1 cup cottage cheese (low-fat is **OK**)
1 cup milk
½ cup celery, chopped

The popular husband-and-wife musical team of Barry and Holly Tashian have done everything from touring with the Beatles to performing on the Grand Ole Opry. Throughout the 1980s, they were members of Emmylou Harris's multi-award-winning Hot Band. The duo is in constant demand for session work on bluegrass, country, and other albums, and in 1995, they formed the nucleus of Emmylou's band that toured in support of her Grammy-winning *Wrecking Ball* album.

Photograph by Florenzo Maffi

½ cup walnuts, chopped
8 tablespoons mayonnaise (low-fat is OK)
1 15-ounce can crushed pineapple, drained

Dissolve the plain gelatin and the lime gelatin in the boiling water. Set aside in the refrigerator to slightly thicken while you mix the remaining ingredients together. Combine the gelatin with the pineapple mixture in a large bowl or mold and refrigerate until set. Serve on lettuce as a side dish.

Makes 6 to 8 servings.

Holly Tashian

THEY'LL BE RUSSIAN FOR THIS SALAD

1 3-ounce package lime gelatin
1½ cups miniature marshmallows
1 cup hot water
1 8-ounce can crushed pineapple, drained
½ pint whipping cream
3 teaspoons sugar
4 ounces cream cheese, softened
1 cup nuts (our choice is pecans), chopped

Dissolve the gelatin and marshmallows in the hot water. Add the pineapple and let cool. Whip the cream until half whipped. Add the sugar and cream cheese to the whipped cream and fold together. Fold in the pineapple/gelatin mixture. Add the nuts and pour into a rectangular Pyrex dish. Chill for 2 to 3 hours before serving.

Makes 4 to 6 servings.

Helen (Mrs. Carl) Story

ALOHA SALAD

1 15-ounce can fruit cocktail, well drained
1 11-ounce can mandarin oranges, well drained
1 3½-ounce can coconut
2 cups miniature marshmallows
1 cup sour cream

Simply mix all the ingredients together after the fruit has drained. Serve.

Makes about 6 to 8 servings.

Molly O'Day

A true guiding force in establishing bluegrass gospel music, Carl Story was one of bluegrass music's important pioneers. He also worked for years as a bluegrass disc jockey in Greer, South Carolina. He is seen here (*on guitar*) with his final band, Danny Arms on mandolin, Brett Dalton on banjo, and Jim Clark on bass.

LOVE OF THE MOUNTAINS CRANBERRY SALAD

A great dish for Thanksgiving and Christmas!

1 cup boiling water
1 3-ounce box cherry gelatin
1 3-ounce box strawberry gelatin
1 cup cold water
1 15¼-ounce can crushed pineapple
1 16-ounce can whole cranberry sauce
½ cup chopped pecans
½ cup shredded coconut (optional)

Mix the cup of boiling water with the cherry and strawberry gelatins. Stir until dissolved. Add the cold water and let cool. Pour the gelatin mixture into a large baking dish and place in the refrigerator until slightly congealed. Next, add the pineapple with juice, cranberry sauce, nuts, and coconut to the gelatin mixture. Mix well with a fork and chill until firm.
Makes 8 to 10 servings.

Deb and Allen Mills
The Lost and Found

MOM'S CRANBERRY SALAD

Mom has a salad for every occasion. This one's a great substitute for the old canned cranberry sauce, and it adds a lot of "zing" and "crunchability" to holiday meals.

1 3-ounce package red gelatin
  (raspberry preferred)
1 cup boiling water
1 16-ounce can whole cranberry sauce
1 8-ounce can crushed pineapple,
  juice and all
½ cup celery, chopped (optional)
½ cup nuts, chopped (optional)
½ cup apple, chopped (optional)
½ cup orange sections (optional)
½ cup miniature marshmallows (optional)

Dissolve the gelatin in the boiling water and allow to cool. Stir in the cranberry sauce and pineapple. Allow the mixture to cool in the re-

frigerator. Before the gelatin is completely firm, gently stir in any of the optional ingredients you like. Place the salad back in the refrigerator to finish solidifying. Serve chilled.
Makes 6 servings.

Claire Lynch

DO RIGHT CHICKEN SALAD

4 chicken breast halves, cooked, boned,
  and chopped
½ cup celery, chopped
½ cup onion, chopped
½ cup green bell pepper, chopped
½ cup pineapple chunks
½ cup raisins (optional)
½ cup grapes (optional)
1 teaspoon curry powder
¾ to 1 cup mayonnaise
Salt and pepper to taste

Combine all the ingredients and chill.
Makes 6 servings.

Lisa Simon
WhiteHouse Harmony

HOT LICKS CHICKEN SALAD

1 whole fryer, cooked, boned, and cut
  into bite-sized pieces
2 cups celery, diced
3 hard-boiled eggs, chopped
½ cup mayonnaise
1 tablespoon lemon juice
2 tablespoons minced onion flakes
1 8-ounce can sliced water chestnuts
1 10¾-ounce can cream of chicken soup
Potato chips

Mix all the ingredients except the potato chips. Put the mixture in a greased 2-quart casserole dish. Crush the potato chips over the top of the casserole. Bake at 350° for 20 to 30 minutes, or until bubbly hot.
Makes 8 to 10 servings.

Glenn Tolbert

They're not in Mayberry anymore. Though the sign on the set says New Mexico, members of the Kentucky Colonels (a.k.a. the Country Boys) are actually posing with Frances "Aunt Bee" Bavier during a break in filming an episode of *The Andy Griffith Show* in 1961. Pictured are (l-r) LeRoy McNees, Billy Ray Lathum, Eric White, Aunt Bee, and Clarence White. (Gone fishing during this photo: Roland White.)

Photograph courtesy of LeRoy McNees

CABO SAN LUCAS CHICKEN SALAD

2-3 medium tomatoes
1 bunch cilantro, chopped
1 avocado
1 large or 2 small red onions
1 bunch romaine lettuce
7-8 ounces jack hot pepper cheese
4 cups grilled chicken
Hidden Valley Taco Ranch dressing, to taste
Crushed tortilla chips for croutons, to taste

Cut the first 7 ingredients into small pieces and mix well with the dressing and chips.

Makes as much as you want.

Janice and LeRoy Mack McNees
Born Again Bluegrass Band

CRAB BOATWRIGHT

1 pound crabmeat or imitation crab, shredded
1 green onion, finely chopped
Garlic powder for light seasoning
Red and green bell peppers to taste, chopped fine
Just enough mayonnaise to make a consistency for serving
Salt and pepper to taste

Mix all the ingredients together. Serve cold. May be served on a mixed lettuce base with Crab Louis dressing. To change the taste, add 4 drops Worcestershire sauce, 1 tablespoon ketchup, and 2 dashes Tabasco.

Makes 4 servings.

Ginger Boatwright

BARRY'S VINAIGRETTE SALAD DRESSING

^{1}/3 cup vinegar (part cider vinegar and part wine vinegar)
^{2}/3 cup olive oil
^{1}/2 teaspoon salt
^{1}/2 teaspoon dry mustard
^{1}/4 teaspoon ground black pepper
2 cloves crushed garlic
1 splash balsamic vinegar (optional)

Combine all the ingredients in a jar and shake well. Let the dressing sit out overnight for extra flavor. Serve on fresh salad greens or as a marinade for potato salad, shish kebab, etc.

Makes about 1 cup.

Barry Tashian

ANDREA'S BALSAMIC VINAIGRETTE

1 6-ounce jar marinated artichoke hearts, finely chopped
1 6-ounce jar marinated mushrooms, finely chopped
½ cup balsamic vinegar
2 tablespoons dill
1 teaspoon oregano

Andrea Zonn started fiddling around at age two and worked at Opryland USA as a teen. She has played in bands with Vince Gill, Pam Tillis, and Lyle Lovett. Her own group is called Twilight Zonn. She's pictured here with Cox Family pals Suzanne Cox (*left*) and Evelyn Cox (*right*).

1 teaspoon basil
1 teaspoon marjoram
½ teaspoon thyme
½ teaspoon rosemary

Combine all the ingredients in a small bowl. Let sit for 15 to 30 minutes to allow flavors to meld. The ideal salad to top with this dressing is one of romaine or another leafy lettuce (not iceberg), sliced red onions, tomatoes, and red bell peppers.

Makes about 1½ cups.

Andrea Zonn

HOME BASS MARINATED SALAD DRESSING

¾ cup sugar
½ cup minced onion
½ cup minced green bell pepper
1 cup vinegar
1 cup salad oil
1 15-ounce can Veg-All mixed vegetables, drained
Lemon juice to taste
Salt and pepper to taste

Combine all the ingredients. Let marinate in a covered container overnight in the refrigerator. Mix with lettuce and tomatoes when ready to use.

Makes about 5 cups.

Sue and George Shuffler

MICHAEL ROWAN'S ROQUEFORT SALAD DRESSING

6 to 8 ounces of the best quality bleu cheese, such as French Roquefort or Maytag bleu
¼ cup mild vegetable oil
1 tablespoon lemon juice or sherry vinegar
1 cup sour cream
½ teaspoon salt

Add all of the ingredients to a food processor.

North Carolinian George Shuffler has been playing music for many years, but he is best known for his stints with the Stanley Brothers during the 1950s and 1960s. At various times, George played both lead guitar and bass with the Stanleys. He is admired for his exciting, syncopated bass runs and for his trademark cross-picking style of guitar playing, which can be heard on such Stanley classics as "Will You Miss Me" and "Beautiful Star of Bethlehem." During the 1970s and 1980s, George toured with his family gospel group, the Shuffler Family. Though now retired from active touring, he is a regular at Ralph Stanley's Memorial Festival and other bluegrass events around western North Carolina. Shuffler (*center*) is pictured here with Ralph Stanley (*left*) and Larry Sparks in 1992.

If Bela Fleck is the Mr. Eclectic of Bluegrass, then Peter Rowan must be the Original Mr. Eclectic. Peter started out playing mostly rockabilly as a teenager. A few years later, he became a member of Bill Monroe's Blue Grass Boys. There, he began to shine not only as a singer, but also as a songwriter. Peter has played both rock-'n'-roll and bluegrass with the Grateful Dead's Jerry Garcia. He has toured with the Doors. And then there were his late '70s groups, the Green Grass Gringos and the Free Mexican Air Force, which played mostly Tex-Mex music. Peter has even been known to play a little reggae. Pictured here are the Rowan Brothers (l-r, Peter, Chris, and Lorin). The three brothers performed together in the mid-1970s and reunited during the early 1990s to record an album.

Process until the dressing is a nice consistency. This dressing works best with strong greens like romaine, iceberg lettuce, or spinach.

Makes about 2 cups.

Candace and Peter Rowan

MOONDI'S ALL-PURPOSE SALAD DRESSING

I mix this dressing in a Ball wide-mouth, 1½-pint pickling jar because my small whisk fits in it, and it makes mixing quick and easy when mixing with that two-handed, fire-making, warming-your-hands technique. The jar also has way-cool ounce and cup markings on it that make it easy to measure all sorts of things.

The order you do this in is fairly important.

1 cup cider vinegar
⅛ to ¼ cup honey
8 medium cloves garlic, pressed or mashed
1 teaspoon salt
2 tablespoons soy sauce
4 shakes (1 teaspoon) sesame oil
Ground black pepper (it's up to you how much)
1 cup olive oil

Whisk all these ingredients together, except the olive oil, until the honey is completely dis-sipated. Then add the olive oil and whisk the mixture again.

Since there is no ingredient here to emulsify this concoction— that is to say, there is nothing to prevent the salad dressing from separating— you will need to shake or whisk it every time it's used. I keep it in a 1½-pint salad dressing bottle with a rubber stopper, so it's easy to shake before using, thus avoiding spraying unmixed salad dressing all over the dining room.

This dressing is also a wonderful marinade for cooked vegetables, such as broccoli, green beans, and asparagus. Put the cooked veggies in a baggie, add a liberal amount of dressing, and leave the mixture in the fridge. It's good for sides at lunch and dinner. Salad dressing for breakfast is probably going a bit too far. Enjoy.

Makes about 2¼ cups.

Seeya, MK.

Moondi Klein
Chesapeake

MIKE AND ALEXIA'S UNIVERSAL SALAD DRESSING

1 clove garlic, pressed
½ teaspoon salt
¼ cup tamari (or dark soy sauce)
½ cup balsamic vinegar
1 teaspoon prepared Dijon mustard

Mix all the ingredients together with a whisk, let set for a few hours, and then strain into a bottle. This dressing keeps indefinitely in the refrigerator, so you can make double the recipe and keep a lot on hand.

To use on a green salad, first toss the greens with olive oil (about 1 tablespoon per big serving), and then add about 1 teaspoon of dressing per serving. The olive oil coating keeps the greens from getting wilted by the vinegar and salt. Adjust the amounts of oil and dressing to taste. You can also keep this dressing in an old vinegar bottle with a perforated inner cap and let everybody shake it on his or her own salad, with as much or as little oil as desired.

This also makes a good dressing for cold cooked vegetables, such as broccoli and green beans—turning leftovers into salad. You can vary your salad flavors by adding different herbs, such as dill or basil, directly to the greens or vegetables before adding the dressing. We got the basic idea for this dressing from our friend Polly Gott, and we have evolved our own ways of using it.

Makes about ¾ cup.

Mike Seeger and Alexia Smith

Mike Seeger, younger half-brother of Pete, was a key figure in linking bluegrass to the folk revival of the late '50s and early '60s. He was also instrumental in first bringing bluegrass performers to college campuses. He produced the pioneering 1959 Folkways album, *Mountain Music Bluegrass Style*, which helped define bluegrass and introduce it to a more mainstream audience.

Nick of Time Quiz

Match the artists to their nicknames.

1. Uncle Dave Macon
2. Mike Auldridge
3. Vern Gosdin
4. Rose Maddox
5. Jimmy Martin
6. Chubby Wise
7. Buck "Uncle Josh" Graves

A. Mr. Good'n'Country
B. King of the Dobro
C. The Voice
D. Larry the Legend
E. The Queen of the West
F. The Dixie Dewdrop
G. The King of the Bluegrass Fiddlers

Answers: 1. F; 2. D; 3. C; 4. E; 5. A; 6. G; 7. B

BREADS

RUBY'S BISCUITS

Lee Jackson, my dad, is known in bluegrass circles as someone who truly loves the music, and also loves to talk about it—and then talk about it some more. My mom, Ruby, simply put, is an angel on this earth who also just happens to make the greatest biscuits this side of the pearly gates. If you don't believe me, just ask one of the many wonderful friends who've paid visits over the years to Lee and Ruby's house in Louisville, Mississippi. Why, I've even mentioned these mouth-watering masterpieces in two or three songs. They are legendary! Of course, there's no way of measuring the love that goes into these. In fact, like most great cooks, Mom doesn't really measure anything. But this should be close for making 10 to 12 of Ruby's biscuits.

1 1/4 cups Martha White self-rising flour
1/3 cup Crisco shortening
1 cup buttermilk

Preheat oven to 500°. Put the flour into a mixing bowl and cut in the shortening. Add buttermilk and mix really well with a large spoon. Pour the contents onto a board and sprinkle with flour. Knead by hand (Mom says this is important!) only until the dough is fully coated. Then roll by hand, cut, and press onto a baking sheet. Bake at 500° until brown on top.

Makes 10 to 12 biscuits.

Carl Jackson

Grammy Award-winning Carl Jackson is a producer, singer, songwriter, and banjoist who has worked in bands for Jim and Jesse, Glen Campbell, Emmylou Harris, and Ricky Skaggs. His song "Little Mountain Church House" won the IBMA Song of the Year Award in 1990.

The New South in early 1996 was (l-r) Greg Luck, Darrell Webb, Curt Chapman, J.D. Crowe, and Phil Leadbetter. (Dwight McCall has since taken over for Darrell Webb on mandolin.)

J.D. Crowe and the New South

One of the world's most respected banjo players, J.D. Crowe grew up around Lexington, Kentucky, listening to both bluegrass and rock 'n' roll. Fascinated by the banjo, he was always in the front row when Flatt and Scruggs came to town to play the Kentucky Barn Dance in the 1950s. By 1956, J.D. was picking banjo with Jimmy Martin's Sunny Mountain Boys, but he continued to be influenced by other music—listening to Fats Domino, Little Richard, and B.B. King, and studying blues guitar.

In the mid-1960s, J.D. formed the Kentucky Mountain Boys, which at various times included folks like Doyle Lawson, Red Allen, and Larry Rice. The music of J.D. Crowe and the Kentucky Mountain Boys was fairly traditional, but J.D. eventually felt the need to take the group in a new direction. By 1973, he had renamed the band the New South and was moving toward a more contemporary sound.

The group's 1975 debut album on Rounder Records, *J.D. Crowe and The New South*, is generally recognized as one of the landmark albums in bluegrass history. J.D. assembled one of his greatest bands of all time for the album, with Tony Rice on guitar, Ricky Skaggs on mandolin, Jerry Douglas on resonator guitar, and Bobby Sloan on bass. They drew material from many sources, including Gordon Lightfoot, Ian Tyson, and Fats Domino, and they infused the traditional bluegrass material with a fresh, hot contemporary feel. The tremendous musicianship and accessibility of that one release led legions of fans and musicians to discover the magic of bluegrass for the first time.

Over the years, the New South has been a school for many top bluegrass and country musicians including Jimmy Gaudreau, Paul Adkins, Diamond Rio's Gene Johnson, Keith Whitley, and Matthews, Wright and King's

Tony King. During Keith Whitley's tenure as lead singer in the late '70s, J.D. experimented with his most progressive sound ever, using electric instruments, pedal steel, and drums on recordings, as well as choosing material with a decidedly country orientation. At various times, he added drums on stage, displeasing many hard-core bluegrassers but bringing just as many new fans into the bluegrass fold.

During the 1980s, J.D. satisfied fans of traditional bluegrass with his participation in the Bluegrass Album Band. This all-star group included Tony Rice, Doyle Lawson, Jerry Douglas, Bobby Hicks, and Todd Phillips. To date, they have released six albums of classic bluegrass music.

J.D. Crowe "retired" in 1990, but by 1992, he was officially unretired and touring with a revitalized New South. This group, which included mandolinist Don Rigsby and guitarist/singer Richard Bennett (disciples of Skaggs and Rice, respectively), came eerily close to reproducing the sound and feel of the original New South of the '70s. In 1994, they released *Flashback*, a straight-ahead bluegrass collection that was nominated for a Grammy and topped the bluegrass charts for several months. That same year, J.D. was named the IBMA's Banjo Player of the Year and was spotlighted on Rounder's twenty-fifth anniversary tour. Today, the New South features Greg Luck on guitar, Phil Leadbetter on resonator guitar, Dwight McCall on mandolin, and Curt Chapman on bass.

J.D. Crowe is widely acclaimed as "the quintessential Scruggs-style banjoist . . . with flawless timing," yet it is likely that his ability to attract top musicians capable of forging a dynamic, exciting, cutting-edge sound that is the key ingredient in his recipe for success.

OLD HOME PLACE
ANGEL BISCUITS

5 cups all-purpose flour
1 teaspoon soda
1 teaspoon salt
3 teaspoons baking powder
3 tablespoons sugar
¾ cup shortening
2 cups buttermilk
2 packages yeast dissolved in ½ cup warm water

Sift the dry ingredients together. Cut in the shortening until mixed. Add the buttermilk and dissolved yeast. Work together with a spoon until all the flour is moistened. Cover and refrigerate until needed. (The dough will keep for up to 2 weeks in the refrigerator.) Roll the dough on a floured board to ½-inch thickness and cut into biscuits. Bake for 10 minutes at 400°.

Makes about 4 dozen.

J.D. Crowe

JERRY BROWN'S FAMOUS
CAT-HEAD-SIZED
BUTTERMILK BISCUITS

2 cups self-rising flour
½ teaspoon baking powder
1 tablespoon Crisco
1 tablespoon butter (unmelted)
½ cup buttermilk
½ cup whole sweet milk

Preheat oven to 450°. Sift the flour and baking powder into a bowl. Then, add the Crisco and butter, cutting them into the mix until it resembles course cornmeal. Next, add the buttermilk and whole milk into the dry flour and mix by hand until mixture becomes a moist dough ball. (You may need to add a little water to get the dough moist enough.) Put the dough on a flat, floured surface and knead it 6 or 7 times. Then take a look at the size of a cat's head and pinch off a comparable amount of dough. Place this (the dough, not the cat's head) on a flat, well-greased pan. Bake for 12 to 15 minutes.

Makes approximately 15 biscuits, depending on the size of your cat's head.

Jerry Brown
The Shady Grove Band

COUNTRY GAZETTE'S
FAVORITE CORN BREAD

Actually, this is the favorite corn bread of only Alan Munde, Roland White, Gene Wooten, and Billy Joe Foster. But I'll bet all those other guys would like it, too. It's also a little bit healthful, but not enough to hurt anyone.— Anne Solomon

¾ cup all-purpose flour
3 teaspoons baking powder
2 tablespoons sugar
¾ teaspoon salt
¾ cup cornmeal (stone-ground*)
1 egg
2 tablespoons oil
¾ cup plain yogurt

Preheat oven to 425°. Mix together the first 4 ingredients. Add the cornmeal. Beat the egg in a separate bowl. Beat the oil and yogurt into the egg. Pour the liquid into the dry ingredients. If the batter seems too thick, add a little skim milk. Beat lightly. Pour into a hot, greased 8-inch skillet and bake for about 25 minutes.

Makes 6 servings.

*Once, Billy Joe Foster brought me some meal that was a by-product of something he brewed at home. That meal made the best corn bread . . . I think.

Anne Solomon and Alan Munde

The North Carolina-based Shady Grove Band got started in 1981, with founders Charles Pettee and Jerry Brown at the helm. Today the band includes Pettee, Brown, John Boulding, and Adael Shinn. In this photo, Brown relies on his trusty assistant, Lewis, for guidance when making his Famous Cat-Head-Sized Biscuits.

ALISON KRAUSS'S WINNING CORN BREAD

1 tablespoon bacon drippings or vegetable oil
¾ cup Martha White self-rising cornmeal mix
¼ cup Martha White self-rising flour
1 tablespoon sugar
1 egg, beaten
1 cup buttermilk
3 tablespoons vegetable oil

Preheat oven to 450°. Grease an 8-inch skillet with the bacon drippings and place in the oven to heat. In a medium bowl, combine the cornmeal, flour, and sugar. Stir in the egg, buttermilk, and oil. Blend well. Sprinkle a small amount of cornmeal into the hot, greased skillet, then pour the batter into the skillet. Bake for 10 to 15 minutes, or until golden brown.

Makes 4 to 6 servings

Note: This recipe may be doubled, then baked in a 10½-inch skillet for about 25 minutes. For corn sticks and muffins, bake for about 10 to 15 minutes.

Alison Krauss
and Union Station

Goodness Gracious, It's Good

The world-famous Martha White bluegrass jingle was written by the late Pat Twitty of Nashville in the early 1950s and immortalized by Lester Flatt and Earl Scruggs. The tune was preserved on their Carnegie Hall album. Flatt and Scruggs's rendition of the song is still played to kick off the Martha White portion of the Grand Ole Opry at 8 P.M. Saturday nights.

Now you bake right (Uh Huh)—
With Martha White (Yes, Ma'am).
Goodness gracious, good and light,
Martha White.

For the finest biscuits, cakes and pies—
Get Martha White Self-Rising Flour,
The one all-purpose flour,
Martha White Self-Rising Flour has got
*   Hot Rize.*

Alison Krauss and Union Station are taking bluegrass to new heights. They have won numerous Grammy and IBMA awards, and Alison received four awards from the Country Music Association in 1995. Alison has recorded with many of country music's contemporary stars and has performed at the White House. Having fun here with tour sponsor Martha White's products are (l-r) Ron Block, Adam Steffey, Barry Bales, Alison Krauss, and Dan Tyminski.
Photograph by Dan Loftin

Alison Krauss and Union Station:
(l-r) Dan Tyminski, Barry Bales, Alison Krauss, Adam Steffey, and Ron Block.

Alison Krauss and Union Station

Few bluegrass bands of the 1990s can match what Alison Krauss and Union Station have done to broaden the worldwide appeal of bluegrass music. The hard-working band's album sales have broken new ground for bluegrass recordings, and their live shows consistently boast standing-room-only audiences. Indeed, with hits like "I've Got That Old Feeling," "Steel Rails," "Baby, Now That I've Found You," "Every Time You Say Goodbye," and "When You Say Nothing at All," there's a lot to stand up and applaud about for this special band—perhaps most notably its angel-voiced leader. (It seems that almost everyone who comments on Alison's beautiful singing eventually uses the word "angel." And why not? It's certainly accurate.)

The band may have toured to giant venues with the likes of Garth Brooks, but they still seem to prefer intimate settings where they can enjoy hearing each other perform. And while they have managed to attract a wider audience for bluegrass, their music has maintained its great depth: their musicianship is as solid as can be found with any band going (Alison herself is a national champion fiddler), and their selection of songs is both steeped in traditional bluegrass music and appreciative of good tunes originating from other influences.

Then there's that voice from heaven that brings the band's sound together as it captivates audiences. It's no wonder that album sales continue to set records while critics and awards shows alike heap praise on the band. In 1993, Alison, at age twenty-one, became the youngest member ever of the Grand Ole Opry.

Still genuinely self-effacing, Alison and the band are routinely nominated for Grammy Awards in one category or another, where they are frequent and well-received winners. Likewise, bluegrass fans knew there was little need to worry about Alison when she won four awards from the Country Music Association in 1995. Such awards are simply a tribute to the group's versatility and appeal—their bluegrass roots are still firmly set. One needs to look no further than the band's current tour sponsor (Martha White Foods) to realize that Alison Krauss and Union Station are right at home making their music rise in the bluegrass kitchen.

Paul "Moon" Mullins started his career playing fiddle with the Stanley Brothers. In 1964, he began a tremendously successful twenty-five-year radio career on WPFB in Middletown, Ohio. He continued to record and perform with many nationally known bluegrass bands as well. In 1983, he helped found the Traditional Grass, a dynamic band that captured the fire of early bluegrass while making major contributions of its own. The Traditional Grass disbanded in 1995, and Mullins returned to the radio microphone at a station owned by his son, Joe. Paul is an avid gardener and grows and grinds his own corn to make his famous corn bread. The Traditional Grass are (l-r) Mark Rader, Joe Mullins, Gerald Evans, Paul Mullins, and Mike Clevenger.

MOON'S CORN BREAD

2 tablespoons lard
1 cup homegrown cornmeal
½ cup self-rising flour
2 teaspoons baking powder
1 teaspoon salt
2 teaspoons sugar
½ teaspoon baking soda
½ cup sweet milk
½ cup buttermilk

Before mixing the batter, put lard in a 10-inch cast-iron skillet and place the skillet in a 500° oven. Combine the next 6 ingredients. Mix all together with sweet milk and buttermilk, adding each milk a little bit at a time until you reach the right consistency (you may not need all of the milk). Pour the batter into the hot skillet

and bake at 450° to 500° for 12 to 15 minutes, until golden brown.

Makes 6 to 8 servings.

Paul "Moon" Mullins
The Traditional Grass

LONESOME RAMBLER OLD-TIME CORN BREAD

Here is an old-time way to fix corn bread. It's my favorite. As my wife, Pam, will tell folks, "This is the only thing Larry knows how to cook."

1 cup Martha White self-rising white cornmeal
½ cup self-rising flour
1 egg
About 1½ cups milk (or enough to make a slightly thin batter)

Preheat oven to 450°. Grease an 8- by 8-inch square baking pan. Mix the ingredients together in a bowl and pour into the pan. Bake for about 25 minutes, or until fluffy and brown on top.

Makes 6 to 8 servings.

Larry Sparks

There are few singers or guitar players with as much soul as Larry Sparks, who is sometimes called the "Elvis of Bluegrass." Larry began his career playing with the Stanley Brothers as a teenager. Following Carter Stanley's death in 1966, Larry was the obvious choice to step in as lead singer for Ralph's Clinch Mountain Boys. A few years later, Larry formed his own group, Larry Sparks and the Lonesome Ramblers, and today, he is a legend in his own right. His hits include "A Face in the Crowd," "John Deere Tractor," "Tennessee 1949," and "Smoky Mountain Memories."

Sa-Lute to Bluegrass—
Oklahoma native Alan Munde (*right*) has been a fixture on the bluegrass scene for nearly thirty years, beginning with his stint as banjo player with **Poor Richard's Almanac** in 1969. He played with **Jimmy Martin and the Sunny Mountain Boys** for a while, then joined **Byron Berline** in forming **Country Gazette** in 1972. Alan is considered one of the world's leading banjo teachers. He has written several books and produced a variety of instructional audio and video tapes, along with serving as a member of the faculty at **South Plains College** in Levelland, Texas. For years, during the school's summer break, he toured with **Country Gazette**, until the group disbanded in 1996. Alan and fellow **South Plains College** faculty/**Country Gazette** member **Joe Carr** (*left*) also take their bluegrass music workshops on the road nationwide. Joe began performing with the east Texas group **Roanoke** in the mid-1970s and was a member of **Country Gazette** for several years. He teaches mandolin, fiddle, and guitar at **South Plains College.** The college's bluegrass music program has state-of-the-art production facilities and topnotch instructors—attracting students from all over the world. Joe and Alan recently published an award-winning book entitled *Prairie Nights to Neon Lights: The Story of Country Music in West Texas.*
Photograph by Bette Meade.

NOT SO HOT CORN BREAD

3 tablespoons margarine, oil, or bacon grease (if your cholesterol number is low)
1 cup yellow cornmeal
½ cup all-purpose flour
½ teaspoon salt
½ teaspoon baking soda
½ teaspoon baking powder
1 tablespoon sugar
1 cup cow milk
1 chicken egg

Put the margarine in a 10-inch iron skillet and place skillet in a preheated 500° oven. Quickly,

before the margarine starts smoking and sets off your alarm, combine the dry ingredients. Add the cow milk and stir. Add the chicken egg and mix. The skillet should be good and hot by now, so remove it from the oven (not with your bare hand) and pour the melted margarine into the batter. Mix quickly and pour the batter back into the skillet. Return the skillet to the oven for 10 minutes, or sing the first 15 verses of "Knoxville Girl." Eat.

Variation: For Joe and Al's Too Swell, Too Hot Corn Bread, add a handful of chopped jalapeños. Serve with lots of iced tea.

Makes 6 pieces, or 4 if you're really hungry.
Joe Carr and Alan Munde

LOVE AND WEALTH CORN BREAD

You'll be Louvin every bite.

1 cup self-rising cornmeal mix
1 egg
1 tablespoon garlic powder
1 teaspoon honey or sugar
Enough buttermilk to mix the dry ingredients

Preheat oven to 450°. Mix all the ingredients together and pour into a hot, greased 8-inch skillet. Bake until brown. You can double everything for a bigger skillet.

Makes 6 servings.
Charlie Louvin

In the 1950s, the Louvin Brothers, Ira (*left*) and Charlie, created some of bluegrass music's most beloved songs, such as "Ashes of Love" and "I Don't Believe You've Met My Baby." Ira was killed in a car crash in 1965, but Charlie continues to perform as a regular on the Grand Ole Opry and has a Louvin Brothers Museum in Bell Buckle, Tennessee.

TENNESSEE SUNSHINE CORN BREAD

This recipe is from my husband (and guitar player), Mike Long.

1 cup water
Pinch of salt
A little butter
1 cup self-rising cornmeal
¼ cup milk

Preheat a greased 8-inch skillet to be very hot. In a saucepan, bring the water to a boil and add the salt and butter. Remove saucepan from the heat and add the cornmeal and milk. Mix well, pour into the skillet, and fry.
Makes 6 servings.

Gloria Belle (Flickinger)

SOUTH BY SOUTHWEST CORN BREAD

You'll love this recipe. It's almost a complete meal by itself.

1 package yellow corn bread mix
1 package Mexican corn bread mix
½ cup vegetable oil
3 eggs, beaten
8½ ounces cream-style corn
1½ cups longhorn cheddar cheese, shredded
1 large onion, finely chopped
2 4½-ounce cans diced green chilies or 1 8-ounce jar mild jalapeños

Combine all the ingredients, mixing well. Heat a well-greased, 10-inch cast-iron skillet for 3 minutes in a 400° oven. Pour the batter into the hot skillet and bake at 450° for 20 minutes, or until the corn bread is golden brown.
Makes 8 servings.

Al Perkins

BAMA-MEX CORN BREAD

1 cup self-rising flour
1 cup self-rising cornmeal
1 cup onion, chopped

3 eggs, beaten
1 cup sweet milk
1 cup cream-style corn
1 cup medium cheddar cheese, grated
½ cup vegetable oil
¼ teaspoon garlic powder
2 jalapeño peppers, chopped (optional)

Preheat oven to 400°. Mix all the ingredients. Bake for about 30 minutes in a greased 10-inch skillet.
Makes 8 servings.

Glenn Tolbert

BRAMBLE AND ROSE CATBIRD CORN BREAD

Quick, easy, low-fat, and with no added sugar, this recipe is moist and delicious!

Al Perkins's career in music has been as varied as the instruments he plays. He started out playing in California. His travels eventually led to cofounding the Flying Burrito Brothers, and then joining Manassas with Chris Hillman and Stephen Stills. As a member of Emmylou Harris's Grammy-winning Nash Ramblers, Al was called upon to play the banjo, resonator guitar, and acoustic guitar, as well as to provide fine harmony vocals.

1 1/2 cups stone-ground cornmeal
1/2 cup all-purpose flour
1 teaspoon salt
1 tablespoon baking powder
2 eggs
2/3 cup applesauce (I prefer the natural kind with no added sugar)
3/4 cup milk (whole, low-fat, buttermilk, or non-fat buttermilk)
1 8-ounce can whole kernel sweet corn (optional)

Preheat oven to 425°. In a bowl, combine the first 4 ingredients and mix thoroughly. In a separate bowl, combine the remaining ingredients, and then add to the mixture in the first bowl. Mix well. Pour the batter into a greased and floured 9-inch glass pie pan. Bake at 425° for 15 to 20 minutes. Brush melted butter (or low-calorie margarine) on top when you take the bread out of the oven. (The center of the corn bread should feel firm to the touch.)

Makes 6 to 8 servings.

Lynn Morris

SIMPLE PLEASURES CUSTARD-FILLED CORN BREAD

I once made this recipe for a party, and Larry Perkins, the great bluegrass banjo player from North Carolina, told me that it was the best corn bread he ever ate. I guess he would know! When it's done, the corn bread will have a creamy custard inside.

2 eggs
3 tablespoons butter, melted
3 tablespoons sugar
1/2 teaspoon salt
2 cups milk
1 1/2 tablespoons white vinegar
1 cup all-purpose flour
3/4 cup yellow cornmeal
1 teaspoon baking powder
1 teaspoon baking soda
1 cup heavy cream

Preheat oven to 350°. Butter an 8-inch square

Marshall Wilborn and Tom Adams

Lynn Morris and Tom Adams

Lynn Morris grew up in west Texas and got an art degree from Colorado College. She played banjo and guitar in various bluegrass bands before forming the Lynn Morris Band in 1988, along with her husband, bass player Marshall Wilborn. Marshall is a fine songwriter, whose material has been recorded by Doyle Lawson and Quicksilver, the Johnson Mountain Boys, and others, as well as the Lynn Morris Band. Lynn and Marshall literally make beautiful music together. Their smooth vocal harmonies are some of the best in bluegrass. Red-hot banjo player Tom Adams looks as though he's about done in the oven. Audie Blaylock rounds out the band with his driving mandolin playing and tenor vocals.

Prior to pursuing a full-time career in music, Alison Brown was a fast-tracking investment banker. After a couple of years of dealing with Wall Street, she decided that a more enjoyable investment of her time would be to follow the backroads of music. She toured with Alison Krauss and Union Station from 1989 to 1991 (during which time she was named Banjo Player of the Year by the IBMA). Her first solo album, *Simple Pleasures,* was nominated for a Grammy in 1991. Alison started her own record label, Compass Records, in the mid-1990s.

baking dish or pan that is about 2 inches deep. Put the buttered dish or pan in the oven and let it get hot while you mix the batter. Put the eggs in a mixing bowl and add the melted butter. Add the sugar, salt, milk, and vinegar, and beat well. In a bowl, sift or stir together the flour, cornmeal, baking powder, and baking soda. Add the flour mixture to the egg mixture. Mix just until the batter is smooth and no lumps appear. Pour the batter into the heated dish, then pour the heavy cream into the center of the batter—don't stir. Bake for 1 hour, or until lightly browned. Serve warm.

Makes 8 servings.

Alison Brown

PENNSYLVANIA APPLESAUCE BREAD

2 cups all-purpose flour
½ teaspoon double-acting baking powder
I teaspoon salt
I teaspoon baking soda
I teaspoon ground cinnamon
½ teaspoon ground nutmeg
½ cup butter
¾ cup sugar
I teaspoon vanilla extract
2 eggs
I cup applesauce
½ cup walnuts, chopped

Sift together the flour, baking powder, salt, baking soda, cinnamon, and nutmeg. Cream the butter. Gradually add the sugar to the butter and cream well. Add the vanilla and eggs. Beat the mixture well. Add the flour mixture to the butter mixture and mix thoroughly. Add the applesauce and walnuts. Mix only until blended. Pour the batter into a well-greased 9- by 5- by 3-inch pan. Push the batter up in the corners of the pan, leaving the center slightly hollow for a well-rounded loaf. Allow the batter to sit for 20 minutes before baking. Bake in a 350° oven for 55 to 60 minutes. Cool completely before topping with glaze and slicing.

Makes 1 loaf.

Glaze:

½ cup confectioners' sugar
½ teaspoon milk (or enough to make a glaze consistency)

Mix together and spread over the bread.
Dale Ann Bradley
The New Coon Creek Girls

STRINGBEAN AND GRANDPA'S FRIED BREAD

Stringbean and Grandpa Jones cooked this when they were out fishing.

I cup cornmeal
I cup water

SOUTHERN SPOON BREAD

1 cup yellow cornmeal
1½ teaspoons baking powder
½ teaspoon salt
2 eggs, beaten
3 tablespoons butter, melted
2¼ cups milk

Preheat oven to 425°. In a mixing bowl, stir together the cornmeal, baking powder, and salt. Next, pour the eggs and butter into a greased 1-quart casserole dish. In a medium saucepan, heat the milk, stirring to prevent scorching. As the milk starts to boil, sprinkle in the dry ingredients, stirring vigorously with a wooden spoon. Cook and stir for 2 or 3 minutes, allowing the mixture to thicken. Pour the mixture into the casserole dish and mix it with the eggs and butter. Bake for 45 minutes. Serve from the casserole dish with a spoon. Eat with a fork.
Makes 4 to 6 servings.

Dale Ann Bradley
The New Coon Creek Girls

BERRIER'S BROCCOLI BREAD

1 stick margarine, melted
1 large onion, chopped
1 11-ounce box frozen chopped broccoli, thawed
4 eggs, beaten
8 ounces cottage cheese
1 box Jiffy corn bread mix, or 2 cups self-rising cornmeal

Preheat oven to 400°. Mix all the ingredients and pour the batter into a greased 9- by 13-inch pan. Bake at 400° for 25 minutes, or until golden brown on top.
Makes 8 to 10 servings.

Barry Berrier
The Lost and Found

This classic pose shows **David Akeman** (originally **Akemon**), better known as **Stringbean**, in 1961. The beloved clawhammer banjo player, singer, and comedian has the distinction of being the first banjo player hired by **Bill Monroe** for his **Blue Grass Boys**. Millions enjoyed Stringbean's humor and musical skills during his many years as a member of the **Grand Ole Opry** and as a favorite cast member on *Hee Haw*.
Photograph by Les Leverett

¼ teaspoon salt
Vegetable oil

Mix the cornmeal, water, and salt together. Put sufficient oil in a frying pan. Form mixture into patties and place in the frying pan. Brown well on both sides. Serve while hot. You may substitute flour for the cornmeal.
Makes enough for dinner for two.

Submitted by Alfred Akemon,
Stringbean's brother

SUMMER WAGES
CORN 'N' PEPPER FRITTERS

1 egg
½ cup milk
1 12-ounce can whole kernel corn with
   sweet peppers, undrained
1 tablespoon oil
1½ cups flour
1 tablespoon baking powder
1 teaspoon salt
Dash of pepper

In a large bowl, beat the egg. Add the milk, corn with liquid, and oil. Beat in the flour, baking powder, salt, and pepper. Heat an oiled, uncovered skillet, then drop the batter by tablespoonfuls into the hot skillet. Fry each fritter for 2 to 3 minutes on each side until golden brown. Drain the fritters on paper towels and serve hot.

Makes about 12 fritters.

Barry Berrier
The Lost and Found

WINCHESTER
APPLE BEER BREAD

This makes a tasty snack with coffee, or it makes a great breakfast. It tastes a little like a yeast bread, but total preparation time is less than 1 hour.

3 level cups all-purpose flour (for wheat
   bread, you can substitute ½ to 1 cup
   whole-wheat flour for equal amount of
   white flour)
1 teaspoon salt
1 tablespoon baking powder
3 tablespoons sugar (more if you like it
   sweet)
12 ounces of any beer (I favor a medium-
   strength, non-light beer for this recipe)
1 Granny Smith apple, peeled, cored, and
   sliced into small pieces
3 tablespoons butter or margarine, lightly
   melted

Preheat oven to 350°. In a large mixing bowl, combine the first 4 ingredients and mix thoroughly with a whisk. (Make sure the flour is measured in level cups; otherwise, the bread will be too dry.) Add the beer and mix thoroughly into the dry mixture, then mix in the sliced apples. Put the batter into a greased and floured glass pie pan (or loaf pan). Because the dough is very sticky, put flour on your hands and on top of the batter in the pan, then pat the top down smooth, as you would with yeast dough. Generously brush the lightly melted butter onto the top "crust" of the loaf. Bake for 45 minutes to 1 hour. If you wish, you can sprinkle a little sugar and/or cinnamon on top before baking. After the bread is baked, remove it from the pan and let it cool for 10 minutes before serving.

Makes about 8 servings.

Lynn Morris

WOODSONGS WHOLE
WHEAT APPLE BREAD

Every winter, my sweet little wife gets in a bread-making mood. I get into a "making" mood, too, but I'm not really thinking of bread. Anyway, Jenny is a farm girl from Quality, Kentucky. She grew up on a dairy farm—big family, cute as a button, and tough as nails. And the best bread maker I know. We got married about five years ago, and I still have trouble believing I haven't blown up to the size of a house. Keeping your weight down when you're married to the Queen of Calories is tough, but I've managed.

This recipe is best tried when it's snowing out. For a manly man like me, working outside in the crisp winter chill, chopping up some wood for the fire stove, coming inside and getting a roaring good blaze going, and then having Jenny serve up a big slice of this bread with some hot chocolate . . . well, man, I fall in love about a hundred times just thinking about it!

Here's what you need:

1 cup whole-wheat flour
1 cup all-purpose flour
1 teaspoon baking powder
1 teaspoon baking soda
1 teaspoon salt
1 teaspoon ground cinnamon
½ teaspoon ground nutmeg
¾ cup real applesauce (the chunkier, the
   better)

½ cup dark brown sugar
½ cup apple juice
1 teaspoon vanilla extract
1 tablespoon grated orange rind (you can eat the orange while you're cooking)
1 tablespoon vegetable oil
1 egg, slightly beaten
½ apple

Preheat your oven to 325° and grease up a bread pan that's about 9- by 5-inches. In a bowl, mix the bread flours, baking powder, baking soda, salt, cinnamon, and nutmeg. Stir it all up. In another large bowl, mix up the applesauce, brown sugar, apple juice, vanilla, orange rind, oil, and egg. Peel, core, and slice the apple into 8 crescent-shaped slices. Whisk ½ the flour mixture into the applesauce mixture until it's fairly gooey, then put the rest in. Note: If you overdo this step, the bread will be too bland. Just mix it up, and you will have a great, homemade texture that you can't buy in a store.

Pour the mixture into the baking pan, lay the apple slices across the top, and then sprinkle a little brown sugar across the top. Pop this into the oven for about 1 hour—just enough time to romance your wife or write a new song. Then, have a slice of homemade bread afterward instead of a cigarette. Sure makes a cold day warm, don't it?

Makes 1 loaf.

Michael Johnathon

REBEL SOLDIER'S ZUCCHINI BREAD

3 eggs
2 cups sugar
1 cup Crisco oil
2 cups shredded zucchini
3 cups all-purpose flour
1 teaspoon baking soda
1 teaspoon baking powder
3 teaspoons ground cinnamon
1 teaspoon vanilla extract
Nuts

Preheat oven to 350°. Beat the eggs. Add the sugar to the eggs and beat well. Add the oil and beat. Add the zucchini and mix. In a separate bowl, mix together the flour, baking soda, baking powder, and cinnamon. Add the flour mixture to the zucchini mixture and mix well. Add the vanilla and nuts. Pour into 1 large or 2 small greased and floured loaf pans. Bake for 60 to 70 minutes. Enjoy!

Makes 1 large or 2 small loaves.

Sachiko and Charlie Waller
The Country Gentlemen

Charlie Waller has spent four decades as leader of the award-winning Country Gentlemen. When he's not on the road, Charlie, his wife Sachiko, and daughter Mina enjoy relaxing in their cabin in the Virginia woods.

RODNEY'S SWEET POTATO MUFFINS

1 stick margarine
1¼ cups sugar
2 eggs
1¼ cups mashed sweet potatoes
1 cup milk
2 cups all-purpose flour
2 teaspoons baking powder
1 teaspoon ground cinnamon
¼ teaspoon ground nutmeg
½ cup raisins
½ cup chopped nuts

Preheat oven to 350°. Cream the margarine and sugar. Beat in the eggs until fluffy. Mix in the potatoes and milk. In a separate bowl, sift the dry ingredients. Add the flour mixture to the sweet potato mixture. Add the raisins and nuts. Stir the batter until the flour is moist. Bake in well-greased muffin tins for 20 minutes.

Makes about 2 dozen muffins.

Beverly and Rodney Dillard
The Dillards

GIBSON CINNAMON PUMPKIN ROLLS

2³/₄ to 3¹/₄ cups all-purpose flour
1 1¹/₄-ounce package active dry yeast
¹/₂ cup solid-pack pumpkin
²/₃ cup milk
2 tablespoons sugar
4 tablespoons butter or margarine
¹/₂ teaspoon salt
1 egg, beaten
¹/₂ cup packed brown sugar
1 teaspoon ground cinnamon

Combine 1½ cups flour and the yeast. Set aside. In a saucepan, heat and stir the pumpkin, milk, sugar, 2 tablespoons of butter, and salt until warm and the butter has almost melted. Combine the pumpkin mixture with the flour and yeast mixture, then add the egg. With an electric mixer, beat on low for 30 seconds. Beat on high for 3 minutes. Add enough additional flour to make the dough stiff. Knead until smooth and elastic. Put the dough in a greased bowl, turning once to grease the top. Cover and let rise for 1 hour. Roll the dough into a rectangle on a board. Melt the remaining butter and brush on the dough. Combine the sugar and cinnamon and brush over the dough. Roll the dough like a jelly roll. Slice into 1-inch rolls and place into a 9-by 13-inch greased baking pan. Cover and let rise for about 30 minutes. Bake at 375° for 20 to 25 minutes.

Caramel Frosting:

2 tablespoons butter or margarine
¹/₄ cup packed brown sugar
1 tablespoon milk
¹/₄ teaspoon vanilla extract
Dash salt
¹/₄ to ¹/₃ cup confectioners' sugar

Melt the butter in a saucepan. Stir in the brown sugar and milk. Cook over medium-low heat for 1 minute. Stir in the vanilla, salt, and confectioners' sugar. Drizzle over the rolls.

Makes about 1 dozen.

Corina and Eric Gibson
The Gibson Brothers

The Gibson Brothers, Eric (*left*) and Leigh, were raised on a dairy farm in upstate New York and began playing banjo and guitar before they were teenagers. In 1991, they formed the Gibson Brothers Bluegrass Band along with resonator guitar player Junior Barber. In 1993, Junior's son, Mike, joined the band on bass. Eric and Leigh are excellent singers—both equally comfortable with lead or harmony parts. They write songs as well, and while steeped in tradition, their original material has a fresh, new sound. Their latest album is *Long Forgotten Dream* on Hay Holler Records.

Photograph by Wayne Dunford; courtesy of Hay Holler Records and Gary Reid

MOMMA'S NOT DEAD* CINNAMON BREAD

*She's just playin' possum.

4 cans Pillsbury biscuits
1 cup sugar
2 tablespoons ground cinnamon
1 stick butter, melted

Preheat oven to 350°. Line 1 can of biscuits in a Bundt pan. Mix sugar and cinnamon, then sprinkle some of the mixture over the biscuits. Repeat until all of the biscuits are used, reserving 2 or 3 tablespoons of the sugar mixture. Bake for 35 minutes. Mix the remaining sugar-cinnamon mixture with the melted butter and pour mixture over the baked bread. Let stand for 5 minutes to cool, then dump the bread onto a serving dish.

Makes about 12 servings.

Kim and Tim White
Troublesome Hollow

Artist and bluegrass musician Tim White poses in front of the mural he painted to commemorate Bristol as the Birthplace of Country Music.

Birthplace of Country Music

During the summer of 1927, Victor Records's Ralph Peer traveled to the heart of the Appalachian Mountains along the Virginia/Tennessee border to make recordings of traditional musicians in the area. What he found was a gold mine of talent, and country music historians now hail the "Bristol Sessions," as those groundbreaking recording sessions came to be known, as the "Big Bang of Country Music." Among the fifteen or so artists recorded for the first time by Peer in Bristol, Tennessee/Virginia, during those sessions were Jimmie Rodgers, the Carter Family, and the Stoneman Family.

Bristol continued to thrive as a country music mecca through the next several decades. In 1946, radio station WCYB hit the airwaves. The station's tremendously popular *Farm and Fun Time* show made its debut about this same time. On December 26, 1946, the newly formed Stanley Brothers and the Clinch Mountain Boys were the first act to perform on the show, which quickly became a launching board for many careers. During the late-1940s and the 1950s, many nationally known and local country and bluegrass acts were featured on the live show. The show began in an hour-long format following the noon news but soon expanded to two hours. Among those who at various times had daily slots were the Stanley Brothers, Charlie Monroe, the Blue Sky Boys, and Flatt and Scruggs. Other musicians featured often included Jim and Jesse, Mac Wiseman, Jimmy Martin and the Osborne Brothers, and Carl Story. Many of these artists used the show to test new songs and arrangements.

The audience response to the *Farm and FunTime* show was tremendous. "We'd get a big pile of mail every day," recalled Ralph Stanley. "We got so many job offers from the program, at times we couldn't meet the demand." Mac Wiseman added, "I've had hundreds of people tell me over the years how they'd get up early and work late out in the fields just so they could come in the house at noon and hear the program."

Through the years, the Bristol area has remained a focal point for bluegrass music. Today, many current artists call the area home, including Doyle Lawson, Ralph Stanley, Tim Stafford, and Adam Steffey. East Tennessee State University in nearby Johnson City even has a nationally recognized program in bluegrass and country music, headed by mandolinist Jack Tottle.

The Birthplace of Country Music Alliance (BCMA) was founded in 1993 to focus attention on the important role the Bristol area has played in country music's history. Its board of directors includes Jack Tottle, Tim Stafford, and Tim White (of Troublesome Hollow and the Beagles). The BCMA's mission is to bring national and international recognition to the people, music, and cultural heritage of the Southern Appalachian region, to the area's role in the development of country music, and to its influence on music around the world. The BCMA frequently promotes concerts at Bristol's historic Paramount Theater and other venues in the area. The organization also offers speakers for civic groups in order to increase community awareness.

For information, contact the Birthplace of Country Music Alliance at P.O. Box 216, Bristol, Tennessee 37620.

SUNNY MOUNTAIN TROPICAL GINGERBREAD

½ cup shortening
½ cup sugar
1 egg
2½ cups sifted all-purpose flour
1½ teaspoons baking soda
1 teaspoon ground cinnamon
1 teaspoon ground ginger
½ teaspoon ground cloves
½ teaspoon salt
1 cup molasses
1 cup hot water
White frosting
Coconut

Preheat oven to 350°. Melt the shortening in a 3- or 4-quart saucepan over low heat. Remove the saucepan from heat and let cool. Add the sugar and egg, and beat well. Sift together the flour, baking soda, salt, and spices. Combine the molasses and water. Alternately add the molasses mixture and flour mixture to the shortening mixture. Pour the batter into a 9- by 9- by 2-inch Teflon-lined pan (or one sprayed with a vegetable spray). Bake for 50 minutes to 1 hour. Cool for 5 minutes. Remove from the pan. Cover with a white frosting and sprinkle generously with coconut.
Makes 9 servings.

Gloria Belle (Flickinger)

ANDREA'S PUMPKIN BREAD

1 stick butter or margarine
1 cup sugar
2 eggs
1 teaspoon baking soda
½ teaspoon salt
½ teaspoon baking powder
2 cups pumpkin
2 cups flour
1 teaspoon vanilla extract
1 teaspoon ground cinnamon
½ teaspoon ground cloves
½ teaspoon ground allspice
½ teaspoon ground ginger
½ cup chocolate chips (optional)

Preheat oven to 350°. Combine the butter and sugar. Add the eggs. Add the baking soda, salt, and baking powder. Alternately add the pumpkin and flour. Add the vanilla and spices. Add the chocolate chips. Grease and flour a 9- by 4- by 4-inch pan. Pour the batter into the pan and bake for 45 minutes to 1 hour, or until a toothpick inserted in the middle of the bread comes out clean.
Makes 1 loaf.

Andrea Zonn

THREE-FINGER ROLLS

2 packages Fleischmann's dry yeast
½ cup warm water
¼ cup butter, margarine, or Crisco
1 cup milk
4 cups Martha White self-rising flour
3 tablespoons sugar

Dissolve the yeast in the water. Heat the Crisco and milk until warm and gradually add to the flour in a large bowl. Then gradually add the water with the yeast in it to the flour. Add the sugar and stir the mixture until it forms a soft dough. Put out on a floured surface and knead until smooth and elastic. Place in a greased bowl and turn over to grease both sides of the dough. Cover and let rise in a warm place until double its size (about 35 to 45 minutes). Take the dough out and punch it down on a floured surface. Divide the dough into 12 equal pieces. Divide each of those pieces into three pieces. Form those pieces into balls and put three balls into each cup of a greased muffin tin. Cover and let rise in a warm place for about 30 minutes. Bake at 425° for about 10 minutes.
Makes 1 dozen rolls.

Louise and Earl Scruggs

HESTER ROLLS

They're dyn-o-mite!

4 tablespoons Miracle Whip
1 cup milk
2 cups self-rising flour

Lester Flatt and Earl Scruggs stand beside their bus with a mid-1950s version of the Foggy Mountain Boys: (l-r) "Little Darlin'" (Charles "Kentucky Slim" Elza), Buck "Uncle Josh" Graves, Curly Seckler, Paul Warren, and Onie Wheeler.

Flatt and Scruggs

Perhaps the most famous bluegrass band of them all, Lester Flatt, Earl Scruggs, and the Foggy Mountain Boys carried bluegrass to larger audiences than ever before. From 1948 to 1969, this pair put out so many great bluegrass tunes that most of them are still "must knows" for new bluegrass bands. These songs include "Roll in My Sweet Baby's Arms," "Blue Ridge Cabin Home," "Doin' My Time," "Salty Dog Blues," "I'll Stay Around," "Some Old Day," "Cabin on the Hill," "Don't This Road Look Rough and Rocky," "Before I Met You," "Down the Road," and many more. Earl Scruggs is regarded as the guru of the five-string banjo, and it would be impossible to find a bluegrass banjo player today who has not been influenced by his mastery. Likewise, Lester Flatt's smooth, distinctive voice and warm, friendly stage demeanor have been often emulated but never duplicated.

The pair were members of Bill Monroe's "original" Blue Grass Boys from 1945 to 1948. In 1948, they began performing on their own. One of their big breaks came in 1953 when they started playing for WSM Radio and Martha White; their Martha White theme was probably their most frequently requested song. The Grand Ole Opry stars took the genre to television and film in the 1960s with the "Ballad of Jed Clampett" (the theme song of *The Beverly Hillbillies*), and "Foggy Mountain Breakdown," which they played for the soundtrack of *Bonnie and Clyde*. Lester and Earl appeared as themselves in about a dozen episodes of *The Beverly Hillbillies* as well. The song "Pearl, Pearl, Pearl," composed especially for that show, became one of their trademark songs. During the '60s, Flatt and Scruggs also had their own syndicated half-hour television show that was sponsored by Martha White and broadcast in many areas of the Southeast.

The duo went their separate ways in 1969. Lester Flatt led the Nashville Grass until his death in 1979, while Earl Scruggs formed the Earl Scruggs Revue with sons Randy, Gary, and Steve. Flatt and Scruggs entered the Country Music Hall of Fame in 1981 and the International Bluegrass Music Association Hall of Honor in 1991.

Preheat oven to 400°. Mix ingredients together and stir for 4 minutes. Grease and flour a muffin tin. Spoon the batter in with a teaspoon. Bake for 10 minutes.

Makes 10 rolls.

Hoot Hester
Flat Creek Skillet Lickers

NOW OR NEVER YEAST ROLLS

2 envelopes active dry yeast
¼ cup warm water
1½ cups buttermilk, heated to lukewarm
¼ cup sugar
½ cup oil
I teaspoon salt
4½ cups bread flour (or all-purpose flour)
½ teaspoon baking soda
Butter

Dissolve the yeast and ¼ teaspoon of the sugar in the warm water. Set aside to double. Combine the heated buttermilk, sugar, oil, and salt. Sift the flour and soda into a large bowl. Mix the yeast with the milk mixture and add to the flour mixture. Mix well with a wooden spoon. (This will be a stiff dough.) Let the dough stand for 15 minutes. Turn out onto a lightly floured counter. Turn the dough to lightly flour it. Pat it out and cut into biscuits.

Melt some butter in the bottom of 2 round cake pans. Place the rolls in the pans, turning each roll over to butter the top. Let stand in a warm place for 45 minutes, then bake at 425° for 10 to 15 minutes, depending on the size of the rolls.

Makes 12 to 15 rolls.

Steve Pye
Highstrung

FRENCH BROAD BREAD

I package yeast
¼ cup warm water (about 80°)
½ cup milk
I cup boiling water
I tablespoon butter
I tablespoon sugar
4 cups plain or bread flour

2 teaspoons sugar
2 teaspoons salt

In a large bowl, dissolve the yeast in the warm water. Scald the milk and add the boiling water. Add the butter and 1 tablespoon sugar to the milk and stir. Let cool to lukewarm. Sift together the flour, 2 teaspoons sugar, and the salt. Combine with the milk mixture and the dissolved yeast, then stir (don't knead). Cover and let the dough rise for 2 hours.

Divide the dough into 3 pieces and roll each into a ¼-inch-thick rectangle. (At this point, I brush mine with melted butter.) Roll each piece up from the side toward you. Place the dough on a buttered baking sheet and cross-cut diagonally at 1-inch intervals along the top of the loaves. Let rise for ½ hour. Preheat oven to 400°. Place a pan of hot water on the lower rack of the oven and put the bread loaves on the top rack. After 15 minutes, reduce the heat to 350° and continue baking for an additional 30 minutes. Sugar and cinnamon may be sprinkled on the dough before rolling to make a nice cinnamon bread.

Makes 3 loaves.

Ginger Boatwright

NEW ORLEANS GARLIC BREAD

½ cup mayonnaise
½ cup margarine, softened
2 cups (½ pound) mozzarella cheese, grated
I cup black ripe olives, pitted and chopped
6 green onions, chopped
½ teaspoon garlic powder
I loaf French bread, sliced in half with a lengthwise horizontal cut

Add the mayonnaise to the margarine. Blend well. Add the remaining ingredients, mix well, and spread onto each piece of bread. Bake at 350° for 10 to 15 minutes until the cheese bubbles. This can be frozen and baked later.

Makes 8 to 10 servings.

Jeff and Sheri Easter

SUE HESTON'S FAMOUS BREAD

These are fast to prepare and very good.

5 cups very warm milk
1 heaping cup sugar
3 heaping tablespoons yeast
14 to 18 cups bread flour
4 or 5 eggs
¾ to 1 pound butter, margarine, vegetable shortening, or a combination
2 tablespoons salt
½ cup butter, melted

In a large bowl, mix the first 3 ingredients until the yeast and sugar are dissolved, then add 5 or 6 cups of the flour. Beat the eggs together and add to the yeast mixture along with the remaining ingredients, except the melted butter. The flour may vary from 14 to 18 cups. The dough should be very soft and elastic. Cover with a towel and let rise until double in size. Then knead to work out the air and put into 6 greased loaf pans. (You can also use muffin pans for rolls.) Cover and let rise until about double in size. Bake in the middle of the oven at 375° for about 22 to 25 minutes. Brush the tops with melted butter. Cool on wire racks.

Makes 6 loaves or a bunch of rolls.

Willia and Melvin Goins

BUSY QUICK BANANA NUT BREAD

3 cups Bisquick
²/₃ cup sugar
¹/₂ cup milk
2 eggs
³/₄ cup English walnuts, chopped
1 cup ripe bananas (about 3), mashed

Preheat oven to 350°. Grease and flour a 9- by 5- by 3-inch pan. Mix all the ingredients well and pour the mixture into the pan. Bake for 55 to 60 minutes. Cool the bread for 10 minutes before removing from the pan.

Makes 1 loaf.

Hoot Hester
Flat Creek Skillet Lickers

Rosa Lee, Doc, and a young Merle Watson pose for a family portrait in the early 1950s, about the time Rosa Lee learned to make Doc's favorite gingerbread. *Photograph courtesy of Sugar Hill Records*

WATSON'S FLAT-PICKIN' GOOD GINGERBREAD

Rosa Lee has been making this gingerbread since Merle was a small boy. It is a family favorite, "hot or cold, in plain or fancy dress." Be sure to use good quality country molasses, not blackstrap from the store!

¼ cup shortening
¼ cup sugar
1 egg
¾ cup good quality molasses
¾ cup milk
2 cups self-rising flour, sifted
1 teaspoon ground ginger
¾ teaspoon ground cinnamon
¼ teaspoon ground cloves

Preheat oven to 350°. Grease an 8-inch square baking pan. In a large bowl, cream the shortening. Add the sugar gradually. Add the egg and beat well. In a separate bowl, stir the molasses into the milk. Sift the dry ingredients together. Add the dry ingredients alternately with the milk mixture to the shortening mixture. Mix until smooth. Pour the mixture into the prepared pan and bake for about 35 to 40 minutes, or until the top is brown and a toothpick inserted in the middle comes out clean. Rosa Lee recommends checking it after 30 minutes to account for variations in different ovens. You can also use this recipe for one large loaf pan or 1½ dozen cupcakes.

Makes 8 to 10 servings.

Rosa Lee and Doc Watson

Doc Watson

Arthel "Doc" Watson was born the sixth of nine children in Deep Gap, North Carolina, in the heart of the Blue Ridge Mountains. Blinded by illness before he was a year old, he grew up surrounded by the sounds of fiddles and banjos, absorbing the traditional Appalachian folk songs of his ancestors. He also immersed himself in the popular music of the day by way of radio and Victrola. When Arthel was eleven, his father made him his first banjo. Watson soon picked up the guitar and began playing on the streets of area towns on weekends. At age eighteen, he got his nickname when a radio announcer had problems pronouncing his given name and someone in the audience shouted, "Call him 'Doc!'"

In 1951, Doc traded his Martin acoustic guitar for a Les Paul electric and began playing in a weekend dance band. Over the next ten years, he honed his skills on the popular country, big band, and rockabilly songs of the time. Then in 1960, folklorist Ralph Rinzler visited the area and discovered Watson's tremendous talent. He recorded Doc playing traditional music with his family and friends, and later brought him to the Newport Folk Festival and other urban venues. Watson set the Les Paul aside for an acoustic guitar and an old-timey banjo, and soon he was one of the most sought-after performers on the folk revival scene.

In 1964, Watson's fifteen-year-old son, Merle, joined his father as a touring partner. In addition to being a highly skilled guitarist in his own right, Merle served as road manager and guide. Through Merle's influence, Doc began playing more mainstream venues, performing alongside many of the folk-rock stars of the '70s. This exposure, coupled with his participation in the Nitty Gritty Dirt Band's historic *Will the Circle Be Unbroken* album, released in 1972, led a whole new set of fans to discover Doc Watson's genius.

In 1985, Merle Watson died tragically in an accident, leaving his grief-stricken father with serious thoughts of retiring. However, the music, and the need to share it with the fans he considers his friends, are in his blood. While Doc has cut back his schedule, he has courageously continued to tour, often accompanied by his longtime friend, guitarist Jack Lawrence.

Though the traditional music of home remains his first love, Watson has developed a vast and eclectic repertoire that includes bluegrass, blues, folk, country, jazz, and rockabilly. He has made dozens of recordings, including five Grammy winners, and a number of instruction and performance videos. His one all-bluegrass release (his last recording with Merle), *Riding the Midnight Train,* won a Grammy in 1986. It features an all-star lineup of pickers, including the Nashville Bluegrass Band, Sam Bush, Jerry Douglas, and Mark O'Connor.

In 1987, the first annual Merle Watson Memorial Festival (a.k.a. MerleFest) was held on the campus of Wilkes Community College in Wilkesboro, North Carolina, just a few miles from Doc's home. This festival has become a living memorial to Merle and a homecoming for many of Doc's musician friends. It has grown to be one of the biggest and most highly acclaimed acoustic music festivals in the country, with hundreds of performers, ten different stages, and annual attendance at close to forty thousand.

Doc Watson

Trivia Sundries

1. **What well-known bluegrass musician appeared in an episode of *Star Trek*?**

2. **Where will you find Johnson Mountain, from which the Johnson Mountain Boys take their name?**

3. **At what venue did instrumental virtuoso Norman Blake perform with Kris Kristofferson and Billy Swann on December 30, 1971?**

4. **What do banjo pickers David Akeman, Earl Scruggs, Hubert Davis, Vic Jordan, Blake Williams, Lamar Grier, Butch Robins, Bill Keith, and Curtis McPeake all have in common?**

5. **What special link do both Tony Rice and Marty Stuart have to the Kentucky Colonels?**

6. **Who was the first female artist to record an album of only bluegrass music?**

7. **What was the first song Bill Monroe sang on the Grand Ole Opry?**

8. **Who were the Dopyera brothers?**

Answers:
1. Byron Berline
2. In Dudley Connell's imagination.
3. Carnegie Hall
4. All have been members of Bill Monroe's Blue Grass Boys.
5. Each is the proud owner of one of the late Clarence White's guitars.
6. Rose Maddox
7. "The Muleskinner Blues"
8. Inventors of the Dobro resonator guitar.

Re-Grouping Matching Quiz

Match the maybe-not-so-easily-remembered group with the artists who were members of the group.

1. East Kentucky Mountain Boys
2. Uncle Bob and the Blue Ridge Partners
3. Whetstone Ru
4. Country Store
5. The Dixie Drifters
6. The Timberliners
7. The Dixie Ramblers
8. Here Today
9. Sundance
10. The Blue Diamond Boys
11. Poor Richard's Almanac
12. Tasty Licks

A. Hylo Brown
B. Vern Gosdin, Chris Hillman, and Don Parmley
C. Bela Fleck, Pat Enright, Jack Tottle, and Mark Schatz
D. Lynn Morris
E. Ricky Skaggs and Keith Whitley
F. Doug Dillard, Rodney Dillard, and John Hartford
G. Keith Whitley, Jimmy Gaudreau, Jimmy Arnold, and Bill Rawlings
H. Sam Bush, Alan Munde, and Wayne Stewart
I. Herb Pedersen, David Grisman, Jim Buchanan, Vince Gill, and Emory Gordy, Jr.
J. Bill Emerson
K. Norman Blake
L. Byron Berline and Vince Gill

Answers: 1. E; 2. J; 3. D; 4. G; 5. K; 6. A; 7. F; 8. I; 9. L; 10. B; 11. H; 12. C

BREAKFAST

FINE FEATHERY EGG OMELETTE

This recipe is from my mother, Caroline Flickinger.

2 tablespoons minute tapioca
³/4 teaspoon salt
¹/8 teaspoon pepper
³/4 cup milk
1 tablespoon butter
4 egg whites
4 egg yolks

Preheat oven to 350°. Combine the tapioca, salt, pepper, and milk in a pan. Cook on medium heat until it comes to a full boil, stirring constantly. Add the butter and remove from the heat. Allow the mixture to cool slightly while beating the eggs. Beat the egg whites stiff. In a separate bowl, beat the yolks to a lemon color. Add the tapioca mixture to the yolks. Mix well and then fold in the egg whites. Put the mixture into a hot and buttered 10-inch skillet. Cover over low heat for 3 minutes, and then bake for 15 minutes. The omelette is done when a table knife inserted into the center comes out clean.

Makes 2 to 4 servings.

Gloria Belle (Flickinger)

BUDDY'S SPIKED OVERNIGHT CHEESE OMELETTE

Great for a brunch or any meal.

1 large loaf Italian bread
6 tablespoons butter, melted
³/4 pound Swiss cheese, shredded
¹/2 pound Monterey Jack cheese, shredded
9 thin slices ham or salami
9 eggs
1 ¹/2 cups milk
¹/2 cup white wine
3 or 4 large green onions, minced
1 tablespoon prepared mustard
¹/4 teaspoon black pepper
¹/8 teaspoon red pepper
1 ¹/2 cups sour cream
1 cup Parmesan cheese, grated

Butter or grease a 9- by 13-inch baking dish. Break the bread into small pieces and spread over the bottom of the dish. Drizzle with melted butter and sprinkle with the cheese and meat. Beat together the eggs, milk, wine, onions, mustard, and peppers. Pour the egg mixture over the cheese. Cover the dish with foil. Refrigerate for up to 24 hours. Remove from the refrigerator 30 minutes before baking. Bake covered at 325° for 1 hour. Uncover and spread sour cream over the top, then sprinkle with Parmesan cheese. Bake uncovered until brown (10 to 15 minutes). Serve with fresh fruit salad and a small muffin.

Makes 9 to 12 servings.

Paula and Buddy Spicher

ONE TOO MANY MORNINGS BAKED OMELETTE

**6 eggs
2 tablespoons melted margarine
I cup milk
¹/₂ teaspoon salt
¹/₈ teaspoon pepper
¹/₂ cup cheddar cheese, shredded
6 slices bacon, cooked and crumbled, or ¹/₂ pound cooked sausage**

Preheat the oven to 400°. Grease a 9-inch square pan. Combine the eggs, margarine, milk, salt, and pepper. Beat with a hand beater until blended. Pour the mixture into the pan. Sprinkle the cheese and bacon over the top. Bake for 20 minutes, or until golden brown.

Makes 4 servings.

*Sandy and Dean Webb
The Dillards*

HILLBILLY JAZZ BRUNCH OMELETTE TORTE

**2 sheets frozen puff pastry, thawed
¹/₄ cup butter
3 cups medium potatoes, cubed
I cup onion ring slices
Salt and pepper to taste
2 tablespoons butter
6 eggs
¹/₄ cup fresh parsley, chopped
2 tablespoons water
¹/₂ pound thinly sliced ham, cooked
2 cups cheddar cheese, shredded
I egg, slightly beaten
I tablespoon water**

On a lightly floured surface, roll each pastry sheet into a 12-inch square. Lay one sheet of pastry into a 10-inch pie plate and set aside. In a

Buddy Spicher (*far left*), one of the all-time great fiddlers, is pictured here fiddling with an elite group of bow masters. Joining Buddy at this 1970s festival are (*l-r, after Buddy*) Charlie Smith, Red Taylor, Dale Potter, and Roy Huskey, Jr., on bass fiddle.

skillet, melt the ¼ cup of butter until sizzling. Add the potatoes, onions, and salt and pepper. Cook the potatoes until crispy and tender and set aside. In a clean skillet, melt 1 tablespoon butter. In a mixing bowl, stir together the 6 eggs, parsley, and 2 tablespoons of water. Pour ½ the mixture into the skillet and cook on medium heat until the mixture sets (2 to 3 minutes). Slide the omelette onto a cookie sheet. Use the remaining 1 tablespoon of butter to regrease the skillet and cook the remaining omelette mixture.

Layer the ingredients onto the pastry sheet in the pie plate in the following order: 1 omelette, ¼ pound of the ham, ½ the fried potatoes, 1 cup of the cheese, then the remaining potatoes, ham, cheese, and omelette. Top with the other pastry and press the pastry edges together. Mix together beaten egg and 1 tablespoon water. Brush egg mixture over top and edges of the pastry just before cooking. Bake in a 375° oven for 30 to 35 minutes, or until golden brown; or cover and refrigerate overnight and bake the next morning. Note: If refrigerated overnight, let the torte stand 30 minutes at room temperature before baking.

Makes 6 servings.

Millie and Vassar Clements

GRAND OLE SCRAMBLED EGGS WITHOUT BUTTER

From the kitchen of the great Metropolitan Opera star and family friend, Lawrence Tibbett.

The Dillards pose on the set of the Taylor house interior on **The Andy Griffith Show** *during the early 1960s. Pictured are: (l-r) Rodney Dillard, Doug Dillard, Andy Griffith, Mitch Jayne, and Dean Webb. The group's appearances on the popular show helped introduce millions of TV viewers to bluegrass music.*

Photograph courtesy of Doug Dillard

The Dillards

It was "everybody on the truck" when the Dillards (Doug Dillard, Rodney Dillard, Mitch Jayne, and Dean Webb) left Salem, Missouri, in 1962 to pursue their dream of making a living in bluegrass. Though the trip was a struggle, the foursome quickly landed a record deal with Elektra Records when they arrived in California. However, their big break arrived in early 1963 when they were selected to play the Darling Boys on *The Andy Griffith Show*.

The Dillards appeared in a total of six episodes of the Griffith show during the next three-and-a-half years. Through the Darling family's visits to Mayberry, all of America came to know classic Dillards bluegrass tunes such as "Ebo Walker," "Dooley," "Hickory Hollow," "Doug's Tune," and "There Is a Time." To this day, reruns of *The Andy Griffith Show* continue to expose millions of people worldwide to the distinctive, beautiful music of the boys from the Ozarks.

While the Dillards were making a big splash on television, they were also rising to prominence on the bluegrass and folk music scenes. On stage, they backed their accomplished musicianship with Mitch's masterful storytelling, and with comedy and humor from all the band members.

The popularity of the Dillards made them an influence for other groups forming at the time. Members of legendary bands such as the Byrds, the Eagles, the Nitty Gritty Dirt Band, and New Grass Revival are among the many musicians who cite the importance of the Dillards's music.

In fact, it was after touring with the Byrds in 1968 that Doug Dillard left the group and joined with Byrds member Gene Clark to form the Dillard and Clark Expedition. Herb Pedersen replaced Doug in the Dillards for four years. When Herb left the group, Billy Ray Lathum and others joined the group, but after a few years, the group disbanded. Mitch Jayne retired to pursue his writing full time (his novel *Old Fish Hawk* was already being made into a movie by Twentieth Century Fox). By then, Rodney was looking to get off the road, and Dean was too, and so in the late '70s, the Dillards unofficially parked their truck. Rodney and Dean hooked up with Earl Scruggs for a couple of highly successful tours, then settled into steady local performances at Silver Dollar City in Branson, Missouri.

The original Dillards reunited for the *Return to Mayberry* movie in 1986 and have subsequently made several more reunion appearances in conjunction with other *Andy Griffith Show* celebrations. The Dillards toured again in the late 1980s (with the addition of Steve Cooley on banjo and, sometimes, Doug Dillard). They released two albums during this reunion period, including the critically acclaimed *Let It Fly*. The original Dillards reunited again in 1996 and 1997 for another successful tour.

This much is certain: Even back in the days when they were headed to California, or Mayberry, on a truck, one thing the Dillards have always done is "let it fly."

Use 2 eggs per person. Whip the eggs with 2 tablespoons cream per each 2 eggs. Heat a frying pan until very hot. Pour in the egg and cream mixture, stirring slowly. When the eggs start cooking, turn the heat to low and stir until the mixture is the consistency of a soft custard. Serve with paprika and fines herbes.

Buell Neidlinger
The Grass Is Greener

Bass player Buell Neidlinger has performed and recorded with a number of jazz musicians and is in great demand as a studio player for movie soundtracks. For over ten years, Buell has worked with Richard Greene in various groups; he is currently the bass player for Richard's bluegrass group, The Grass is Greener. Buell comes from a long line of cooks and uses recipes dating back to the early 1800s.

BLUE DIAMOND BREAKFAST BURRITOS

4 flour tortillas
4 eggs
2 tablespoons olive oil
Sour cream
Salsa

Salsa Ingredients:

½ cup scallions, chopped
¼ cup cilantro, chopped
3 tomatoes, chopped
1 red bell pepper, chopped
1 tablespoon rice vinegar
½ teaspoon peanut oil
½ teaspoon Tabasco sauce
Salt and pepper to taste

Mix all the salsa ingredients together in a bowl. Steam the tortillas. Fry the eggs in the olive oil. Wrap the eggs in the tortillas and serve with the salsa and sour cream on the side.

Makes enough salsa for 4 servings.

Dudley Connell
The Seldom Scene

CHARLIE'S RANCHO DEVILLE MIGAS

Back in the later part of the nineteenth century and into the twentieth, south Texas became a new home for many Eastern European immigrants. Polish, Czech, and German families settled in and around Texas towns such as Boerne, Fredericksburg, and San Antonio—bringing with them a rich culture that was infused into the already-rich Mexican-American culture of the region. The sounds of the accordion now melded with the sounds of the cowboy and Mexican guitars and became the music we know as Tex-Mex or conjunto. This Eastern European influence had a huge effect on the local cuisine as well. Because of this wonderful blending of cultures, we now include cheese and sour cream in recipes we call Tex-Mex.

2 tablespoons cooking oil
12 corn tortillas
4 fresh whole tomatillos, husks removed
14 ounces canned salsa verde (Herdez brand from Mexico is the best)
4 cloves garlic
12 green onions, chopped
Fresh cilantro
2 avocados
2 ripe tomatoes
10 free-range brown eggs

Though originally from Texas, guitar player Charles Sawtelle went to college in Colorado and decided he liked it there enough to stay. He played around the Denver/Boulder area with various bands—including the Monroe Doctrine, the Drifting Ramblers, and the Rambling Drifters—before joining with Pete Wernick and Tim O'Brien to form Hot Rize in 1978. After Hot Rize disbanded in 1990, Charles went on to produce projects by several Colorado groups; he has also toured and recorded with Peter Rowan and the Panama Red Riders. Charles currently fronts his own group, the Whippets.

Dash salt and pepper
1/8 cup half-and-half or milk
1/2 cup Monterey Jack cheese, grated

1. Warm up the hi-fi. Place a Flatt and Scruggs record on the turntable and play it.

2. Heat the oil in a skillet on medium heat; cook the tortillas one at a time until they become soft. Cool the tortillas on paper towels to soak up the excess oil. Cut 8 tortillas into 1-inch squares. Save 4 whole tortillas for later. Keep the skillet warm.

3. Blend the tomatillos and salsa verde in a food processor or blender; add the garlic, 6 of the chopped green onions, and a few sprigs of cilantro and blend again to make a thick sauce. Heat in a saucepan on low heat.

4. Cut the avocados in half, remove the seeds, and peel. Chop the avocados, tomatoes, and about 3/4 cup cilantro. Set aside.

5. Place some ovenproof serving plates in a warm oven with one whole tortilla per plate. Mix the eggs in a bowl using a fork; beat in the half-and-half and salt and pepper until smooth (scrambled eggs!). Pour the mixture into the warm skillet and cook over medium heat; use a spoon to blend in a little sauce and add the tortilla squares. Continue mixing to avoid burning. The eggs are done when they are light and fluffy—don't let them get rubbery or too dried out!

6. Spoon some of the green sauce onto each whole tortilla; heap the eggs onto the tortillas. Smother with more sauce. Grate the cheese over the eggs and top with the chopped avocados, tomatoes, remaining green onions, and cilantro. Serve immediately.

Makes 4 servings.

Charles Sawtelle

SKILLET CAMP BREAKFAST

1/2 pound sausage or bacon
6 red potatoes
1 medium onion
6 extra large eggs
Salt and pepper to taste

Cut the meat into bite-sized pieces and brown in a skillet over medium-high heat. "A good cast-iron skillet is best for cooking and later licking." Remove the meat from the skillet, leaving a little grease but draining most of it. Cut the potatoes and onion into bite-sized pieces that even Opie could eat. Cook the potatoes and onion in the skillet grease over medium-high heat until golden brown like the color of a Mayberry dirt road. Add salt and pepper to taste. Stir the meat into the potatoes and onion. Beat the eggs as if to scramble and pour into the skillet mixture. Stir frequently until the eggs are cooked. Serve while hot right from the skillet.

Some folks like ketchup on their Skillet Camp Breakfast, so put a bottle on the table. When you've scraped all you can, and if you don't choose to do the lickin', call your favorite dog and let it do the skillet lickin' for ya. You'll have a friend for life.

Makes 2 to 3 servings, plus leftovers for man's best friend.

Bruce Keedy
Flat Creek Skillet Lickers

JOHNSON MOUNTAIN CHEESE GRITS

4 cups milk
2 cups water
1½ cups quick grits
10 tablespoons butter
1 teaspoon salt
½ teaspoon cayenne pepper
1 cup cheddar cheese, grated
3 eggs, beaten

Preheat oven to 350°. Butter a 2-quart casserole dish. In a large saucepan, boil the milk and water. Add the grits and cook for 5 to 7 minutes. Mix the rest of the ingredients into the grits, then pour the mixture into the buttered dish. Bake for 30 to 40 minutes, or until the top is lightly browned.

Makes 8 servings.

Dudley Connell
The Seldom Scene

COUNTRY BOY CHEESE GRITS

4 cups boiling water
1 teaspoon salt
1 cup quick grits
½ stick margarine
2 cups (or more) sharp cheddar cheese, grated
3 eggs, well beaten

Cook the grits with the boiling water and salt for 2½ to 5 minutes. Remove from heat and stir the margarine, cheese, and eggs into the cooked grits. Pour the mixture into a greased 1½-quart baking dish. Bake at 350° for 30 to 40 minutes.

Makes 6 to 8 servings.

Glenn Tolbert

PENNY AND MIKE'S GRANOLA

If you want only certain items in your granola, it's easy to make your own. Experiment, using this as a starting point. My sister Penny gave me the basic recipe, which I have changed slightly.

3 cups rolled oats
1¼ cups (approximately) of a mixture of the following (Use roughly an equal amount of each. Sometimes I use only three of these—deleting either the wheat or the coconut.):
    Sunflower seeds (raw)
    Pumpkin seeds
    Wheat germ and bran
    Coconut
¼ cup canola, sunflower, or corn oil
¼ cup honey or maple syrup (a mixture of both is OK)
¼ teaspoon salt

Optional:

½ teaspoon ground cinnamon
½ teaspoon ground cardamom
¼ to ½ teaspoon ground nutmeg

Mix the grains and seeds in a shallow pan. The pan should be equivalent to about 15- by 12-inches. The grains should be about ½- to ¾-inch deep. Mix the oil, sweetening, and salt (and optional spices), then pour over the grains, mixing thoroughly. Bake at approximately 300° for 15 to 25 minutes, stirring about every 5 minutes, until toasted light brown. Allow the mixture to cool in the pan before putting in a storage canister. Note: Seeds can go rancid in warm weather, so use fresh stuff and either refrigerate or consume granola soon.

Makes about 8 to 10 servings.

Penny and Mike Seeger

SAIL AWAY BUCKWHEAT CAKES

1 package dry yeast
2½ cups buttermilk
1 teaspoon salt

2 cups buckwheat flour (old-fashioned, not
   self-rising)
½ cup cornmeal
1 teaspoon baking soda

Dissolve the yeast in lukewarm buttermilk.
Add salt. Stir in the buckwheat flour and cornmeal. Cover the bowl with a clean cloth and let
stand in a warm place overnight. The next morning, add the soda and beat well. Cook on a hot
griddle or skillet that has been slightly greased.
Turn when golden brown on the bottom, then
brown on the other side. Refrigerate left over
batter and use in the next making.
   Makes about 6 servings.

Tommy Jarrell

LEROY'S WILD RICE PANCAKES

While on the road in Minnesota, we heard of
a cafe that served "Wild Rice Pancakes." We
went out of our way to find the cafe, only to be
told they are only made on Friday. This was a
Monday. So LeRoy created his own recipe. It
has been a favorite of ours ever since, and while
on the road, LeRoy makes them at least once a
week.

1 cup "Krusteaz buttermilk pancake mix"
   (just add water)
¾ cup water
¾ cup cooked wild rice
½ package Sweet & Low
¼ cup pinon nuts

Mix all the ingredients. Heat a lightly oiled
pan to the point that a drop of water skittles
across the pan. Use ¼ cup of batter per 'cake
and make yummy pancakes.
   Makes 6 4-inch pancakes.

Janice and LeRoy McNees
Born Again Bluegrass Band

GINGER'S BANNA WAFFLES

½ cup self-rising flour
1 egg
1 teaspoon sugar

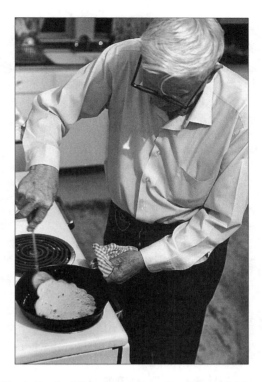

North Carolina's Tommy Jarrell was largely responsible
for a major resurgence of interest in old-time fiddle
playing among young musicians. In addition to being a
powerful fiddle player, Tommy also sang and played old-
time banjo. Born in 1901, he grew up in a time before
the advent of radio and recordings, and learned much of
his repertoire from the oral tradition of his community.
Tommy never performed as a professional but played
often in his home and for community events such as
dances and parties.

After he was "discovered" in the late 1960s, Tommy
Jarrell did make several recordings for County Records,
and in 1982 he received a National Heritage Fellowship
award. He was best known for his unique renditions of
regional tunes such as "Sail Away Ladies," "Drunken
Hiccups," and "Fortune." He is remembered as a
charismatic personality who readily opened his home to
the flood of young musicians who made the pilgrimage
to hear him play. Tommy's skill with a fiddle bow was not
lost in the kitchen. Here he serves up one of his famous
buckwheat pancakes for a hungry visitor.

Photograph by Alice Gerrard

½ cup milk
1½ tablespoons vegetable oil
1 small, peeled banana

Blend the flour, egg, sugar, and milk in a
blender on high. Add the vegetable oil and blend
again. Toss in the banana and blend until smooth.

Pour the batter into a heated waffle iron and bake. Serve hot with homemade maple syrup.

Makes 3 waffles.

Homemade Maple Syrup:

½ cup boiling water
I cup granulated sugar
I teaspoon maple flavoring or mapleine

To the boiling water, add the sugar and stir until dissolved. Remove from heat and stir in the maple flavoring. Serve on the hot banana waffles.

Ginger Boatwright

NEW LOST CITY CORN PANCAKES

1½ cups cornmeal
½ cup oat, whole wheat, or a similar flour
¾ teaspoon soda
1½ teaspoons baking powder
½ teaspoon salt
4 teaspoons Butter Buds butter flavoring
    (optional)
Grated peels of 2 medium oranges
    (preferably organic)
Juice of 2 oranges
Buttermilk (to supplement orange juice)
2 tablespoons canola, sunflower, or corn oil
2 egg whites, beaten almost stiff

To mix: Sift all the dry ingredients into a mixing bowl and blend thoroughly with a spoon. Wash and dry the oranges and then grate the peels down to the white—not too far, as you will juice the oranges next. Juice the oranges. Put the orange juice in a measuring cup and add enough buttermilk to make almost 1¾ cups.

Next, add the grated orange peel, orange juice mixture, and oil to the dry ingredients. Mix with as few strokes as possible—don't beat. (Note: Flours and buttermilks vary a lot, so you'll have to adjust the liquid amount a little. The batter should be a little thinner than vanilla pudding.) Add extra buttermilk, if necessary, and let sit for a couple of minutes, then fold in the beaten egg whites and cook immediately. I prefer a cast-iron pancake griddle. About 5 minutes before the batter is ready, set the heat at low to medium, so as to cook the cakes slowly. Put some canola oil (or other oil that you prefer) on a paper towel and spread evenly on the griddle. (This is a modern version of the old time "meatskin" that folks used to grease pans.)

Pour ¼ cup or so of the batter for each pancake. Turn once after the edges show slight evidence of cooking and the bottom is browned. Do not pat the pancake with your turner. Remove each pancake from the griddle after a minute or two, or when brown on the bottom. Don't turn it again. Eat it! Re-grease the griddle very lightly between each pancake. Eat 'em as they come off the griddle.

The orange rind and juice make the pancakes pretty tasty as they are, and a little butter or margarine can help them along, too. If you like, honey is a good sweetener, and a fancy addition can be a sprinkle of good white liquor with the honey. In absence of liquor, Grand Marnier will do OK.

Alexia and I find this recipe to be sufficient for our two healthy appetites.

Mike Seeger

KELEN'S BUBBLE BREAD

These are delicious sticky buns that are simple to make.

Mix the following:
½ stick butter or margarine, melted
½ cup brown sugar
½ to 1 cup pecans, chopped

Pour this mixture into the bottom of a Bundt or tube pan.

In a separate bowl, mix:
¾ stick butter or margarine, melted
¾ cup white sugar
I tablespoon ground cinnamon

You will also need:
I package frozen yeast rolls

Roll each of the dinner rolls in the second mixture. Place the rolls on top of the pecan mixture in the pan. Cover with waxed paper and let

Performing at the Merle Watson Festival are (l-r) Jimmy Gaudreau, Moondi Klein, T. Michael Coleman, and Mike Auldridge. Since they were all working in other bands at the time, this foursome originally formed Chesapeake as a second band where they could stretch out, experiment, and have fun. But Chesapeake proved to be more successful than they had dreamed, becoming a full-time group in 1995.

sit at room temperature overnight. In the morning, bake at 325° for 30 minutes.

Makes 8 to 12 servings.

Robin and T. Michael Coleman
Chesapeake

BLUE KENTUCKY GIRL COFFEECAKE

Cake ingredients:

1 stick butter
1 cup sugar
2 eggs
1 cup sour cream
2 cups all-purpose flour
1½ teaspoons baking powder
½ teaspoon baking soda
½ teaspoon salt
1 teaspoon vanilla extract
1 21-ounce can blueberry pie filling

Topping ingredients:
¼ cup butter
½ cup all-purpose flour
½ cup sugar

Preheat oven to 325°. In a large bowl, cream the butter and sugar. Add the eggs and sour cream and beat well. Sift together the flour, baking powder, baking soda, and salt. Add the dry ingredients and vanilla to the egg mixture. Pour ½ the batter into a greased 9- by 13-inch pan. Cover with the pie filling. Pour the rest of the batter on top of the filling. Take a knife and swirl it through the mixture. Mix the topping ingredients and sprinkle over the cake. Bake for 45 minutes.

Makes 9 to 12 servings.

Andrea Zonn

TWIN MOUNTAIN BLUEBERRY COFFEECAKE

A favorite from the *Great Island Cook Book*, New Castle Congregational Church (1965).

2 cups all-purpose flour
1 cup sugar
3 teaspoons baking powder
¼ teaspoon salt
½ cup shortening
2 eggs, beaten
1 cup milk
1½ cups blueberries
1⅓ cups flaked coconut

Doyle Lawson has a knack for unearthing hot young pickers and singers for his tight Quicksilver sound. When he's not playing music, Doyle likes to watch old Western movies. He's a member of the Roy Rogers fan club and is pictured here with his Roy Rogers, Trigger, and Dale Evans cookie jars (and his Happy Trails Christmas tree).

Preheat oven to 375°. In a large bowl, mix and sift the flour, sugar, baking powder, and salt. Cut in the shortening. Combine the eggs and milk; stir the mixture into the dry ingredients. Fold in the blueberries. Divide the batter between 2 greased 9-inch layer cake pans. Sprinkle coconut evenly on the tops. Bake at 375° for 25 minutes, or until brown on top. Serve warm as coffeecake or for dessert. (We like it warm the best.)

At our house, if all 4 of us are present, it serves 4.

Suzanne and Doyle Lawson

THE ART AND APPRECIATION OF WEEKEND MORNING PANCAKES

For me, pancakes are soul food. Some of my earliest and happiest memories are of Saturday mornings eating the pancakes my dad made while we listened to Big John and Sparky on the radio. By the time I was around nine, my dad showed me the treasured family recipe, which as it turns out is about the same as most pancake recipes. Many weekend mornings since then have carried on the tradition, complete with the fine smells from the griddle and the fun and challenge of well-executed monogrammed pancakes.

The recipe (about right for 3 medium-hungry people or one voracious one):

1 cup all-purpose flour
1 egg
1 cup milk (can be whole, skim, or made from dry mix)
1 tablespoon sugar
1 teaspoon baking powder
½ teaspoon salt
1 tablespoon melted butter or margarine

The sugar, salt, and baking powder can be altered for differing degrees of sweetness, saltiness, and fluffiness. The butter or margarine is necessary for the cakes not to stick to the griddle (oil is not used in the cooking). Add more to taste or limit it in the interest of not having to "wear it" tomorrow!

Before combining the ingredients, I start heating the griddle. I use a family heirloom, a magnesium griddle big enough to cover two burners. A big cast-iron frying pan is OK too, or any frying pan'll do in a pinch. Heat on high for a minute, then pull down to a shade under medium. The griddle is ready when drops of water dance on it, not just sizzle and fizzle in one place. While the griddle is heating, blend the ingredients.

I add all the ingredients right into a quart pitcher—flour first, and then the rest of the dry ingredients. Then, use the flour measuring cup to add milk (and get any stray flour). Before beating the egg and adding it, put the unmelted butter in a small dish in the microwave. It's melted and not burned in about 10 to 15 seconds, long enough to beat and add the egg before adding the butter. Mix the batter with a large spoon, mashing out the bigger lumps on the side of the pitcher. The batter should be well mixed, but small lumps are no problem.

One thing I like about making pancakes is that you can have them on the griddle about 5 minutes after you decide to make them.

Griddle Techniques

If you mixed the batter in a pitcher, you can just pour out your cakes while catching drips with the mixing spoon (though drips can be fun too—they have their appeal as garnishes next to the full cakes). As you pour, be aware that the cake will grow a little after you stop pouring. With time and experience, your aim and finesse will improve so that you can achieve the ideal of eight 4- to 5-inch-diameter cakes not touching on a two-burner griddle.

On the first pour, be especially aware of griddle temperature. If it's too hot, the batter will be a little noisy and splatter a bit as it lands. If it's not hot enough, it will seem to take forever before the little bubbles appear on the tops. Adjust the burner temperature as soon as you're aware it needs it, and keep your eye on it throughout cooking. The right temperature will give you fine-looking golden brown cakes.

When the top of a cake has been pretty well bubbled and has even started to look a little dry, it's time to flip. You can peek to check, but if it's not ready to flip, you'll find it won't cook as well or as quickly after you've checked it. It's better to go just by looking at the tops.

Flipping technique comes with experience. Larger cakes are harder to land evenly and accurately. All pancake chefs have had to deal with a raw underside messing up a perfectly good, almost-done cake on the griddle. The consolation for these inescapable occasional blunders is that at least they taste good, and they can be stuck somewhere in the middle of the stack. Don't ask, don't tell.

A folded cake on the griddle should be corrected as quickly as possible by maneuvering it so that the entire uncooked side is face down. Again, it's ugly, but it's edible. Cooked, splattery-thin edges can be trimmed and given to Fido. Any batter on the spatula should be rinsed off pronto.

The Monogrammed Cake

For that someone special (yourself included, if that's the way you feel), a monogrammed cake at the top of the stack is a special surprise and honor that always gets a happy reaction—especially when the letter is well executed.

For the letter to come out right, of course, it must be poured backwards onto the griddle. It's also important that the thickness of the letter's lines be fairly uniform and not blobby. This is not easy, especially when pouring from a pitcher or using a large spoon. A small spoon is preferred—or, for the really ambitious (it's almost cheating), a paper funnel or a regular funnel with a small hole.

Once again, experience is a great teacher when

Pete Wernick (a.k.a. Doctor Banjo) is a jack of all bluegrass trades. He is president of IBMA, has written several bluegrass instruction books and songbooks, and conducts regular banjo camps (where students can spend a week of intensive study in a cool place.) A member of the acclaimed band Hot Rize for twelve years, he continues to perform with various groups, including Live Five, a group that combines Dixieland jazz with Colorado bluegrass. Members of Live Five are (l-r) Rich Moore, Kris Ditson, Pete Wernick, Joe Lukasik, and George Weber.

it comes to well-formed letters. Remember, as before, that the batter spreads a bit after pouring. Keep the pour thin and uniform, and keep moving. One big blob and the letter will be indiscernible, or bogus at best, so give up and just pour a regular cake over your mishap, then try again. Drips are OK—just clear them after they've cooked a little.

If you've got a good letter down, be sure not to get too eager. Take your time and let it cook even a little more than a regular cake. Many a great monogram has been rendered inconsequential due to poor contrast. You want the letter rather brown to allow it to stand out from the surrounding cake.

When it's finally time, pour carefully to cover and surround the letter. You want some fresh batter around all the edges of the letter, but not so much as to make a huge, hard-to-flip cake. Also, beware of odd shapes created by careless over-pouring. The standard circle, not oversized, is ideal. For best results, start with a thin pour of the border, then fill in.

If all has gone well thus far, the main thing to do is stay confident and patient. Wait the normal time and look for the bubbly top of the second pour (not the monogram), without premature checking. I often reserve half the griddle space for a monogrammed cake, while working the other half as normal. The last thing you want is for a flipping error to mess up a carefully crafted monogrammed cake.

Finishing Touches

True maple syrup is my favorite, but there are many good choices. In any case, don't use it straight out of the refrigerator. Either take it out early or warm it in a pitcher in the microwave. You can add butter, but remember there's already butter in the cakes; the goodness of pancakes needn't create a high-fat situation.

If the pancakes are hot and good, hell, you don't need syrup. And there's nothing one bit wrong with grabbing one and eating it in the way you would a piece of fresh bread. In fact, it's the cook's prerogative. I'm sure Big John and Sparky would agree.

Pete Wernick

Mark Your Calendar Matching Quiz

Match the bluegrass artist to his birthday.

1. Bill Monroe	A. January 6, 1924
2. Lester Flatt	B. February 25, 1927
3. Carter Stanley	C. February 13, 1927
4. Jesse McReynolds	D. August 10, 1927
5. Sonny Osborne	E. September 13, 1911
6. Charlie Waller	F. May 17, 1925
7. Don Reno	G. June 19, 1914
8. Ralph Stanley	H. October 29, 1937
9. Mac Wiseman	I. December 7, 1931
10. Jim McReynolds	J. August 27, 1925
11. Doc Watson	K. February 21, 1927
12. Earl Scruggs	L. January 19, 1935
13. Bobby Osborne	M. May 23, 1925
14. Red Smiley	N. July 9, 1929
15. Jimmy Martin	O. March 3, 1923

Answers: 1. E; 2. G; 3. J; 4. N; 5. H; 6. L; 7. K; 8. B; 9. M; 10. C; 11. O; 12. A; 13. I; 14. F; 15. D

ENTREES

MOTHER MAYBELLE'S STUFFED CHICKEN WITH VEGETABLES

2 cups water
1 3½-pound chicken (pullet) with giblets and liver
2 ribs celery, chopped
2 large onions, chopped
½ tablespoon olive oil
½ pound bulk mild country sausage, cooked
1½ cups white bread or corn bread crumbs (use corn bread left over from the night before)
1 teaspoon fresh parsley, chopped
Pinch of ground allspice
Salt and pepper
1 tablespoon sage
1 stick butter
8 small onions (for just being pretty)
6 or 8 small potatoes or 4 large potatoes, peeled and cubed
4 slices good quality lean bacon

Boil the giblets and liver in water; reserve cooking water. Chop the cooked giblets and liver. Sauté the celery and chopped onion in olive oil until onion is tender. Mix the celery and onion with the sausage, bread crumbs, parsley, allspice, salt, pepper, and sage. Stuff this in the cavity of the chicken with the cooked giblets and liver. Pour the 2 cups of reserved cooking water over the stuffing to soften it.

Melt the butter in a large baking dish or Dutch oven. Put the chicken in center. Place the whole onions and potatoes around the chicken. Cut the bacon in ¼-inch squares and dot over the vegetables. Season the vegetables with salt and pepper. Cover and cook in a 350° oven for 1 hour and 20 minutes.

Makes 4 servings.

Mother Maybelle Carter

In 1927, Mother Maybelle Carter performed as one-third of the original Carter Family, along with brother-in-law A.P. and his wife Sara, on one of the first commercial recordings of country music in Bristol, Tennessee. Maybelle's unique guitar style was as much a trademark of the legendary Carter Family sound as was A.P.'s prolific songwriting and the women's distinctive mountain harmonies.
Photograph courtesy of the Vicki Langdon Collection

Mother Maybelle Carter and the Carter Sisters became an all-female band in 1943. Three years later, they became stars of the Old Dominion Barn Dance in Richmond, Virginia. Later, they were members of the Tennessee Barn Dance, the Ozark Jubilee, and then the Grand Ole Opry. Pictured here are (l-r) June Carter, Mother Maybelle, Anita Carter, and Helen Carter posing with the autoharp, guitar, bass, and accordion.
Photograph courtesy of the Vicki Langdon Collection

HELEN'S DRUNK CHICKEN

I serve the chicken and gravy over hot cooked rice.

I 3-pound broiler-fryer chicken, whole or
   cut up
Seasoned salt
4 potatoes, cut up
2 onions, quartered
6 carrots, quartered
¼ cup white wine
I or 2 tablespoons cornstarch (depending
   on amount of drippings)
Enough water to make a paste with
   cornstarch
I 6-ounce can sliced mushrooms, drained
   (optional)

Sprinkle the chicken all over with seasoned salt. Bake in a casserole dish at 350° for 40 minutes. Remove the casserole dish from the oven and add the potatoes, onions, and carrots. Return the casserole dish to the oven.

After about 30 minutes, add the wine. Continue cooking the chicken for about 15 minutes. Remove the chicken and vegetables to a platter.

In a tightly covered jar, shake the cornstarch and water to blend, then gradually stir mixture into the drippings in the casserole dish. Bring to a boil; boil and stir for 1 minute until gravy is thickened. Stir in the mushrooms.

Makes 4 servings.

Helen Carter

GINGER'S ROWDY CHICKEN RANCHERO

I medium onion, chopped
I stick butter or margarine
4 large chicken breast halves (boil about I
   hour and 15 minutes, then bone)
I 10¾-ounce can cream of mushroom soup
I 10¾-ounce can cream of chicken soup
I 12-ounce can evaporated milk
I to 2 tablespoons juice from jalapeño
   peppers
I package flour tortillas
2 cups cheddar cheese, grated
2 tablespoons canned jalapeño peppers,
   sliced

In a large skillet, sauté the onion in the butter. Add the chicken, soups, milk, and juice from the jalapeño peppers. Simmer 15 minutes. Line a buttered casserole dish with tortillas. Add a layer of the soup-and-chicken mixture and top with cheese. Repeat. Decorate the top with sliced jalapeños. Bake at 350° until the cheese melts, about 20 minutes.

Makes 6 servings.

Ginger Boatwright

EVERY WEDENSDAY NIGHT GRILLED CHICKEN SAUCE

Also good for every Thursday, Friday, and Saturday night.

I cup cider vinegar
2 tablespoons salt
½ stick butter
½ cup cooking oil
4 teaspoons Tabasco sauce
5 teaspoons Worcestershire sauce

Combine all the ingredients and bring to a boil. Put the chicken on the grill and baste with this sauce.

Makes about 2 cups of sauce.

Hubert Davis

JOSH'S GENIE IN THE WINE CHICKEN WELLINGTON

I 13¼-ounce can chicken broth
¾ cup white wine
I teaspoon seasoned salt
6 chicken breast halves
I package Pepperidge Farm frozen pastry
    shells, thawed
Garlic powder, optional
I½ cups cheddar cheese, shredded
3 tablespoons butter
4 tablespoons flour
Dash of ground nutmeg
2 tablespoons lemon juice
3 cloves garlic, crushed

In a large pan, combine the broth, wine, and seasoned salt. Heat wine mixture. Add the chicken and simmer for 20 minutes. Remove the chicken and save the broth. Remove the chicken from the bone and cut into bite-sized pieces. On a floured board, roll out pastry shells about 3 inches larger than original size. In each shell, put a handful of chicken, then sprinkle with garlic powder and cheese. Fold dough over and pinch edges together like a turnover. Bake on an ungreased baking sheet at 400° for 30 minutes, or until brown. To make sauce, melt the butter and stir in flour. Add the broth, nutmeg, lemon juice, and garlic. Cook the sauce over medium heat, stirring until thickened. To serve, pour some sauce on a plate, add a pastry, and cover with more sauce. (This may not be that easy to make, but the taste is well worth the effort.)

Makes 6 servings.

Robin and T. Michael Coleman
Chesapeake

FIDDLIN' MAN'S FABULOUS CHICKEN

4 boneless chicken breast halves
I package dry onion soup mix
I 12-ounce can whole cranberry sauce
½ cup creamy French dressing
2 tablespoons vinegar
3 or 4 tablespoons brown sugar

In a non-stick skillet, brown the chicken on each side. Lay the chicken in a single layer in a greased baking dish. Mix together the onion soup mix, cranberry sauce, French dressing, vinegar, and brown sugar. Pour the mixture over the chicken. Cover and bake at 350° for approximately 1 hour. Uncover, baste, and return to the oven for 15 minutes until well glazed. Serve with your favorite vegetables.

Makes 4 servings.

Paula and Buddy Spicher

THE DIXIE DEWDROP'S CHICKEN AND DUMPLINGS

Uncle Dave Macon was my grandfather. We affectionately called him "Pap." He was well known for his love of country ham, but it was his favorite breakfast meat. His favorite dinner food was chicken and dumplings.

Early Grand Ole Opry superstar Uncle Dave Macon rears back and plucks another tune in this 1940 photo of the "Dixie Dewdrop."

I remember the delicious Sunday dinners we ate with Pap and my grandmother when I was a girl. My grandmother was afflicted with severe asthma and was unable to perform household chores. A hired cook and housekeeper would be on duty with instructions to cook by the recipes my grandmother had always used.

In the summertime, there were always plenty of fresh vegetables, pone corn bread, and home-made custard and fruit pies.

After our meal in winter, we would sit by a fireplace in the family room. If it was in the summertime, Pap and the rest of us would go outside and sit under a big oak tree. Often he would read his fan mail that he had picked up at the Opry on Saturday night. If we requested, he would entertain us with his banjo. Sometimes he would lie down and rest in a lounge chair on the porch because he knew come Monday morning, he would be on the road again to do what he loved best—playing and singing for his fans.

I am happy to note that he appeared on the Grand Ole Opry, singing and playing his beloved banjo, until three weeks before his death in 1952 at age eighty-one. My grandfather truly had a long and rewarding life.

1 large fryer chicken, cut up
1 teaspoon salt
1 rib celery, chopped (optional)
2 tablespoons butter
1 chicken flavored bouillon cube
1½ cups warm water

Place the chicken in a stewing pot and cover with water. As the water starts to boil, skim off scum. Add the salt and celery, cover the pot, and boil for about 1 hour, or until chicken is fork-tender. While the chicken is cooking, dissolve the bouillon cube in the 1½ cups warm water. Remove the chicken from the broth. Add the butter and dissolved bouillon to the broth. Leave the broth on the heat and bring to a rolling boil. Then add the dumplings.

Dumplings:

3 cups all-purpose flour
1 teaspoon baking soda
1 teaspoon salt
3 tablespoons shortening
¾ cup chilled water (approximately)
Black pepper

Sift the flour, baking soda, and salt into a mixing bowl. Cut in the shortening with a pastry blender. Slowly add chilled water until no flour is left dry, but be cautious that the dough doesn't get too wet. Divide the dough and roll thin on a floured board. Cut dough into strips about 1-inch wide and 4-inches long. Repeat for the remaining half of dough. Slightly stretch each strip before dropping into boiling broth. Sprinkle black pepper over the top, put the lid on, lower the heat, and gently boil for 15 minutes. Remove the bone and skin from the chicken and cut the meat into pieces. Add the meat to dumplings in the broth.

Makes 6 servings.

Mary Macon Doubler
Granddaughter of Uncle Dave Macon

CHICKEN IN THE PIE PAN

6 chicken leg quarters
I small jar dried beef (optional)
3 boiled eggs
I 15-ounce can green peas and carrots (drained)
I 10¾-ounce can mushroom soup
I 10¾-ounce can celery soup
2 soup cans water

Boil the leg quarters. Take out the bones and place the meat in the bottom of a large greased casserole dish. Sometimes I place dried beef over the chicken. Slice the eggs and place the egg slices on the chicken. Mix the vegetables, soups, and water, and pour this mixture over the chicken.

Mix:

I stick melted margarine
2 cups flour
2 cups milk

Pour this mixture over the chicken mixture and bake in a 400° oven until it is slightly brown on the edges. (I like to cook this in a large oven pan because it seems to brown better, but don't overcook it.)

This is a very favorite of my children, grand-children, and husband.

Makes about 8 servings.

Polly Lewis Copsey
The Lewis Family

MOONLIGHTER CHICKEN POT PIE

This is one of my previous cookbook entries. It's from 1988, when my son, Kegan, was in kin-dergarten. All of the children were asked to give their own version of their mom's recipe. Those were my "Moonlighter" days—guess it shows.—Claire Lynch

"She gets it from Kroger and she takes it out of the box and puts it in the oven and cooks it for 3 hours. Then she takes it out and puts it on the table and lets it cool. It's real hot. It has peas and chicken and sometimes beef inside."

Kegan Lynch

FINGER-ROLL CHICKEN BREASTS

This is Jeff's favorite.

4 to 6 chicken breast halves
I 4-ounce package dried beef
½ pint sour cream
I 11-ounce can cream of mushroom soup

Wrap some dried beef around each chicken breast. Place the chicken in a buttered baking dish. Spread a layer of sour cream over the beef and chicken. Spread cream of mushroom soup on top of the sour cream. Bake uncovered at 300° for 1½ hours.

Makes 4 to 6 servings.

Jeff and Sheri Easter

Husband and wife Jeff and Sheri Easter form an incredible blend of bluegrass and Southern gospel. Jeff is not only noted for his singing, but can play almost every stringed instrument. Sheri, who was born into the legendary Lewis Family, has twice been named Favorite Female Vocalist by the Society for the Preservation of Bluegrass Music in America.

Virtuoso John Hartford's solo show is as fine as any in bluegrass. He accompanies his singing with the banjo, fiddle, and guitar—usually while dancing on a piece of sand-covered plywood. Widely known for penning the often-recorded and performed "Gentle on My Mind," John, a licensed riverboat captain, is perhaps most at home when he's near the water with a banjo on his knee.

IMPERIAL CHICKEN ROMP

4 boneless chicken breast halves
$^3/_4$ cup margarine, melted
2 cloves garlic, pressed
I cup fine dry bread crumbs
$^2/_3$ cup grated Parmesan cheese
$^1/_4$ cup fresh parsley, minced
I teaspoon salt
$^1/_4$ teaspoon pepper
Juice of 2 lemons
Paprika

Flatten the chicken out between two pieces of waxed paper. Combine the margarine and garlic, stirring well. Set aside. Combine the bread crumbs, cheese, parsley, salt, and pepper, then stir well. Dip the chicken in the margarine mixture and coat with the bread-crumb mixture. Fold the long sides of the chicken together, bring the short ends over, and secure with a toothpick. Place the chicken rolls, seam side down, in a greased 9- by 13- by 2-inch pan. Sprinkle the chicken with lemon juice and paprika. Bake at 350° for 1 hour, or until done.

Makes 4 servings.

Marie and John Hartford

HAPPY VALLEY CHICKEN DELIGHT

4 chicken breast halves
I 10$^3/_4$-ounce can cream of mushroom soup
I 14$^1/_2$-ounce can chicken broth
$^1/_2$ teaspoon onion flakes

Combine all the ingredients in a medium-sized pot and cook over medium-high heat, stirring occasionally, for about 1 hour, or until the chicken is done. Serve over rice.

Makes 4 servings.

Charles Bailey
The Bailey Brothers

The Bailey Brothers, one of the pioneering groups of bluegrass, were being influenced by the music of Bill Monroe as early as the late 1940s. With Charlie on mandolin and Danny on guitar, the brothers and their Happy Valley Boys made many popular recordings. They performed for years on the Grand Ole Opry and later on Knoxville radio stations. Charlie continues to lead the Tennessee-based band and carry the bluegrass torch.

New Jersey native Ralph Rinzler was a major player in revitalizing bluegrass and traditional music during its most difficult years–following the advent of rock 'n' roll in the 1950s. Rinzler was a musician himself, playing mandolin with the Greenbriar Boys, but he is remembered today more for introducing such relatively unknown artists as Bill Monroe and Doc Watson to a whole new audience during the folk revival of the '60s. Rinzler not only helped Monroe and Watson gain an extensive new fan base by booking them at events like the Newport and Chicago folk festivals, he also brought them to the attention of popular folk-oriented musicians of the day, such as Joan Baez and Bob Dylan. After relocating to Washington, D.C., Rinzler became active in bringing bluegrass artists to that area and served for a number of years as director of the Smithsonian Institute's annual Festival of American Folklife. Rinzler's contributions to bluegrass, folk, and traditional music are too numerous to list. He remained an active scholar, supporter, player, and fan of the music until his death in 1994.

HOW FAR TO LITTLE ROCK CORNISH GAME HENS WITH ORANGE GLAZE

Cornish game hens
Orange slices
Frozen orange juice concentrate
New potatoes
Carrots or squash, cut into chunks
Onions, cut into chunks
Celery, cut into chunks

Stuffing:

Pre-cooked wild rice and brown rice in equal proportions (about 1 cup per hen)
Chopped onion and game hen giblets fried in olive oil
Raisins (I like them; Ralph did not)
Chopped parsley
Poultry seasoning (very little)

Chestnuts, split, boiled, peeled, and crumbled (optional)

Cook one bird per person (you'll have leftovers). After stuffing the hens, place them in a large baking pan. Cover them with sliced oranges and pour a few tablespoons of partially defrosted frozen orange juice over the birds. Bake at 350° for about 1 hour, along with new potatoes, carrots or squash chunks, onions, and celery. Baste with the orange juice mixture from the pan. Do not crowd the hens, or they'll take longer to cook. Serve with a mixed-greens salad.

Since I was an inveterate improviser, Ralph occasionally had to eat one of what he called my "peanut butter and fish" recipes. At other times, we wished that I had written down my ingredients. This was one meal that always met with a warm approval.

Kate (Mrs. Ralph) Rinzler

CHICKEN REEL MARINADE

This marinade can be used on chicken sections, with or without skin, on roast leg of lamb, or on thinly sliced chicken or beef.

Garlic clove, pressed through a garlic press
Low sodium soy sauce
Worcestershire sauce
Lemon juice
Honey
Olive oil

You know best what proportions suit your taste. Ralph liked the garlic to predominate. I use about equal portions of soy sauce and lemon juice, with a dash of Worcestershire. The honey provides a slight sweetening and helps to brown the meat as it broils. The olive oil aids moisture retention. For a more oriental flavor, use toasted sesame oil. This marinade works rather fast, even 10 minutes imparts flavor, and it can be used to baste the meat as it broils. It is also delicious when the meat is marinated for longer periods of time. A leg of lamb would take overnight.

Ralph often cooked with me, and one way that he broiled chicken was with a coating of Gulden's or Grey Poupon mustard mixed with a little honey. Fresh lemon wedges provided additional flavor.

Hazel Dickens tells this story on Ralph and me: Early in our marriage, Ralph invited Ralph Stanley and the Clinch Mountain Boys over for dinner. (He typically gave me little or no notice on such occasions, and I took it in stride. I was either Mrs. Cool, or ignorance was bliss.) When the entourage arrived, there was no food in evidence, and I announced that I was going shopping for chicken and leeks. This contrasted gravely with Hazel's perception of what was required—fried chicken, beans, potato salad, coleslaw, and homemade cake, at least, and well on the way to the table. She says that Ralph was visibly upset. In due course, and much faster than Hazel had imagined it could be done, I produced broiled, marinated chicken and leek soup with accompaniments. Hazel is very polite, and she says that the dinner was eventually delicious. The above recipe, along with the leek soup recipe on page 27, reflects what I probably cooked.

Kate (Mrs. Ralph) Rinzler

CONSENSUS CORNMEAL-CRUSTED OVEN-FRIED CHICKEN

We were served this at the home of Tom and Lenora White while visiting Charleston, South Carolina. We loved it so much that we begged for the recipe! It takes a little work, but if you like something with a little spice, Cajun-style, you won't be sorry you tried this.

³/4 cup buttermilk
1 teaspoon lemon zest, freshly grated
¹/3 cup fresh lemon juice
¹/4 cup olive oil
2 shallots, minced
1 tablespoon fresh thyme leaves
2 teaspoons salt
1¹/2 teaspoons cayenne pepper
1 3-pound chicken, cut into 8 pieces (works with 8 boneless chicken breast halves as well)
³/4 cup yellow cornmeal
¹/2 cup fine dry bread crumbs
¹/4 cup Parmesan cheese, freshly grated
2 tablespoons fresh parsley leaves
¹/2 teaspoon paprika
Egg wash, made by beating 2 large eggs with 2 tablespoons cold water and 1 tablespoon fresh lemon juice
3 tablespoons unsalted butter, melted

The night before:

In a large bowl, whisk together the buttermilk, lemon zest, lemon juice, oil, shallots, thyme, 1 teaspoon of salt, and 1 teaspoon cayenne. Add the chicken, stirring to coat it with the marinade. Cover and refrigerate chicken. Let chicken marinate overnight, stirring occasionally. (If you decide that you want to fix it the same evening, let it marinate at least 3 hours.)

The night of the dinner:

Preheat oven to 425°. In another large bowl, combine the cornmeal, bread crumbs, Parmesan cheese, parsley, the remaining 1 teaspoon salt, paprika, and the remaining ½ teaspoon cayenne. Remove the chicken from the marinade with a slotted spoon, letting the excess marinade drop

One of the most dedicated bridge-builders in bluegrass music is the group Special Consensus, led by banjo-playing founder Greg Cahill. The group, nominated for multiple Grammy Awards and now working on its third decade together, gracefully spans the bluegrass waters with a crisp repertoire of both traditional and contemporary sounds that can connect well with any audience. Pictured here are Special Consensus members (l-r) Colby Maddox, Greg Cahill, Diana Phillips, and Bobby Burns.

off. Dip the chicken in the egg wash and dredge it in the cornmeal mixture, shaking off the excess. Arrange the chicken in one layer on a rack and let it dry for 30 minutes. The chicken may be prepared up to 6 hours in advance and kept chilled and covered loosely. Arrange the chicken, skin side up, in one layer on a lightly-oiled glass dish. Drizzle the butter over the chicken and bake in the middle of the oven for 35 minutes, or until it is crisp and golden. Transfer the chicken to paper towels to drain. Serve immediately, or at room temperature.

Makes 4 to 6 servings.

Jackie and Greg Cahill
Special Consensus

GOLDEN COUNTRY FRIED CHICKEN

1 fryer chicken, cut up
Seasoning: salt, pepper, Accent (approx.
 ½ tsp. each)
1 cup buttermilk
1½ cups flour
Vegetable oil

Season the cut-up fryer chicken with salt, pepper, and Accent. Put chicken in a large bowl and cover with buttermilk. Remove the chicken from the buttermilk and roll it in flour. Drop the chicken into a fryer of hot oil. Cook until golden brown.

Makes 4 to 6 servings.

John "Doodle" Thrower
and the Golden River Grass

SOUND AND CURRY CHICKEN

Signifrying nothing.

1 small onion, chopped
½ green and/or red bell pepper, chopped
3 cloves garlic, chopped
1 tablespoon olive oil or seasoned oil
1 fryer chicken, cut up and skinned, or 5
 skinned chicken breast halves
Pinch of saffron
2 cups instant brown rice, uncooked
2¼ cups water
2 teaspoons curry powder

Preheat oven to 350°. Lightly spray a 9- by

In 1980, John "Doodle" Thrower and the Golden River Grass included (l-r) Bill Kee, Gene Daniell, Doodle Thrower, James Watson, and Lynn Elliott. Thrower was a Georgia humorist, harmonica player, instrumentalist, and singer who led his musical group for over forty years and was featured in *Appalachian Journey* on PBS.

Photograph courtesy of Randall Franks Collection

13-inch casserole dish with cooking spray. In a skillet, sauté the onion, pepper, and garlic in oil until tender. Add the chicken and sauté until just browned. Remove the chicken from the skillet and arrange in the casserole dish. Sprinkle the pinch of saffron on the sautéed onion mix and cook for just a minute to release the flavor. Mix the rice, water, and curry powder in a bowl. Add the rice mixture to the onion, pepper, and garlic. Mix thoroughly and pour over the chicken. Cover with foil and bake for approximately 40 minutes. During cooking time, check to make sure the rice is not drying out.

Makes 4 to 6 servings, usually with some leftovers, unless they're really big eaters.

Taffy and Gary Ferguson

CURRIED KISSIMMEE CHICKEN AND RICE

4 tablespoons butter
1½ teaspoons salt
¼ teaspoon lemon juice
Curry powder to taste
2 pounds chicken pieces, or 5 breast halves
½ cup sliced almonds
1 cup cream
1 cup uncooked rice
2 cups hot chicken stock

Preheat oven to 350°. Melt the butter in a casserole dish. Stir in the seasonings. Add the chicken, turn, and coat well with the seasoned butter. Cook on the stove over medium heat for 5 minutes. Stir in the almonds and cream. Cover and bake for 30 minutes. Add the rice and chicken stock. Recover and bake 20 minutes longer. Uncover and continue baking for 10 minutes. Remove from the oven and serve.

Makes 4 to 5 servings.

Millie and Vassar Clements

BEPPE'S CHICKEN WITH ARTICHOKES (POLLO AI CARCIOFI)

This is a personal recipe inspired by Zia Maria (Aunt Mary), my great cooking "guru," who supervised the compilation of my cookbook, *Beppe Cooks*.

Pennsylvanian Gary Ferguson is a tasty singer who has contributed a number of strong original songs to the contemporary bluegrass repertoire, including the powerful Civil War song "Last Day at Gettysburg," also recorded by Larry Sparks. The Gary Ferguson Band includes (l-r) James Bailey on banjo, Gary on guitar, Tom Gray on bass, and Ron Pennington on mandolin.

2 pounds boneless, skinless chicken breasts
2 cups black olives with pit
2 cloves garlic
1 large onion
8 tablespoons extra virgin olive oil
Salt and pepper to taste
1 bottle dry white wine
5 medium artichokes
Juice of 2 lemons
1 bunch parsley
½ cup pine nuts

Cut the chicken breasts into bite-size pieces. Pit ½ of the olives and chop them. Chop the garlic and ½ of the onion. Brown the chicken breasts in a skillet with at least 4 tablespoons oil. Add the garlic, chopped onion, chopped olives, salt, and pepper. Add a glass of white wine and the rest of the olives, then reduce the flame.

Meanwhile, clean and trim the artichokes to the tender hearts, cut them into 8 pieces, and store the hearts in water with the lemon juice to avoid turning black. Chop the remaining onion, the parsley, and the pine nuts (some may stay whole). In a separate skillet, sauté the artichokes with at least 4 tablespoons of oil, along with the remaining onion, parsley, and pine nuts. When the artichokes are well sautéed, add the whole contents of the skillet to the pan with the chicken. Stir all together and cook at medium heat for at least 45 minutes while adding white wine and stirring from time to time (the food needs to be only half submerged in liquid).

Toward the end of the cooking time, adjust the salt and pepper and let liquid reduce a little without adding more wine. (If the ingredients aren't tasty enough, add 1 tablespoon chicken bouillon.) Turn off the heat and wait 5 minutes before serving with Italian-style bread.

Makes 4 servings.

Time: 1½ hours
Level of difficulty: quite easy
Suggested wines: Gutturnio, Barbera, or Bonarda.
Suggested listening: Hot Rize's *Radio Boogie*, Dreadful Snakes' *Snakes Alive*, or Beppe Gambetta's *Good News From Home*.

Beppe Gambetta

KIM'S THANKS A LOT CHICKEN

1½ to 2 pounds boneless chicken pieces
3 sleeves Ritz crackers
2 sticks butter
8 ounces sour cream
1 10¾-ounce can cream of chicken soup
½ cup chicken broth

Boil the chicken for approximately 10 minutes. Crush the Ritz crackers in a large bowl. Melt the butter and mix with the crackers. Put ½ of the cracker mixture in the bottom of a 9-by 13-inch pan. Bake at 350° until browned (approximately 10 to 15 minutes). Mix the sour cream, soup, and broth. Cut the chicken into bite-sized pieces and mix into the sour cream mixture. Pour the mixture onto the Ritz crackers in the pan. Cover with the remaining crackers. Bake at 350° for ½ hour. Great with Mexicorn.

Makes 6 servings.

Ronnie McCoury
The Del McCoury Band

HILLBILLY ROCKIN' CHICKEN CASSEROLE

3 or 4 chicken breast halves, boiled, cooled, boned, and cut into bite-sized pieces.
Salt and pepper to taste
1 10¾-ounce can cream of chicken soup
1 10¾-ounce can cream of celery soup
1 10¾-ounce can cream of mushroom soup
1 cup uncooked white rice
2 cups water
Butter

Guitarist Beppe Gambetta was born in Genoa, Italy, and began his career in a classical music orchestra. In 1977, he founded the Italian bluegrass group Red Wine. He tours frequently in the United States and has released several albums on U.S. labels. In 1995, Beppe's first instructional video was released by Homespun video, and in 1996, his first cookbook, *Beppe Cooks! Recipes from the Homeland*, was published by Herring Press. *Beppe Cooks!* not only includes tantalizing recipes like the one he's cooking here in Charles Sawtelle's kitchen, but also suggested listening for your dinner party.
Photograph by Maria Camillo

Season the chicken pieces with salt and pepper to taste. Combine the soups, rice, and water. After mixing well, add the chicken. Pour into a greased 2-quart casserole dish. Dot with butter and bake at 350° for 45 to 60 minutes. This is Marty's favorite casserole.

Makes 4 servings.

Hilda Stuart,
mom of Marty Stuart

SWEETHEART'S MAN-CATCHER CHICKEN

½ pound boneless chicken breasts
1 11-ounce can cream of mushroom soup
¼ cup dry white wine
1 cup Swiss cheese, grated
1 cup dry herb stuffing mix
¼ cup melted butter

Preheat oven to 350°. Spray a small casserole dish with non-stick cooking spray. Cut the chicken into strip-sized tenders. In a small bowl, mix the soup and wine together and set aside. Layer ½ of the chicken strips in the bottom of the casserole dish. Sprinkle ½ of the cheese over the chicken, then pour ½ of the soup-and-wine mixture over the cheese. Repeat the layers. Top with the dry herb stuffing mix. Pour the melted butter over the top of the casserole. Bake at 350° for 45 minutes.

Makes 2 to 4 servings.

Kristine Arnold and Janis Gill
The Sweethearts of the Rodeo

WHITEHOUSE CHICKEN RATATOUILLE

4 boneless chicken breast halves, cut into chunks
Cooking oil
3 zucchini, sliced
1 large onion, sliced in large pieces

A youthful Marty Stuart wanted to be a cowboy (*above*), before making bluegrass his music as a teen (*right, in 1974*). Marty got his first taste of bluegrass when he heard Bill Monroe and the Sullivan Family perform in Mississippi. Marty was later a member of the Sullivan Family group himself. He played mandolin and lead guitar for Lester Flatt and the Nashville Grass in the '70s and has been a member of the Grand Ole Opry since 1992. He was entrusted with the mandolin playing for Bill Monroe's funeral service at the Ryman Auditorium in 1996.

The Sweethearts of the Rodeo are sisters Janis Gill (*right*) and Kristine Arnold. Their pinpoint harmonies and heartfelt renditions, such as those found on their recent *Beautiful Lies* release, have made them one of the most enduring and endearing duos performing today. While the Sweethearts are obviously at home in virtually any musical setting, their bluegrass performances are among their most inspiring.

Texas natives Buck White and the Whites (*daughters Cheryl, left, and Sharon*) have been performing bluegrass and country music for twenty years. Originally known as Buck White and the Down Home Folks, they became Grand Ole Opry members in 1984.

1 bell pepper, sliced in thin pieces
1 teaspoon garlic salt
1 teaspoon basil
1 teaspoon parsley
Dash black pepper
1 20-ounce can tomatoes, or use fresh
   tomatoes, chopped
Cooked rice

In a large skillet, sauté the chicken in the oil for 2 or 3 minutes, then add the vegetables. Cover and cook for 15 minutes. Add the seasonings and simmer for about 8 minutes, then add the tomatoes. Serve over rice.

Makes 4 servings.

Nina White
WhiteHouse Harmony

BUCKWHITE'S DOWN HOME BAKED CHICKEN

1 fryer chicken
1 stick margarine
1 bag potato chips

Wash, skin, and cut up the fryer. Melt the margarine in a small pan. Crush one bag of potato chips while in the bag. Dip the chicken pieces in melted margarine and roll in the potato chips. (Not you! Roll the dipped chicken in the chips.) Bake at 350° until tender and brown you-all. Yow suh!

Makes 4 servings.

Buck White

PARMESAN CHICKEN RAINWATER

1 cup Parmesan cheese, grated
2 cups bread crumbs
1/3 cup butter or margarine, melted
1/2 cup Dijon mustard
6 chicken breast halves, boned and skinned

Combine the cheese, bread crumbs, and butter. Coat the chicken with mustard, then dip into the crumb mixture. Place the breaded chicken in a greased 9- by 13-inch baking pan. Bake at 425° for 15 minutes, or until done.

Makes 6 servings.

Emma and Jody Rainwater

HEAVENLY TREASURES
CHICKEN PACKAGES

2 tablespoons butter
Aluminum foil cut in long enough pieces to
    fold in half and make 4 big envelopes
4 chicken breast halves
4 peeled potatoes, cut in chunks, or
    unpeeled new potatoes
4 onions, cut up coarsely
Lots of carrots, peeled and cut in rounds, or
    use the baby carrots whole
Salt and pepper to taste
Parsley

Lay the foil pieces out and spray each one with
cooking spray or grease with butter. Place the
chicken breast halves meat-side-down on foil and
add the potatoes, onions, and carrots on top. Salt
and pepper to taste, sprinkle with parsley, and
dot with butter. Fold each piece of foil in half,
then fold up the front edge several times to seal
and fold up side edges several times to seal. Place
the packages on cookie sheets and bake at 375°
for 1 to 1½ hours. Place each package on a plate
and slit the package carefully with a knife, avoiding the steam. Eat right from the package. I sometimes add fresh mushrooms, green pepper, and
fresh herbs (if Doyle hasn't mowed them down).
Doyle used to be able to fix these himself, but
he seems to have forgotten how. I guess he can
read it in this cookbook.

Makes 4 servings.

Suzanne and Doyle Lawson

FIVE SPEED
APRICOT CHICKEN

2 or more boneless, skinless chicken breast
    halves, cut up in small pieces and
    sprinkled with garlic powder and pepper
Vegetable oil
1 large onion, thinly sliced
8 ounces apricot preserves
8 ounces Wishbone dark Russian dressing
12 ounces dried apricots, chopped
6 ounces chicken broth

In a heavy skillet, preferably a cast-iron Dutch
oven, brown the chicken pieces in a little oil.
Once the chicken is browned on all sides, remove it from the pan and place on a plate with
paper towel to drain.

Keeping all bits and oil in the pan, add the
sliced onion and cook until brown.

To the onions in the pan, add apricot preserves,
Russian dressing, and dried apricots. Mix well.
Add the chicken broth last and bring it to a slow
boil for a few minutes.

Return the chicken pieces to the mixture and
place in a 350° oven for at least ½ hour to 1
hour. The sauce will get nice and dark, and it
should be quite thick.

Serve over white rice with a green vegetable
on the side.

Makes 2 or more servings.

Richard Underwood
Bob Paisley and Southern Grass

Maryland native Richard
Underwood (*left*) spent a
number of years playing
banjo and singing with the
Johnson Mountain Boys,
along with Dudley Connell
(*right*). Richard currently
picks with Bob Paisley and
Southern Grass.

Doyle Lawson and Quicksilver: (l-r) Barry Abernathy, Owen Saunders, Doyle Lawson, Dale Perry, and Barry Scott.

Doyle Lawson and Quicksilver

Doyle Lawson began his career in 1964 at age eighteen, playing banjo with Jimmy Martin and the Sunny Mountain Boys. A few years later, he became the guitar player for J.D. Crowe and the Kentucky Mountain Boys. In 1971, Doyle joined the Country Gentlemen, and it was during his eight-year stint in that vanguard group that he established himself as a renowned tenor singer, mandolin player, producer, and arranger.

In 1979, Lawson changed the face of bluegrass music with the formation of his ground-breaking band, Quicksilver. At a time when the influences of "newgrass" and "new acoustic" music had pushed instrumental prowess to the forefront, Doyle brought harmony singing back into the bluegrass spotlight. The Doyle Lawson and Quicksilver sound—which emphasizes smooth, intricate, astonishingly perfect vocal harmonies, innovative song arrangements, and sparkling instrumental work—has been the model for countless progressive bluegrass bands of the 1980s and 1990s.

Gospel-quartet singing has always been an integral part of the Quicksilver repertoire, and Doyle is a master of discovering and revitalizing great obscure material from old hymn books and early recordings. The band's unprecedented all-a cappella release, 1987's *Heaven's Joy Awaits*, set the standard for bluegrass gospel quartet singing. The album remains a top seller today. In 1993, Doyle Lawson and Quicksilver were nominated for two Gospel Voice Diamond Awards. The band has received a host of other awards as well, including multiple honors from SPBGMA, and Song of the Year (for "Little Mountain Church") and Gospel Recording of the Year (for *There's a Light Guiding Me*) from the IBMA. In 1994, Doyle Lawson's first video, *Treasures*, was released. It contains biographical segments highlighting Doyle's thirty-year career, as well as live concert footage from a show in Bristol, Tennessee.

Fans of Doyle Lawson and Quicksilver always know where they can catch the group live. In addition to hundreds of other performances, each July Doyle headlines the renowned "Doyle Lawson and Quicksilver Family Style Bluegrass Festival" in Denton, North Carolina.

B.J.'S BARBECUE CHICKEN

4 chicken halves
1 28-ounce bottle Carolina Treat Barbecue
   sauce
2 teaspoons vinegar
3 ounces Texas Pete hot sauce
Salt and pepper to taste

Boil the chicken until almost tender. Leave or remove the skin. Cut small slits in the thicker part of chicken. Dip the chicken in the barbecue sauce, which has been mixed with the vinegar and the Texas Pete. Place on the grill and let brown slightly. Add salt and pepper to taste. Turn and baste several times with the barbecue sauce until the chicken is well done. The longer you baste and cook the chicken, the spicier it becomes; but do not let it burn.

Makes 4 to 8 servings.

Benny Jarrell

MOM'S
CHICKEN-OKRA GUMBO

My Mom (Linda Stewart of Dallas) makes this when I come home for a visit. She used to make this when we had bluegrass jams at our house. It's one of my favorite dishes of this kind. There's never any left over.

2 tablespoons oil
2 tablespoons flour
1 14½-ounce can chicken broth
1 whole chicken or 6 to 8 thighs, boiled,
   boned, and strained (saving the liquid)
1 20-ounce can diced tomatoes
2 cups fresh or frozen okra, sliced
Seasonings

Cut in bite-sized pieces and set aside:

1 cup celery
1 medium onion
1 medium green bell pepper

Make a dark roux using 2 tablespoons oil and 2 tablespoons flour (preferably in a deep iron skillet). To make the roux, sprinkle flour on heated oil and stir constantly over low heat un-

Benny Jarrell, named after his fiddle-playing grandfather, Ben Jarrell, began playing fiddle when he was thirteen. He turned "pro" at sixteen. Through the years, he played in old-time and bluegrass bands with artists such as Jim Eanes, Hubert Davis, Bobby Hicks, and Allen Shelton. He also fronted his own band, Benny Jarrell and his Flint Hill Playboys. He worked as a disc jockey on country station **WRXO** in Roxboro, North Carolina, from 1955 to 1965. Here Benny (*left*) is pictured listening to some tall tales from his famous dad, Tommy Jarrell (*middle*), and Mike Seeger.

Photograph by Alice Gerrard

til very dark brown. If you burn it, start over because it will ruin the taste.

Turn fire to medium heat and stir in 1 can of chicken broth and ½ can of the saved liquid from the chicken.

Add the tomatoes, okra, celery, onion, green pepper, and seasonings (if available, use Cajun seasonings for blackened fish or salt, pepper, garlic powder, and hot sauce to taste).

Let simmer for at least 30 minutes, adding

Jon Randall (Stewart) grew up in a bluegrass music family in Dallas (mother Linda and father Ron are songwriters). He first caught the ears of the national acoustic music scene as a member of Emmylou Harris's Grammy-winning Nash Ramblers during the late '80s and early '90s. When the Nash Ramblers dissolved, the one-two punch of Jon's impressive picking on lead guitar and his beautiful harmony landed him a record deal with RCA.

Fiddler James Price played for several years with the Goins Brothers before joining Ralph Stanley's Clinch Mountain Boys in 1995. He is one of the finest and most tasteful of the young fiddlers playing in the traditional style. He's no slouch as a singer either, and they say he took lessons from a couple of big country stars. Anyone who's been to Ralph Stanley's Memorial Weekend Festival knows that James can serve up the best lemonade and fried bologna sandwiches this side of Norton.

more liquid if necessary (it should be soupy). Add the chicken during the last 15 minutes.

Serve with rice and garlic bread.

Makes 6 servings.

Jon Randall

ter on them. Cook the rice according to its package instructions. Add the sausage to the beans approximately ½ hour before the beans are done. Add the rice to the bean mixture in a serving dish.

Makes 4 to 6 servings.

James Price
Ralph Stanley and the
Clinch Mountain Boys

THE OLD MOUNTAINEER'S BLACK BEAN GUMBO

16 ounces black beans
2 cups cooked minute rice
½ pound smoked sausage (or your favorite pork)
Salt and pepper to taste

Cook the beans according to the package instructions, making certain to have enough wa-

CLAY JONES' AMAZING GOULASH

1 pound ground beef
½ Vidalia onion, chopped
2 11-ounce cans cream of mushroom soup
1 12-ounce can sliced mushrooms
Several large potatoes

In a large skillet, brown the ground beef and

sauté the onion. Throw the ground beef, onion, soup, and mushrooms in a large pot and cook on high until it boils. In a separate pot, cook your potatoes and mash them up. After everything is cooked, pour the goulash over the mashed potatoes. Then it's m'mm so good!

Makes about 4 servings.

Clay Jones
Lou Reid and Carolina

HEIRLOOM SLOPPY JOE SAUCE

This is Jan and Jill's mother's recipe.

2 pounds ground beef
1 cube beef bouillon
1 cube vegetable bouillon
1 teaspoon parsley flakes
½ cup brown sugar
¾ cup ketchup
2 teaspoons prepared mustard
1 tablespoon dried vegetable flakes
1 small onion, chopped

In a large skillet, brown the ground beef and drain the grease. Add all the remaining ingredients and simmer for 25 minutes, or until the dried vegetable flakes are soft. Serve on a sandwich bun. This can also be served as a Coney dog sauce.

Makes 6 servings.

Jan Harvey, David Harvey, and Jill Snider
Wild and Blue

Bass player **Wayne Taylor** is having the time of his life playing with award-winning **Blue Highway**. Though Wayne had been picking, singing, and writing songs for years, **Blue Highway** is his first chance to tour nationally—he even quit his job as a truck driver! Now we know he was one of bluegrass's best-kept secrets. His crystal clear voice and powerful songs have helped make **Blue Highway** one of the hottest new bands of the 1990s.

PERFECT BLUEGRASS LUNCH

Drive ½ mile to the Burger King. Order 2 regular burgers and 1 medium Diet Coke. Then drive 5 miles to my favorite spot and tune in to 1 hour of bluegrass for lunch with Tim White on WGOC radio in Blountville, Tennessee.

Makes 1 happy meal.

Wayne Taylor
Blue Highway

David and Jan Harvey formed **Wild and Blue** along with Jan's sister, Jill Snider (*right*), in 1988. The band's trademarks are David's dazzling instrumental work and Jan and Jill's stunning vocal harmonies. In 1992, **Wild and Blue** was named Best New Band of the Year by SPBGMA.

Jan and Dave were really cooking at the 1995 IBMA Fan Feast.

MOUNT AIRY MEATBALLS

2 pounds ground beef
2 eggs, beaten
1 medium onion, chopped
1 green bell pepper, chopped
2 garlic cloves, chopped
20 crackers, crumbled
¼ teaspoon sugar

Mix the above ingredients and roll into meatballs.

2 tablespoons oil
2 teaspoons salt
4 15-ounce cans tomato sauce
5 cans water

Brown the meatballs in the oil and salt. Add the tomato sauce and water. Cook slowly for 2 to 3 hours.
Makes 6 servings.

Barry Berrier
The Lost and Found

BIG WILBUR'S MEATBALLS

1½ pounds ground beef
¾ cup quick oats
1 cup milk
¾ tablespoon onion, chopped
¼ teaspoon pepper
1 egg, slightly beaten
Lard

Mix the first 6 ingredients all together, form into balls, and brown in the lard. Drain off the excess grease. Place in a baking dish and cover with a sauce made of:

2 tablespoons Worcestershire sauce
2 tablespoons brown sugar
3 tablespoons vinegar
1 cup ketchup
6 tablespoons onion, chopped
1½ cups water

Simmer in a 350° oven for 1 hour.
Makes 4 servings.

Willia and Melvin Goins

FESTIVAL FAMOUS MILLS MEATLOAF

A favorite meal of the Osborne Brothers, the Lewis Family, and the Traditional Grass.

3 pounds lean ground beef
1 large green bell pepper, chopped
1 large white onion, chopped
2 eggs, beaten
1 4½-ounce can chopped mushrooms
1 cup oats (may need more or less to get consistency)

Season to taste with:

Salt
Pepper
Onion powder
Garlic powder
Sugar

Gravy:

2 10¾-ounce cans Campbell's Beefy Mushroom soup

Mix all the ingredients together (except the soup). Mold into a loaf, cover, and bake at 350° for approximately 1½ hours. Remove from oven and drain. Cover the loaf with the soup and reduce heat to 300°. Bake uncovered for approximately 30 minutes to thicken the gravy. Enjoy!
Makes 8 to 10 servings.

B.J. and Jim Mills
The Bass Mountain Boys

Banjo player Jim Mills has performed and recorded in a number of fine groups, including Summer Wages, Doyle Lawson and Quicksilver, and the Bass Mountain Boys. For his day job, Jim manages the shipping department at Sugar Hill Records. He is an avid banjophile and collector, and he has all of the Flatt and Scruggs episodes from *The Beverly Hillbillies* on video.

THE RESOPHONIC MEATLOAF

The name, of course, is mine. The recipe is my grandmother's, from the 1920s, about the time the Dopyera brothers were making the first Dobro resophonic guitars.

2 pounds ground chuck
1 large onion, chopped
1 egg, beaten
1¾ teaspoons salt
3 teaspoons horseradish
½ teaspoon pepper
1½ teaspoons sugar
½ cup bread crumbs
4 tablespoons ketchup
1 tablespoon Worcestershire sauce

Combine all the ingredients in a bowl. Form into a ball and beat most of the air out (this is a really important step). Shape into a "football." Bake in a roasting pan at 350° for 1½ hours.
Makes 6 servings.

Mike Auldridge
Chesapeake

BEEF GOULASH BEAGLES

Unleash your taste buds!

¹/₃ cup onion, chopped
¹/₃ cup green bell pepper, chopped
¹/₃ cup celery, chopped
1 pound ground chuck
8 ounces tomato sauce
1 cup water
¹/₂ teaspoon salt
¹/₂ teaspoon black pepper
1¹/₂ tablespoons chili powder
8 ounces cooked macaroni

Cook the onion, green pepper, and celery with the ground chuck in a skillet until browned lightly. Add the tomato sauce, water, and seasonings. Simmer 20 to 30 minutes. Add the drained macaroni, simmer for about 10 minutes, and serve.
Makes 4 servings.

Kim and Tim White
The Beagles

One of Mike Auldridge's biggest musical inspirations was his uncle, Ellsworth Cozzens, who played steel guitar with Jimmie Rodgers and wrote several of Rodgers's hit songs. Mike got his start as a professional musician in the 1960s with Cliff Waldron and The New Shades of Grass. He was a founding member of The Seldom Scene in 1971, and went on to help found acoustic group Chesapeake in the early '90s. Though known primarily as a resonator guitar player, Mike also plays lap steel, pedal steel, acoustic guitar, and his own invention, the eight-string resonator guitar. Mike is in great demand as a studio musician and has performed on recordings with Linda Ronstadt, James Taylor, Emmylou Harris, Hank Williams, Jr., and many others.

CORDLE'S FAMOUS BLUEGRASS BEEF STROGANOFF

1 to 2 pounds lean stew beef
1 medium onion
½ to 1 pound fresh mushrooms
Vegetable oil
1 quart water
4 beef bouillon cubes
1 stick butter
1 pound sour cream
1 pound cooked wide egg noodles, or 1 package cooked rice (white or wild)

Trim all the fat from the meat and cut into bite-sized pieces. Chop the onion and slice the mushrooms. Place the meat, onion, and mushrooms into a large pot and sauté in a little vegetable oil for about 5 to 7 minutes. Add 1 quart water and cook for about 15 minutes. Add the bouillon cubes, butter, and sour cream. Cook over low heat until the meat is tender, adding water to thin the consistency as desired. This may be served over the egg noodles or rice. Delicious either way. Happy eating!
Makes 4 to 8 servings.

Larry Cordle

Larry Cordle grew up pickin' and grinnin' with his boyhood pals Ricky Skaggs and Keith Whitley in Cordell, Kentucky. The picker, singer, and tunesmith was lead vocalist in Lonesome Standard Time. He wrote "Highway 40 Blues," a number one hit for Skaggs in 1983, while his "Lonesome Standard Time" was a hit for Kathy Mattea in 1992 and the IBMA Song of the Year in 1993.

FLAT CREEK CRAB-STUFFED STEAK

1 8-ounce rib eye steak, thick cut
½ cup French salad dressing
¼ cup Heinz 57 Sauce
3 tablespoons lemon juice, divided
Paprika to taste
4 ounces shredded crabmeat

Butterfly cut the rib eye and perforate evenly with an ice pick or fork. Prepare a marinade of French salad dressing, Heinz 57 Sauce, 2 tablespoons of lemon juice, and paprika. Completely cover the steak in marinade and allow to marinate in refrigerator for 2 to 3 hours. Preheat oven to 400°. Broil the crabmeat in a pie pan with remaining tablespoon of lemon juice for 4 minutes. Remove the crabmeat from the oven. Open the steak and fill with the crabmeat and marinade. Close and secure with wooden toothpicks. Place in a covered pie pan with marinade and bake at 400° for 7 to 10 minutes.

Makes 1 serving.

Shane Green
Flat Creek Skillet Lickers

REUBEN REUBEN I'VE BEEN THINKING

1 12-ounce can corned beef, or ¾ pound fresh corned beef, chopped
¼ cup thousand island dressing
1 16-ounce can sauerkraut
½ pound Swiss cheese, grated
½ cup butter, melted
6 slices Pepperidge Farm rye bread, cubed

Crumble the beef and place it in a buttered 2-quart casserole dish. Spread on the dressing. Drain the sauerkraut and spread it on top of the dressing. Add the grated cheese. Top with bread cubes that have been tossed with butter. Bake uncovered for 30 minutes at 350°, or until hot and bubbly. This is good for a quick Sunday night supper.

Makes 4 servings.

Hairl Hensley
Host of The Orange Possum Special
WSM Radio (650 AM)

Country music deejay great Hairl Hensley has spent over a quarter of a century with WSM Radio in Nashville. In 1996, the Society for the Preservation of Bluegrass Music in America named him the Bluegrass Deejay of the Year. He hosts *The Orange Possum Special* every Monday night on WSM.

VASSILLIE BEEFTIPS AND RICE

2 pounds round or sirloin steak, cut into 1-inch cubes
2 tablespoons oil
3 cups beef broth
$1/2$ teaspoon salt
1 teaspoon basil
$2/3$ cup burgundy wine
2 tablespoons soy sauce
2 cloves garlic, minced
1 tablespoon onion powder
4 tablespoons cornstarch
$1/2$ cup water
Cooked rice

In a skillet, brown both sides of the meat in the oil. Stir in the remaining ingredients, except the cornstarch, ½ cup of water, and rice. Cover, reduce heat, and simmer until the meat is tender. When the meat is done, mix the cornstarch and water together, then stir into the meat. Stir until the mixture thickens. Continue to cook for 3 minutes. Serve over cooked rice.

Makes 6 servings.

Millie and Vassar Clements

UNCLE'S ORANGE-GLAZED GRILLED STEAK

I picked up the name "Uncle" about ten years ago for some strange reason, while I worked as a nurse. It just seemed to stick. Stick this steak in your mouth and it'll cure what ails you!

¼ cup soy sauce
2 cloves garlic, pressed
1 teaspoon coarsely ground black pepper
1 top round steak, 1¼ inches thick (about 2 pounds)
$1/3$ cup orange marmalade

Mix the soy sauce, garlic, and pepper in a glass baking dish. Add the steak to the mixture, turning to coat. Cover and refrigerate for 30 minutes, turning once. Place the steak on a grill over medium heat. Spoon the remaining marinade over the steak. Cook to desired doneness (about 25 minutes for medium-rare), turning occasionally. Brush with orange marmalade during the last 10 minutes of cooking, turning once.

Makes about 5 servings.

Phil Leadbetter
J.D. Crowe and the New South

Fiddler Vassar Clements started out at age fourteen with Bill Monroe and his Blue Grass Boys. Vassar has also performed with Jimmy Martin, Jim and Jesse, John Hartford, and the Earl Scruggs Revue. He has lent his musical talents to hundreds of records and was on the Grammy-winning *Will the Circle Be Unbroken* album. His latest solo recording, *Vassar's Jazz*, was released in 1996.

LONESOME HONEY ORANGE GLAZED HAM

1 6-ounce can frozen orange juice
   concentrate, thawed
1¾ cups water
¾ cup honey
1½ tablespoons cornstarch
1 5- to 7-pound ham

Combine the juice, water, honey, and cornstarch in a saucepan. Cook until thick. Cut slits in the ham, pour half of mixture over the ham, and partly bake at 325°. Then pour the remaining mixture over the ham and finish baking. Total lonesome standard baking time should be about 20 minutes per pound, or until the internal temperature reaches 160°.

Makes 10 to 12 servings.

P.S. Cloves can be placed here and there and stuck in the top half of the ham for additional flavor.

Larry Cordle

OLD-TIME CANNED OR JAR SAUSAGE

The last long visit I had with my grandmother, we talked about the farm, the way it was back then, etc. The subject of canned (or jar) sausages came up. I asked her why they tasted so good. She told me about her "secret" recipe. Then she looked at one hand and said, "They say, they might be bad for you." She was a month away from her ninety-ninth birthday!!

2 pounds ground pork
2 teaspoons salt
1 teaspoon black pepper
1 teaspoon sage
½ teaspoon red pepper, finely ground

Mix all the ingredients well. Form the sausage into golf-sized balls. Place the sausage balls in a cold frying pan. Cook on moderate heat for about 10 minutes, or until brown on each side. Place the sausage in a hot, sterilized jar, covering with the sauce that was cooked when browning the sausage. Seal the jar. Turn the jar upside down until it is ready for serving. (It's best to allow to stand a minimum of 10 days.) Heat in an oven or frying pan.

Makes about 6 servings.

Jack White

In 1996, singer/songwriter Jack White of Columbia, Tennessee, went into the studios with Helen and Anita Carter to record *Southern Songbook*, his debut album for Daywind Records. He was also a frequent performer on the Mountain Opry in Signal Mountain, Tennessee, in the late '80s.

PAT'S TWICE-COOKED PORK WITH NAPALM SAUCE

It's a devil's dream!

This dish is a variation of a common dish served in Chinese restaurants. The fermented black beans are usually available in oriental grocery stores. Sometimes they're hard to find, but they're worth the search. The healthy portions of fresh ginger, garlic, and habanero pepper make the dish happen, too. I'm assuming that folks who may want to try this are already familiar with the rudiments of stir-fry cooking and that they own a wok. Everybody should own a wok.

1 pound lean pork (butt, shoulder, or tenderloin)
Water
3 tablespoons peanut oil
1 heaping tablespoon fermented black beans, or canned Szechuan hot-bean sauce
1 tablespoon ginger root (fresh!), finely minced
1 tablespoon garlic (fresh), finely minced
1 cup cabbage, cut into 1-inch strips
1 green bell pepper, cut into thin strips
½ cup pork stock (reserved from cooking pork)
3 tablespoons soy sauce
2 or more habanero chile peppers, minced
4 scallions, cut into ½-inch pieces
1 tablespoon liquid cornstarch (dissolve ½ tablespoon cornstarch in a little cold water)
Steamed rice

Place the pork in a pot and add enough water to cover. Bring the water to a full boil, then reduce the heat and let it simmer until it's done (jam a chopstick in the pork to test for doneness; it should slide right in). Remove the pork from the water, let it cool a bit, remove the fat (or not!), and slice the pork into thin pieces across the grain—chopstick size.

Heat a wok (or a big iron skillet) over high heat for 1 minute, or until it's plenty hot, Mon! Add the peanut oil and heat it until it's smokin'. Add the pork, black beans, ginger, and garlic, and mush it all together for about 30 seconds. Add the cabbage and green pepper, then stir (with vigor) for 30 seconds.

Add the pork stock, soy sauce, and minced habaneros. Blend well; then add the scallions and liquid cornstarch. Add a dash of oil for appearance. Serve immediately with plenty of steamed rice and a beer.

Makes about 4 servings.

Pat Enright
Nashville Bluegrass Band

Prior to helping found the **Nashville Bluegrass Band**, Indiana native **Pat Enright** performed with Laurie Lewis in the Phantoms of the Opry and with Jack Tottle, Bela Fleck, and Mark Schatz in Tasty Licks. During the 1980s, Pat became a regular jammer at Nashville's Station Inn. There he joined with Jerry Douglas, Bela Fleck, Roland White, Blaine Sprouse, and Mark Hembree to form the in-house, part-time band, the Dreadful Snakes. The group made a highly successful recording for Rounder, *Snakes Alive*, released in 1984. Soon after that, the Nashville Bluegrass band was born.

The **Nashville Bluegrass Band** got its start in 1984, when Alan O'Bryant called some picking buddies from the Station Inn to organize a group to tour on a package show. Alan, Pat Enright, Mike Compton, and Mark Hembree soon realized that their music was special and decided to continue as a full-time band. The NBB immediately turned heads with its powerful vocal harmonies, bluesy arrangements, and emphasis on material drawn from the great black gospel quartets. The Nashville Bluegrass Band was named IBMA Vocal Group of the Year for four years straight (1990–93), and in 1996, they received a Grammy Award for their *Unleashed* recording on Sugar Hill. Today, the Nashville Bluegrass Band includes (l-r) Stuart Duncan, Alan O'Bryant, Gene Libbea, Pat Enright, and Roland White.

FIDDLER'S GRILLED SAUSAGE PATTIES ON RYE

8 sausage patties
8 slices onion
8 green bell pepper slices
8 slices caraway rye bread
4 slices mozzarella cheese
6 tablespoons butter

Cook the sausage patties until brown and thoroughly done. Add the onion and green peppers. Continue cooking until the veggies are crisp and tender. Remove the patties and veggies from the skillet. Pour off the fat. Assemble each sandwich: take 4 slices of bread and place 2 sausage patties, 2 onion slices, 2 green pepper rings, and 1 slice mozzarella cheese on each slice. Top the sandwich with a slice of bread. Melt the butter on a griddle or in a skillet and brown each sandwich on both sides. Serve hot.

Makes 4 servings.

Millie and Vassar Clements

BACK PORCH BARBECUE PORK RIBS

1 pack Caesar salad dressing mix
½ cup olive oil
1 tablespoon lemon juice
1 pound boneless, country-style pork ribs
Garlic salt
Parmesan cheese, grated
Any kind of outdoor grill

Mix the Caesar dressing mix, olive oil, and lemon juice together to make a marinade. Place the ribs in the marinade and let them marinate overnight in the refrigerator. Place on the grill and sprinkle on a little garlic salt, or as much as you like. When the ribs are done, sprinkle with Parmesan cheese and let set for 5 minutes on the grill, covered. This is some good eatin'. Don't be afraid to fire up your grill in the winter either.

Makes 2 to 4 servings.

Dale Reno
The Reno Brothers

PORK DISGUISED AS LAMB

1 boneless pork loin roast (10 inches long, 4 inches thick)
8 to 10 cloves garlic, minced
1 6-ounce can concentrated frozen pineapple juice
3 ounces water
¼ cup cider vinegar
2 tablespoons fresh rosemary, chopped
3 pounds fresh spinach
6 slices provolone cheese
Black pepper to taste—I like lots

On every pork loin I have seen, there is a side of it that has a thick piece of fat. Cut it off if you want. I don't. I leave it on the outside of the finished product so that the baking process helps it to baste the roast while it cooks away. Also, it tastes real gooood.

The first thing to do is the hardest part. Flatten the pork loin, not by pounding but with a very sharp knife. It might take you 15 minutes on your first try.

Select your favorite long, very sharp knife. Place the pork loin on the counter fat side down, with the grain of the meat perpendicular to the edge of the counter. I am a righty, so I start cutting on the right. Suit yourself. Begin a continuous cut ¼ to ⅜ of an inch above the counter top, keeping the cut as even as possible. When you near the left side, be careful not to slice through. Gradually pick up the remaining pork loin with your left hand while you cut with the right and flop it over when you can. Go slow. "Unrolling" a pork loin is tricky business. Continue this lifting and flopping process until there

The Reno Brothers are (l-r) Dale, Don Wayne, and Ronnie

Moondi Klein got his nickname in childhood from a babysitter, and it stuck! Moondi comes from a musical family, and he and his brother sang with the Metropolitan Opera's children's chorus for several years. Moondi moved to Washington, D.C., in 1984 and played in the bluegrass band Rock Creek prior to joining Mike Auldridge, Jimmy Gaudreau, and T. Michael Coleman to form Chesapeake. Moondi also performed with The Seldom Scene in 1994 and 1995.

picks in the last edge to keep it from curling in the heat. Place the roast in a deep baking dish, uncovered, and put in the oven for 1 hour and 45 minutes, or until done. It is always a good idea to use a meat thermometer to check the interior temperature of pork. Let it cool for as long as you can, at least 2 minutes, then place the meat parallel to the counter's edge and slice $3/8$- to $1/2$-inch-thick pieces of this "log," so that you see the pretty spirals of the pork and the spinach. This makes a fantastic lunch meat when cold and sliced very thin. It does not remotely taste like lamb; that's just what my wife calls it.

Suggested side dishes are potatoes (however you like them), steamed asparagus (use the water you steamed the spinach in), and a tossed salad with Moondi's salad dressing.

Makes 6 to 8 servings.

Seeya, MK.

Moondi Klein
Chesapeake

is no more meat to lift and flop. What you should have now is a $2^1/2$- to 3-foot-long, 10-inch-wide, $3/8$-inch-thick unrolled pork loin. Rub this exposed side with minced garlic, fold in half, then half again, and put in a Ziplock freezer bag. To the bag, add the frozen pineapple juice with only $1/2$ can of water, $1/4$ cup of cider vinegar, and a whole mess of fresh chopped rosemary or your favorite pork herb. Cilantro is interesting, but you need a lot of it. Get as much air out of the baggy as you can and leave it in the fridge overnight.

Two hours and 15 minutes before you want to eat, clean and steam the spinach. Drain well. Preheat oven to 350°. Remove the loin from the marinade and place it on the counter all opened up. Distribute the spinach evenly across the entire pork loin, then lay the provolone cheese slices down the middle. Grind black pepper over the whole thing. Starting from one side, roll it up as tightly as possible. Make sure the thick fat piece ends up on the outside. Put 2 or 3 tooth-

MOM LEWIS'S GEORGIA HASH

2 pounds pork
I pound beef
I whole, deboned chicken, cooked (save the broth)
I 20-ounce can tomatoes
I slice bread
I small onion (optional)

Grind the meats, tomatoes, bread, and onion all together.

Add:

Enough chicken broth for the right consistency
I stick margarine
¼ cup vinegar
I tablespoon black pepper
Salt to taste
A little sugar
I 15-ounce can shoepeg corn (small kernel)

Mix all the ingredients in a large pot. Simmer a long time. Hash can be frozen.

½ **stick margarine**
¼ **cup sugar**
I **cup vinegar**
½ **cup water**
I **teaspoon salt**
Black pepper to taste

Mix all the ingredients and bring to a boil. Serve vinegar sauce with hash.

Makes about 12 to 15 servings.

Mom and Miggie Lewis
The Lewis Family

MAMA MITCH'S VENISON STEAKS WITH GRAVY

When we were on the road, the other three Dillards all called me "Mama Mitch" because I was trying to look out for their nutrition. I remember that Rodney wouldn't eat a medium-rare steak because you cooked meat until it was DONE back home, and he had never seen an artichoke. He wouldn't eat Parmesan cheese because it smelled like gym socks. I remember that Doug Dillard would eat anything you put before him as long as it looked familiar, and I'd love to tell about the knapsack of grub he packed to take to Japan (Dinty Moore Beef Stew, chili, peanut butter, Cheese Whiz, and a bale of crackers) because he heard that the Japanese had never even heard of gravy and ate things like raw fish and dogs. He never ate one Japanese thing in the two weeks we were there.

2 pounds venison round or sirloin steaks
   (You can fix tenderloin this way too, if it's
   a big deer.)
Marinade (see below)
Flour
½ **cup oil**
½ **cup water**

Marinade:

I **cup white port wine**
¼ **cup teriyaki sauce**
I **tablespoon garlic salt**
I **teaspoon ground black pepper**
¾ **cup water**

Remove all the fat before placing the meat in the marinade. Marinate in the refrigerator for at least 2 hours, turning the meat periodically. Take the meat out of the marinade and drain, retaining the marinade. Pound the steaks with a tenderizing mallet on both sides and dip in flour. Fry in a large skillet with ½ cup oil, browning well on both sides.

Make gravy by putting 1 tablespoon of flour into a 1 cup vessel containing ½ cup marinade and ½ of cup water. Stir until thick. Pour over frying meat (canned or packaged beef gravy can also be added to increase the amount and deepen color). Add additional marinade as needed while cooking. With a spatula or spoon, loosen the steaks and shift them around to make sure they are smothered. Simmer until time to serve. Serve over mashed potatoes or biscuits.

Makes 4 to 6 servings.

Mitch Jayne
The Dillards

The original Dillards got back on the truck again as the Darlings during an *Andy Griffith Show* cast reunion at Opryland USA in 1991. Pictured are (l-r) Dean Webb, Mitch Jayne, Rodney Dillard, and Doug Dillard.
Photograph by Karen Mol

BLUE RIDGE MOUNTAIN PAN-FRIED VENISON STEAKS

2 pounds venison steak
4 tablespoons flour
3 tablespoons shortening
1¼ cups water
1 cup celery, chopped
½ cup onion, diced
Salt and pepper
1 9-ounce jar whole mushrooms with liquid

Cut the meat into serving pieces, then dredge in the flour. Brown the meat well in the shortening in a skillet over medium-high heat. Add the water, celery, onion, salt, and pepper. Cover and simmer 1 hour. Add the mushrooms with liquid. Cover and simmer for ½ hour.
Makes 4 to 6 servings.

Shawn Lane
Blue Highway

SLADE'S ROASTED ROADKILL

A favorite at the Eat Cafe in Wyoming, Montana. Good with red-eye gravy.

Run over 1 possum or armadillo on the highway. Clean it and put it on the engine of your car. Drive 80 miles an hour for 50 miles. Get out, turn the possum (or armadillo) over, and drive for another 50 miles at 80 miles an hour. Then your possum or armadillo will be done and you have dinner. Cooking time will vary depending on whether you have a 6-cylinder engine or a V-8.
Makes 1 to 3 servings, depending on whether you have a 6-cylinder engine or a V-8.

Slade
Red Knuckles and the Trailblazers

WIDOW MAKER FRIED RABBIT AND GRAVY

Rabbit, dressed
Flour
Grease
Salt and pepper
Milk

Boil your rabbit for about 30 minutes. Take it out and wash it off. Then you dredge it in flour and put it in a hot skillet with grease. Add pepper and salt, and then fry it. After the rabbit is done (about 30 to 40 minutes), take the rabbit out. Put some flour in the gravy and grease. Let the flour fry for 5 to 10 minutes, then pour milk on top. Stir and let come to a boil until the gravy has a little thickness. Now you have good country-fried rabbit and gravy.
Makes 4 servings.

Jimmy Martin

HOLD WHATCHA GOT GROUNDHOG

Groundhog, dressed
2 onions, quartered
4-5 carrots, cut in 3-inch sections
3-4 medium potatoes, quartered

Take your groundhog and boil it for about 10 minutes. Pour the water off, put the groundhog in clean water, and boil for 10 more minutes. Pour that water off and put him in a big skillet like you fix a roast. Put onions, carrots, and potatoes around it and bake like a roast until it is done. Then you have got the best eatin' you ever popped your teeth in.
Makes 6 servings.

Jimmy Martin

A favorite part of every Hot Rize show was when those guys who traveled in the back of the tour bus took the stage for a few numbers. Red Knuckles and the Trailblazers, who got their name from Martha White's Trailblazer dog food, played that good ole country music from the 1950s and 1960s that you don't hear much anymore. And one thing's for sure: you never heard anything else like the Trailblazers. Pictured are (l-r) Waldo Otto, Wendell Mercantile, Slade, and Red Knuckles. (Waldo, by the way, also ran a donut shop in their hometown of Wyoming, Montana.)

Jimmy Martin was already entertaining his siblings at an early age (pictured here with his brother Roy, left). This photo, circa 1939, was used on the graphics for the excellent bluegrass documentary, High Lonesome, which was released in 1991.

Nicknamed "the King of Bluegrass," Jimmy Martin has one of the purest voices in the world of bluegrass. He formed his Sunny Mountain Boys in 1955. One of his greatest achievements was performing six of his original songs on the Grammy-winning Will the Circle Be Unbroken album.

Jimmy Martin

One of bluegrass's greatest performers, Jimmy Martin has been nicknamed "the King of Bluegrass." In 1949, the singer/guitar picker left Sneedville, Tennessee, and headed to Nashville. There, he got his break by singing and playing for Bill Monroe in the alley behind the Ryman after an Opry show. Monroe hired Martin immediately.

During the early '50s, Martin helped record some of Monroe's greatest hits, including "I'm on My Way Back to the Old Home," "Memories of Mother and Dad," "Sitting Alone in the Moonlight," and "On and On." In 1954, Martin teamed with the Osborne Brothers; a year later, he formed the Sunny Mountain Boys.

For his first band, Martin recruited banjo player Sam "Porky" Hutchins and mandolinist Earl Taylor (who in 1959 was the first bluegrass artist to play Carnegie Hall). After a few months, Hutchins left and a teenage prodigy named J.D. Crowe came aboard in 1956. In the fall of 1957, mandolinist/tenor singer Paul Williams (Humphrey) joined the band and the Sunny Mountain Boys really took off. With this group, Martin recorded some of his biggest hits, including "Ocean of Diamonds," "Rock Hearts," "Hold Whatcha Got," and "Sophronie."

Over the next decade, a string of great musicians would come through Martin's band, including Bill Emerson, Paul Craft, Vernon Derrick, Vic Jordan, Vassar Clements, Gloria Belle Flickinger, Doyle Lawson, and Alan Munde. Among Martin's most popular and enduring songs from this period are "Tennessee," "Widow Maker," "20-20 Vision," "Sunny Side of the Mountain," "Freeborn Man," and "Hey Lonesome."

In 1972, Martin's music reached a huge audience when he lent his voice and six of his songs to the Nitty Gritty Dirt Band's million-selling album *Will the Circle Be Unbroken*.

The IBMA Hall of Honor member continues to play a dozen or so concerts a year, and his songs are still recorded by bluegrass and country music greats. When he's not making music, Martin is hunting or working with his coon dogs and rabbit-tracking beagles near Hermitage, Tennessee. Among the dogs are Hank Williams, Minnie Pearl, Marty Stuart, Tom T. Hall, and George Jones, named after some of Martin's favorite country music folks.

JETHRO'S KOSHER CHITLINS

3 pounds chitlins or 1 3-pound chitlin
1 6-pack Coors Light beer
1 pint cheap vodka
1 pint prune juice

The chitlins should be machine-washed using a harsh detergent, then tumble-dried for 30 minutes while sipping a cold Coors beer. Mix the vodka with the prune juice. Place the chitlins under the broiler for 10 minutes. At this time you will notice an odor similar to that of Magic Johnson's old gym shoes. You will feel the urge to sneeze. Now you drink the vodka and prune juice. (Comedians call this a pile driver.) This will prevent sneezing. Actually, at this point, you will be afraid to sneeze! This recipe serves 4. I suggest Barry Manilow, Wendy O. Williams, Ozzy Osborne, and Dick Cavett. Leftovers should be sent to Iran.

The Chief Chitlin,
Jethro van Burns

The legend of Homer and Jethro (seen here in 1965) began when Kenneth C. "Jethro" Burns (*left*) and partner Henry "Homer" Haynes began performing together on Knoxville's **WNOX** Radio in 1932. The duo's blend of comedy and music entertained generations and garnered numerous awards, including a 1959 Grammy. "How Much Is That Hound Dawg in the Winder?" was one of their biggest hits.

LET THE WHOLE WORLD TALK PAD THAI

½ pound dried rice noodles
½ pound shrimp, chicken, pork, or a combination
¼ cup fish sauce
¼ cup sugar
¼ cup white vinegar
1 teaspoon paprika
4 green onions
½ cup vegetable oil
1 teaspoon finely chopped garlic
2 eggs
¼ pound bean sprouts
2 tablespoons ground roasted chilies
¾ cup ground roasted unsalted peanuts
Lime wedges

Cook the noodles according to package directions and drain thoroughly. Peel and devein the shrimp, or slice the chicken/pork into strips ⅛-inch thick and 1 to 2 inches long. Mix the fish sauce, sugar, vinegar, and paprika in a bowl and stir until the sugar dissolves. Slice the onions diagonally into pieces that are 1½ inches long. Heat the wok and add the oil. Add the garlic and stir fry until golden. Add the meat and stir fry until it is no longer pink. Add the cooked noodles and toss to coat them with oil and distribute the meat and garlic. Add the fish sauce mixture and bring to a boil. Fold the noodles into the sauce, trying not to break the noodles, until they have absorbed the liquid.

Next, lift the noodles with a scoop or spatula to one side and pour a little oil along the other side of the wok. Break 1 egg and slip it onto the oiled side of the wok. Break the yolk and cover with noodles. Repeat on the other side with the second egg. When the eggs are almost dry, fold them gently with the noodles. Add the bean sprouts and sliced green onion, then toss the entire mixture. Cook for 2 minutes, or until the sprouts and onions are crisp and tender. Place on a large warm platter and sprinkle with ground chilies and peanuts. Squeeze lime juice over the top.

Makes 3 to 4 servings.

Dudley Connell
The Seldom Scene

Dudley Connell helped found the Johnson Mountain Boys, the hottest new traditional bluegrass group of the 1980s. In 1995, he joined The Seldom Scene. He is one of the most expressive vocalists in bluegrass, as well as a fine songwriter and guitarist. Dudley is also a great cook and likes to experiment with many types of ethnic food, such as Thai, Indian, and Vietnamese. When he's not playing music or cooking, Dudley works as office manager for Smithsonian/Folkways Records in Rockville, Maryland.

FIRECRACKER SHRIMP

Here's a great dish that's quick and easy. All you need is a companion that doesn't mind getting a rich, spicy sauce on his or her hands.

½ to 1 pound medium shrimp in shells
1 tablespoon Cajun spice mix
Fresh ground black pepper
1½ tablespoons olive oil
Juice of 2 lemons
¾ cup heavy cream
½ cup fresh parsley, chopped
Hot sauce

Have biscuits or lots of crusty bread ready for the sauce. In a bowl, season the shrimp with the cajun spices (there are many at the grocery to choose from) and lots of fresh ground pepper. Heat the oil in a large skillet over high heat. Sauté the shrimp for 1 minute. Add the lemon

You have to be careful around quiet Roger Rasnake or his talent will sneak up and surprise you. Equally at home on bass guitar or acoustic guitar, Roger performs regularly as a member of both the Doug Dillard Band and the Brother Boys. Even so, perhaps his best musical instrument is his voice. And with songwriting credits that include the likes of "Endless Highway," Roger is a quadruple threat who's a four-leaf clover for any performance.

juice and the cream. When the shrimp begin to turn pink (1 to 2 minutes), add the parsley and several good hits of your favorite hot sauce. Stir another 2 minutes. Plate the shrimp with lots of sauce for each person. Soak the bread, peel the shrimp, eat, and enjoy!

Make 2 servings.

Roger Rasnake

SIDEMAN SHRIMP SCAMPI

2 pounds medium shrimp, unpeeled
8 ounces fettuccine or linguine, uncooked
1 cup butter or margarine
8 cloves garlic, pressed
2 shallots, minced, or 1 medium onion, finely chopped
$^1/_3$ cup dry white wine (optional)
3 tablespoons fresh lemon juice
$^1/_4$ cup fresh parsley, chopped
$^1/_4$ teaspoon salt
$^1/_8$ teaspoon freshly ground pepper

Del McCoury (left) and son Ronnie demonstrate that they know the important follow-up to cooking is ... eating! Ronnie can play anything on the mandolin, from the straightest syncopated Bill Monroe melody to the hottest jazzy riff, and he frequently borrows from both to create his distinctive style. Ronnie and brother Rob released their first duet recording in 1995.

Peel the shrimp and set aside. Cook the pasta; drain. Place the pasta in a large serving bowl and keep warm. Melt the butter in a large skillet over medium-high heat. Add the garlic and shallots. Cook, stirring constantly for 5 minutes, or until tender. Add the shrimp and cook over medium heat for 3 to 5 minutes, or until the shrimp are pink. Add the wine and remaining ingredients. Pour the shrimp mixture over the pasta and toss.

Makes 4 servings.

Ronnie McCoury
The Del McCoury Band

SAUCEMAN CRAWFISH FETTUCCINE

8 ounces egg noodles
½ stick butter or margarine
1 package frozen Dulaney seasoning mix
Salt, pepper, and red pepper to taste
Creole seasoning to taste
A little garlic powder
A little onion powder
A little paprika
2 pounds peeled crawfish or shrimp tails
1 10¾-ounce can cream of mushroom soup
2 tablespoons lemon juice
2 tablespoons Worcestershire sauce
2 tablespoons evaporated milk
1½ to 2 cups water

Boil the egg noodles in a pot. Drain the noodles and keep warm. In a separate pan, sauté the seasonings in the butter. Add the crawfish or shrimp and smother down. Add the cream of mushroom soup, lemon juice, Worcestershire sauce, evaporated milk, and water. Bring to a boil and then let it simmer down for about 15 minutes. Add the boiled egg noodles and stir together.

Makes 4 to 6 servings.

Carl Sauceman
The Sauceman Brothers

DRILLED GUITAR SALMON

Fresh salmon fillet
1 cup teriyaki sauce
1 teaspoon brown sugar
1 tablespoon lime juice

Make sure the salmon is scaled very well. Grill it skin side down for 3 minutes. Then, flip and grill it until done. Mix the teriyaki sauce, brown sugar, and lime juice and spread on salmon when done. Ready to go.

Makes 3 servings per pound of salmon.

Clay Jones
Lou Reid and Carolina

POACHED PLECTRUM PLATTER

(Plectrum? Darn near killed him.)

1 banjo, pre-war Gibson Mastertone preferred (strap optional)
3 old rusted Black Diamond strings
1 cardboard box Franzia chablis
1 tablespoon nail clippings
2 cups bong water
1 teaspoon aged fret cheese
2 white National medium thumb picks

Carl Sauceman and the Green Valley Boys pose before the camera at WTOK-TV in Meridian, Mississippi, around 1953. The banjo picker/comedian in front is Fred Richardson. Other members of the group include (*l-r*) Monroe Fields, Jimmy Brock, Sr., J.P. Sauceman, Carl Sauceman, and Dickey Mauldin. "All we knew was hillbilly music; then it became bluegrass, because we had a banjo, I guess," says Carl. "We were just hillbilly singers, somewhere between the Delmore Brothers and Charlie and Bill Monroe." The Sauceman Brothers began their career on radio station WWNC in Asheville, North Carolina, in 1944. In 1946, they moved on to WGRV in Greeneville, Tennessee. Members of *The Cas Walker Show* in Knoxville from 1948 to 1949, they then replaced Flatt and Scruggs in Bristol, Virginia, on WCYB's *Farm and Fun Time* show. (Some of those performances are available on the *Early Days from WCYB Farm and Fun Time* album on Rebel Records.) The Sauceman Brothers then took their music to Carrollton, Alabama, from 1952 into the mid–1960s. In 1976, Carl Sauceman put the band back together for a few bluegrass festivals. Over their career, the Sauceman Brothers recorded for Rich-R-Tone, Mercury Records, Capital Records, and United Artists.

Page 143 of *Roy Clark's Big Note Banjo Book*
1 cake rosin, diced

Remove the resonator from the banjo, carefully destring, and discard all nubs. Place the liquid in a stockpot and bring to a full rolling boil. Add the plectrum and reduce heat to simmer, covering tightly with the resonator. Simmer until tender, or all the length of one "Foggy Mountain Breakdown" solo. Strain through a Dobro resonator, reserving the liquid, and place the banjo on a preheated platter in 350° oven to keep warm. Reduce the liquid by one half, add the diced rosin, and stir until thickened. Pour the sauce over the banjo and garnish with a sprinkling of Dill Monroe. Served with Fiddlehead Fricassee and Salty Dog biscuit. Bone aperteet!
Makes enough.

Jonathan Yudkin
and Kathy Mattea

Sideman Jonathan Yudkin (*third from the left*) is red hot on the mandolin and fiddle. While he has his own group, the Chain-Smoking Altar Boys, Yudkin also performs regularly with Kathy Mattea, and he's a former member of the Doug Dillard Band. Pictured here, with Jonathan, is a vintage Doug Dillard Band: (*l-r*) Ginger Boatwright, Doug Dillard, and Kathy Chiavola.

OWEN'S CORNED GROUPER

Before the icemaker, Florida fishermen salted fish to keep them from spoiling, and since there was no commercial market for grouper, they ate grouper. This is what I am hungry for while writing this, but the recipe is good with any big, white-meated fish such as cobia, amberslicks, striped bass, etc.

Marinate 5 pounds grouper fillets in:

**I cup salt
Juice of one lemon
I teaspoon brown sugar
I teaspoon prepared mustard**

Add enough water to cover and let stand in refrigerator overnight, or until it's corned. Then prepare with:

**Potatoes
I pound bacon
Onion, diced
Garlic, diced
Mayonnaise or sour cream**

Boil the potatoes and slice. Fry the bacon, reserving the drippings. Sauté the onion and garlic in the bacon drippings until soft. Poach the grouper in a little water until flaky. (I prefer mine rare.) Serve like a salad: Layer the fish, potatoes, bacon, and onions with mayonnaise or sour cream.
Makes 12 servings.

*Owen Saunders
Doyle Lawson and Quicksilver*

MOUNTAIN PRAISE EGGPLANT PARMIGIANA

**2 large eggplants
2 eggs, beaten
Flour
Vegetable oil
Spaghetti sauce
Mozzarella cheese, sliced
Parmesan cheese, grated**

Peel and slice the eggplants like cucumber. Dip

After stints with the Gillis Brothers and James King, Owen Saunders joined Doyle Lawson and Quicksilver in 1994. He plays fiddle in the "long-bow" style of Benny Martin and Scotty Stoneman. Being from Florida, Owen has done a lot of fishing in his time, and he knows how to cook 'em up right.

the sliced eggplant first in the eggs, then in flour. Heat vegetable oil in a skillet and brown eggplant until golden. Layer some of the browned eggplant in a glass cooking tray. Add a layer of spaghetti sauce, then a layer of mozzarella cheese. Layer again the same way until all the eggplant is used. Top with a layer of Parmesan cheese. Bake at 375° until the cheese is melted (about 20 minutes). Enjoy.
Makes 6 servings.

*Lily Isaacs
The Isaacs*

SUPERPICKER'S RED LEMON SNAPPER

**I fresh lemon
3 tablespoons vegetable oil
2 tablespoons soy sauce
I medium onion, chopped
I fresh green bell pepper, chopped
2 red snapper fillets
Salt and pepper**

Slice ½ the lemon into thin, ¼-inch slices and set aside. Combine the vegetable oil, soy sauce, and the squeezed juice of the other lemon half, then cover the bottom of a frying pan with this mixture. Turn the pan's heat to medium (just a light sizzle) and drop in the onion and pepper pieces, stirring lightly until covered with the sauce. After a couple of minutes, clear out a place

In recent years, gospel group The Isaacs has gained recognition in bluegrass circles by playing bluegrass festivals and through their 1995 recording with Ralph Stanley, *A Gospel Gathering*. The group's patriarch, Joe Isaacs, has enduring ties with traditional bluegrass, dating back to his short stint as one of Stanley's Clinch Mountain Boys in the 1970s. Joe's 1996 recording, *Heartfelt Pickin' & Singin',* is solid bluegrass gospel, with guests including Ralph Stanley, Ricky Skaggs, and Charlie Louvin. The album features the gorgeous harmonies that are an Isaacs family trademark. Pictured here are (*l-r*) Becky Isaacs Bowman, John R. Bowman, Lily Isaacs, Ben Isaacs, Joe Isaacs (*on porch*), Tim Surratt, and Sonya Isaacs Surratt.

in the middle of the pan and put in the fillets (one or both, depending on pan size). Fry the fillets 1 to 1½ minutes, then turn the fillets over. Fry on this side until tender throughout at the touch of a fork. Add salt and pepper to taste. Serve with your choice of salad, rice, or potato. Garnish with lemon slices.

Makes 2 servings.

David Johnson

WOOLWINE FLOUNDER BAKE

My favorite!

1 pound frozen flounder fillets
1 10¾-ounce can cream of celery soup
Cheddar cheese, grated

Thaw the fish and blot dry with paper towels. Place the fillets in a greased baking dish. Pour the cream of celery soup over the fillets. Bake at 325° for 20 minutes. Remove from the oven and cover with cheese. Bake 10 minutes more. Serve hot.

Makes 4 servings.

Allen Mills
The Lost and Found

Superpicker David Johnson can play just about any stringed instrument you put in his hand. David is a regular studio musician on many of the bluegrass gospel releases on the Horizon/Mountain Home label. On his solo recording, *Wooden Offerings*, which was released on Mountain Home in 1995, he plays every instrument except the bass.

Allen Mills helped form The Lost and Found in 1973. With his tireless energy and outgoing personality, Allen is the driving force behind The Lost and Found's popularity and longevity. In addition to booking the band, acting as emcee, playing bass, and doing much of the lead and tenor singing, Allen is a fine songwriter. His "hits" include "Love of the Mountains" and "Peaceful Dreams."

LEMON FISH LEROY

2 fish fillets
2 lemons
Salt

Squeeze 1 lemon's juice on both sides of fish fillets. Put salt in the bottom of the baking dish. Place the fish on top. Refrigerate for several hours.

Combine for sauce:

½ teaspoon basil
Salt and pepper
¼ cup mayonnaise
¾ cup sour cream
4 green onions, chopped
Seasoned salt, optional

Spread the sauce over fish. Thinly slice remaining lemon and place slices over top of the sauce. Bake uncovered at 350° for 35 minutes. Makes 2 servings.

Janice and LeRoy McNees
Born Again Bluegrass Band

PEEWEE AND FERN SPINACH QUICHE

A good frozen 9-inch pie crust
3 large eggs
¼ teaspoon salt
Pinch ground nutmeg
Pinch black pepper
½ cup half-and-half
¾ cup Swiss cheese, grated
⅔ 10-ounce package frozen chopped
   spinach, completely thawed and drained
6 teaspoons butter

After thoroughly pricking the pie crust, bake it at 400° for 5 minutes. Whisk together the eggs, spices, and half-and-half. Put ½ of the cheese and all the drained spinach in the bottom of the crust, then pour the liquid mixture over it. Sprinkle the rest of the cheese over the liquid mixture and put 6 pats of butter on top. Bake at 375° for 35 minutes, until bubbly and golden. Makes 6 servings.

Claire Lynch

LeRoy Mack McNees, former member of the Kentucky Colonels, has been playing resonator guitar for nearly four decades. For the last three decades, LeRoy has played with the group he cofounded, the Born Again Bluegrass Band. LeRoy says that Josh Graves is the biggest musical influence of his life, and LeRoy himself is considered to be one of the world's finest practitioners of the Josh Graves style of playing. LeRoy has made lots of good friends in the world of bluegrass; his 1996 release, *LeRoy Mack & Friends*, is an outstanding musical testimony to the range and talents of LeRoy and some of his pals. Throughout the 1990s, LeRoy has conducted resonator guitar workshops—helping new players get started and sharing licks and tricks with intermediate and advanced players.

DIXON CASSEROLE

We arrived at dinnertime at the Dixon, Missouri, Annual Picking Time Bluegrass Festival. Typical of Southern hospitality, they were having an all-festival potluck. Janice quickly created this casserole from anything she could lay her hands on in the motor home. The casserole was a great hit! Many people came knocking on our motor home door and asked for the recipe. Not even having a name, it was called "Dixon" after the place where it was created.

First Layer:

1 5-ounce box scalloped potatoes, any flavor

Follow the directions for microwave cooking (but use ¼ cup less water). Cook as directed in the microwave.

Second Layer:

1½ pounds ground beef, browned and drained
1 medium onion, diced
3 red chile peppers, diced (optional)
Dash of salt and pepper

Third Layer:

1 cup corn
1 cup green beans, fresh, frozen, or canned

Fourth Layer:

1 11-ounce can cream of mushroom soup
    mixed with ½ cup milk or water

Fifth Layer:

2 cups cheddar cheese, grated

Spread the layers into a 2-quart greased casserole dish. Bake for 45 minutes at 350°, or microwave on high for 20 minutes.
   Makes 6 to 8 servings.

Janice and LeRoy Mack McNees
Born Again Bluegrass Band

CALIFORNIA EARTHQUAKE

Butter
3 cups sour cream
2 4-ounce cans chopped green chilies
1 tablespoon Worcestershire sauce
1 teaspoon salt
4 cups rice
1 pound Monterey Jack cheese, grated
¾ cup cheddar cheese, grated

Butter a 3-quart casserole dish. Combine the sour cream, chopped green chilies, Worcestershire sauce, and salt in a bowl. Cook the rice. Layer the casserole dish as follows: ½ of the rice, ½ of the cream mixture, ½ of the Monterey Jack, and ½ of the cheddar cheese. Repeat the layers, ending with the cheddar cheese. It's great to add a little hot pepper cheese. Bake at 300° for 45 minutes.
   Makes 8 servings.

Ben Eldridge
The Seldom Scene

For twenty-five years, Ben Eldridge has been a banjo player with The Seldom Scene by night and a mathematician by day. Growing up in Richmond, Virginia, Ben spent many evenings in the audience at the Old Dominion Barn Dance as a boy. Ben's first professional picking job was with Cliff Waldron and the New Shades of Grass in 1970. In the fall of 1971, he and Mike Auldridge left that group, and a few weeks later, they got together with John Starling, John Duffey, and Tom Gray to form The Seldom Scene.

HOT PICKIN' MEAT (FOR TACOS AND BURRITOS)

1 medium onion, sliced
1 cup pickled or fresh jalapeño peppers,
    sliced
2 green bell peppers, quartered
1 clove garlic
1 fresh tomato, quartered
1 tablespoon Tabasco sauce
1 teaspoon salt
1 teaspoon black pepper
1½ pounds boneless pork, chicken, or beef;
    ground or chopped

Place all the ingredients, except the meat, in a food processor and chop extra fine. Brown the meat in a non-stick skillet over low heat. Drain off the fat. Add the vegetable mixture from the food processor to the skillet and simmer for 30 minutes, stirring occasionally. Serve in soft (flour tortillas) or hard (corn) shells with toppings of your choice (lettuce, tomato, cheese, onion, etc).
   Makes 6 servings.

Don Rigsby
The Lonesome River Band

Mandolin player Don Rigsby joined The Lonesome River Band in 1995 following stints with J. D. Crowe and the New South and the Bluegrass Cardinals. Pictured here with Don are Lonesome River Band members (l-r) Ronnie Bowman on bass, Sammy Shelor on banjo, and Kenny Smith on acoustic guitar.

COLLEGE GROVE CORN, CHILIES, AND CHEESE CASSEROLE

We lick casserole dishes too.

1 15-ounce can cream-style corn
1 cup Bisquick
1 egg
¼ cup melted butter
1 4½-ounce can chopped green chilies
Monterey Jack cheese, grated

Mix the corn, Bisquick, egg, and butter together. Take ½ the corn mixture and put it in the bottom of a greased casserole pan. Layer ½ the green chilies over the corn mixture and ½ the cheese over the chilies. Then layer the rest of the corn mixture, another layer of chilies, and another layer of cheese. Bake at 350° for approximately 1 hour, or until the top is golden brown. Serve hot.

Makes about 4 servings.

Danny Potter
Flat Creek Skillet Lickers

MAMA'S CHICKEN ENCHILADAS

4 large chicken breast halves
1 medium onion
1 4-ounce can chopped green chilies
8 ounces sour cream
8 ounces grated Monterey Jack cheese (with peppers is OK)
2 tablespoons salsa
1 teaspoon salt
2 10¾-ounce can cream of mushroom soup
10 large flour tortillas
½ stick butter

Cook the chicken breast halves. Cool, debone, and chop the chicken. Chop the onion and add the green chilies, then add the mixture to the chicken. Mix thoroughly with sour cream, cheese, salsa, salt, and ½ can of soup. Warm the tortillas one at a time. Put some of the mixture in each tortilla and roll up. Place seam side down in a buttered, 9- by 13-inch Pyrex dish. Heat the remaining mushroom soup with butter until melted. Pour over enchiladas. Bake at 350° for 30 minutes. Serve with rice and a salad of lettuce, apples, and mayonnaise. Guacamole is also good with this dish.

Makes 5 servings.

Terry Smith
The Osborne Brothers

Members of the Flat Creek Skillet Lickers hail from middle Tennessee, where their skilled licks have made them a popular band in an area where you have to be able to flat do some picking to get noticed. Pictured are Hoot Hester on fiddle, Gary Francis on banjo, Danny Potter on guitar, Shane Green on bass, and Bruce Keedy on mandolin.

The Osborne Brothers of the mid-1990s are (seated, l-r) Terry Smith, Terry Eldridge, David Crow, and Gene Wooten, and (standing, l-r) Bobby Osborne and Sonny Osborne

The Osborne Brothers

Sonny and Bobby Osborne have been playing bluegrass music professionally since they were teenagers in the Appalachian hills of Kentucky. In 1949, at age seventeen, Bobby joined the Lonesome Pine Fiddlers. Sonny was just fourteen when he became the banjo player for Bill Monroe's Blue Grass Boys in 1952. The brothers became a team in 1953, following Bobby's discharge from a two-year stint with the Marine Corps in Korea. During the 1950s, Sonny and Bobby toured and recorded with various partners, including Jimmy Martin and Red Allen. When they separated from Allen in 1958, they continued to work as the Osborne Brothers. In 1964, the Osbornes became members of the Grand Ole Opry and relocated to Nashville.

The Osborne Brothers trademark sound centers around the smooth, tight vocal harmonies led by the clear, powerful tenor voice of Bobby Osborne. Rather than following the usual pattern for bluegrass trios, which is characterized by a lead voice with one harmony part above and one below it (or alternately, with two parts above), the Osbornes use a high lead with two parts below it. This enables them to feature their strongest singer, Bobby, while allowing Sonny to pursue the instrumental improvisation which is his forte.

Throughout their career, the Osborne Brothers have been known for broadening the horizons of bluegrass music. They were the first group to introduce bluegrass on college campuses in 1959, during the folk revival, and the first bluegrass band to play at Harrah's in Lake Tahoe. During the '70s, when the Nashville country music establishment sought to divorce itself from the acoustic sound of bluegrass, the Osborne Brothers were one of the few bluegrass groups that were able to maintain a strong presence in the Nashville arena. They did this partly by electrifying their instruments and using drums, a compromise which angered bluegrass purists at the time. However, the move paid off. In 1971, they were named the Country Music Association's Vocal Group of the Year, and they were finalists in this category for six years. Readers of the Nashville-based *Music City News* voted the Osborne Brothers the Top Bluegrass Group for nine years straight. They continued to bring bluegrass to mainstream country audiences around the world as part of giant country music package tours throughout the '70s. During the mid-1980s, they pioneered a successful program of bluegrass accompanied by symphony orchestras, engaging a whole new set of fans.

Many of the Osborne Brothers's songs have gone on to become bluegrass classics. In 1982, their hit single, "Rocky Top," was named the state song of Tennessee; their recording of "Kentucky" led to its adoption as Kentucky's state song in 1992. Other classic hits include "Midnight Flyer," "Ruby," "Listening to the Rain," "Georgia Pineywoods," "Once More," and "Roll Muddy River." Many of these are included in two, four-CD boxed sets available from Bear Family Records. In 1994, the Osborne Brothers were inducted into the IBMA Hall of Honor, the ultimate nod to the success and popularity of these bluegrass legends.

Hot Rize formed in Boulder, Colorado, in 1978. The group adopted its name from the secret ingredient in Martha White flour, and fans ate up their music like fresh biscuits. Hot Rize's "secret ingredient" pleased crowds the world over, as was evidenced by their IBMA Award for Entertainer of the Year in 1990. The members of Hot Rize parted ways in 1990 to pursue other musical endeavors, but they continue to get together each year for reunion shows. Pictured here are (l-r) Pete Wernick (banjo), Tim O'Brien (mandolin and fiddle), Nick Forster (bass), and Charles Sawtelle (guitar).

ENCHILADAS A LA RAMSEY

This dish is every bit as tasty as it is simple. I learned it from my wife, Kit, who learned it from Steve Ramsey, a good friend of ours from Denver. Steve's not only a great cook, but also a great photographer who's done several album cover shots for Hot Rize and me over the years. These enchiladas are different in that they're flat instead of rolled. Kit modified the recipe a bit; I'll explain below.

8 to 10 ounces Monterey Jack cheese, grated
5 to 6 scallions
12 corn tortillas
½ pound leftover pot roast or roast chicken, shredded into small pieces (optional)
1 10-ounce can enchilada sauce, or 1 bag dried large red chile peppers and 3 cloves garlic

Grate the cheese and dice the scallions, then place these ingredients, along with the tortillas and meat, near the stovetop where you'll be heating the enchilada sauce. Get out enough oven-proof plates for however many are eating (you'll be making the enchiladas right on the plates you serve them on).

You can get canned enchilada sauce at most grocery stores. The kind I like best is made of just red chile peppers and water. Las Palmas makes a good one. Ramsey makes his own this way: Break up the peppers and shake out the seeds. Next, cover the peppers with water in a saucepan. Bring the peppers to a boil and then cook them for 15 to 20 minutes, until the chilies are soft all the way through. Purée them in a food processor in the water they were boiling in, along with 3 peeled garlic cloves. Pour the purée (or the canned sauce, if that's what you're using) into a frying pan that's a little bigger than the tortillas. Simmer until you have the right consistency—sort of thin gravy.

Take a tortilla and dip it in the sauce, coating both sides, then lay it flat on a plate. Put some scallions and cheese on top, then some of the meat (if you're using it), then a bit more cheese. Coat another tortilla with enchilada sauce and place it on top of the other one. Sprinkle a bit more cheese on top, then spoon a little more enchilada sauce on top of the whole thing. Repeat the whole process, one enchilada per plate, as many times as you have plates. Put the plates in a 300° oven just long enough to melt the cheese.

Steve makes his enchiladas in, and serves them from, a frying pan, but we use the plate-in-the-oven method at our house so everyone can eat at the same time. He also heats the tortillas in a little oil before dipping them in the enchilada sauce, but Kit skips that step to reduce the fat content.

Serve immediately with some ranch beans, guacamole, and a little dollop of sour cream on top of each enchilada. These are also really good with a fried egg on top as "Enchiladas Rancheros."

Makes 6 servings.

Tim O'Brien and Kit Swaggert

Multitalented North Carolinian Lou Reid has performed with many of the top names in bluegrass and country music, including Doyle Lawson and Quicksilver, The Seldom Scene, IIIrd Tyme Out, Ricky Skaggs, Vern Gosdin, and Vince Gill. He is proficient on just about every bluegrass instrument and is known for his stratospheric singing and dynamic energy. Lou currently fronts his own group, Lou Reid and Carolina, pictured here in 1996: (l-r) Gena Britt, Alan Bibey, Lou Reid, and Randy Barnes. (Clay Jones returned to the band in late 1996, replacing Alan Bibey.)

GREEN CHILE CHICKEN ENCHILADA CASSEROLE

1 pound boneless chicken breasts
1 medium onion, chopped
1 clove garlic, minced
Salt and pepper to taste
12 ounces sour cream
Cilantro
2 4½-ounce cans chopped green chilies
1 package corn tortillas
Vegetable oil
1 8-ounce bag shredded cheddar cheese

Cook the chicken until done, then shred. Put the shredded chicken in a pan along with the onion and garlic, then cook until heated well. Remove the chicken from heat. Add salt and pepper to taste. In a blender, blend the sour cream, about 3 sprigs of cilantro, and the green chilies until smooth. In a skillet, cook the tortillas, one at a time, in oil for about 15 to 20 seconds on each side. When the tortillas are finished, fill them with meat. Pour some of the green chile sauce over the meat, then roll up each tortilla. Place the tortillas in a greased casserole dish. Pour any leftover sauce on top and sprinkle with cheddar cheese. (Cheese inside the tortillas is optional.) Cook for 20 minutes at 350°, or until the cheese is melted thoroughly. Now, pull up a chair and enjoy.

Makes about 4 to 6 servings.

Lou Reid
Lou Reid and Carolina

DESERT ROSE ENCHILADAS

1½ cups extra sharp cheddar cheese, grated
1 10-ounce jar enchilada sauce
Safflower oil
12 corn tortillas
¹/₃ cup onion, chopped

Set aside the grated cheddar cheese in a bowl. Pour ¼ cup of the enchilada sauce into a pie pan. Heat safflower oil in a frying pan until hot. Dip 1 tortilla at a time into hot oil for several seconds, remove, and drain on paper towels.

Dip the tortilla into the pie pan with the enchilada sauce, then transfer to a greased rectangular casserole dish until you have a layer of 3 enchiladas across (they can slightly overlap). Generously sprinkle on some of the cheese and onion. Repeat the procedure until you have four layers of enchiladas.

The remaining cheese, onions, and enchilada sauce should be spread over the top of the 4 tortilla layers. Heat the casserole dish in an oven at 350° for approximately 20 minutes. Cut into quarters for serving.

Added Suggestions: If you are having guests over to your house to listen to the new Chris Hillman/Herb Pedersen record, include a do-it-yourself buffet featuring cooked chicken, ground beef, sour cream, guacamole, salsa, olives, tomatoes, extra cheese (different styles if you prefer), extra onions, and slices of jalapeño peppers.

Also: Prepare a basket of warm flour and corn

tortillas next to a bowl of hot refried beans and a bowl of cooked Mexican rice, so guests can prepare mini-burritos to eat with their enchiladas.

Makes 4 servings.

Chris Hillman

Californian Chris Hillman got his start performing bluegrass music in such obscure West Coast bands as the Scottsville Squirrel Barkers, the Golden State Boys, the Blue Diamond Boys, and the Hillmen. In 1964, he traded his mandolin for an electric bass and joined folk-rock band the Byrds. After leaving the Byrds, Chris formed the Flying Burrito Brothers with Al Perkins and Gram Parsons, followed by a stint with Manassas, led by Stephen Stills. That venture was followed by a band called Souther-Hillman-Furay, with J.D. Souther and Richie Furay. In the early '80s, Chris returned to his roots with *Morning Sky*, a bluegrass- and folk-flavored recording on Sugar Hill Records. In the late '80s, he found commercial and critical success once again with the Desert Rose Band, with John Jorgensen, Herb Pedersen, J.D. Maness, and Bill Bryson. In the '90s, Chris has come home once more to his roots with recordings with Pedersen for Sugar Hill and Rounder.

The Hillmen

In 1964, California producer Jim Dickson produced the first and only recordings by the Hillmen. The group featured Chris Hillman, country singers Vern and Rex Gosdin, and banjo player Don Parmley (who went on to found the Bluegrass Cardinals). The album was not released until 1969, after the group had disbanded. Sugar Hill Records unearthed the masters and reissued the recording on LP in 1982 (a CD was released in 1995).

藍草水餃

BLUE GRASS DUMPLINGS

As bluegrass is now played worldwide, it seems only fitting to include a recipe that reflects this fact. This recipe is a special favorite of my wife, Lin, and mine. It comes to us from our friend Xiaoping Wang, owner of the Magic Wok Restaurant in Johnson City, Tennessee. The only problem with the dumplings is that they are so good, you can eat more than a reasonable amount if you aren't careful.

Skin:

2½ cups flour
½ cup cold water

Add the water to 2 cups of flour, mix well, and knead into a smooth dough. Use additional flour as needed to prevent sticking. Cover with a damp paper towel and let dough stand for at least 10 minutes. Roll the dough into a long baton-like roll and cut it into 30 to 40 pieces. With a rolling pin, roll each piece into a thin, round wrap.

Filling:

VEGETARIAN VERSION

1 to 1¹/₂ cups cabbage, finely chopped
(squeeze to remove most of the juice;
chives or celery may be substituted for
variety)
1 teaspoon ginger root, finely chopped
(optional)
4 eggs, scrambled
¹/₄ teaspoon salt
¹/₄ teaspoon ground black pepper
1 teaspoon sesame oil
2 tablespoons soy sauce
1 teaspoon sugar

MEAT VERSION

1 pound lean ground beef

1 bunch green onions, finely chopped
1 teaspoon ginger root, finely chopped
(optional)
1 egg, beaten
2 tablespoons water
¹/₄ teaspoon salt
¹/₄ teaspoon ground black pepper
1 teaspoon sesame oil
3 tablespoons soy sauce
1 teaspoon sugar

Other ingredients:

2 tablespoons vegetable oil
¹/₃ cup water
¹/₄ soy sauce
2 tablespoons vinegar
¹/₃ cup sesame oil

*ETSU students join in a grand finale jam
session with the pros at a concert sponsored
by the Birthplace of Country Music Alliance.
The event was held to honor bluegrass
pioneer Benny Sims, who played fiddle on
numerous Flatt and Scruggs classics. Ralph
Stanley, Jim and Jesse McReynolds, Curly
Seckler, Bonnie Lou and Buster Moore, Mac
Wiseman, and John Hartford donated their
time to establish a scholarship fund for
bluegrass students at ETSU in Benny's name.*
Courtesy of ETSU Photo Lab

The Bluegrass and Country Music Program at East Tennessee State University

The Bluegrass and Country Music Program at East
Tennessee State University was founded in 1982 by Jack
Tottle, who continues to serve as its director. The program
is the only one of its kind in the nation at a four-year college
or university. Offered through ETSU's department of music
and the school's Center for Appalachian Studies, the
program offers a variety of courses, including instruction on
bluegrass instruments, vocal harmony, theory for acoustic
players, sound reinforcement, and playing in a bluegrass
band. As part of the program, students engage in private
and group lessons, ensemble performances, and academic
course work.

Alumni of the program include Barry Bales and Adam
Steffey of Alison Krauss and Union Station; Tim Stafford of
Blue Highway (who also teaches guitar and banjo at ETSU);
Rounder recording artist Beth Stevens; Warren Amberson
and Kelly Green (founders of Acoustic Endeavors); Jennifer
McCarter of the McCarters; and country music's Kenny
Chesney.

For information about the program, contact Jack Tottle at
(423) 929-4270, or write to Bluegrass and Country Music
Program, ETSU Department of Music, P.O. Box 70661,
Johnson City, Tennessee 37614-0661.

Add all the filling ingredients together in a bowl and mix well.

Place 1 spoonful of filling in the center of each skin. Fold the skin in half. Starting from one end, use your index finger and thumb to bring the sides together, pleating one edge while keeping the other edge smooth. Continue until reaching the other end and seal. Repeat the procedure for the other dumplings.

Heat an electric skillet or pan to 400° (or over the highest heat) and add 2 tablespoons cooking oil. Arrange the dumplings, flat side down, to line the skillet. Fry the dumplings for about 2 minutes, or until golden brown. Add 1/3 cup of water to the skillet and cover. Cook for 5 to 7 minutes, or until the water is gone. Remove the cover and cook for 2 or 3 minutes more. Remove the dumplings and serve, if desired, with a dip consisting of soy sauce, vinegar, and sesame oil.

Makes 30 to 40 dumplings.

Jack Tottle

BENNY MARTIN COUNTRY CORN BREAD AND BEANS

Pinto Beans:

10 ounces pinto beans
12 cups water
3 ounces fatback or salt pork
1/2 teaspoon salt

Wash and sort the beans, then place in a crockpot with the water, pork, and salt. Cook on high for about 8 hours.

Corn Bread:

2 tablespoons lard or vegetable oil
2 1/2 cups self-rising cornmeal (I use Martha White self-rising cornmeal mix)
1 1/2 cups buttermilk
1 egg, beaten

Place a 10-inch iron skillet in a 450° oven with 2 tablespoons of hog lard or 2 tablespoons of cooking oil. Heat until the skillet is very hot (this keeps the bread from sticking to the pan). Mix the cornmeal with the buttermilk and the

Bluegrass fiddle pioneer Benny Martin played with Bill Monroe's Blue Grass Boys and Flatt and Scruggs's Foggy Mountain Boys before going solo forty years ago. Many of the great young fiddlers of today, such as the Del McCoury Band's Jason Carter, name Benny as one of their biggest influences.

egg. Remove the skillet from the oven. Pour the oil from the skillet into the batter and mix. Add more milk if the batter seems too dry. Pour the batter into the hot skillet and place in the oven for 20 to 25 minutes. Check the bread. If it is good and brown, Bingo: You've got lip-smacking good Benny Martin Corn Bread. Serve the corn bread with the beans.

Makes about 4 servings.

Benny Martin

"CORN BREAD AND BEANS" LYNAM-STYLE

This has always been one of my favorite dishes. It is based on a recipe of my mother's, although she's never really written it down (typical of a good "down-home" cook). As it's cooking, it fills the house with an aroma that really takes me back to when I was a kid at home. I make it as a crockpot dish and usually put it on before heading out for the day, so that it will be done when I return (and so I won't be so tempted to "dig in" before it's really ready). In order to mostly avoid the unpleasant aftereffects of beans, the night before you make this, boil the beans for about five minutes, then let them soak overnight.

In a 2-quart crockpot, place the following:

3 cups dried navy beans, soaked as described above
1 pound hamhocks, trimmed of fat
1 onion, diced
1 clove garlic, minced
1 bay leaf
Salt and pepper to taste (go slow on the salt)
Water to fill the crockpot to within an inch of the top

Cook on low for 10 to 12 hours.

Corn Bread:

Mix:
¾ cup whole-wheat flour
1¼ cups cornmeal (preferably stone-ground)
2½ teaspoons baking powder
½ teaspoon salt

In a separate bowl, mix:
1 cup milk
1 egg
2 to 3 tablespoons canola oil

Mix the dry and wet ingredients together with a few brisk strokes, then bake in a greased baking dish or muffin pan at 425° for 15 to 20 minutes (slightly less if you're making muffins) until it begins to brown on top.

The correct way to eat this is to break up some corn bread in a bowl and then ladle the beans over the top. It doesn't hurt to have some buttered corn bread on the side, too. I'm getting hungry just thinking about this!

Makes 6 to 8 servings.

Ron Lynam
Front Range

INTERSTATE EXCHANGE CHUCK WAGON MACARONI

1 5½-ounce package Kraft Macaroni & Cheese dinner
1 pound ground beef
½ cup celery, chopped
¼ cup green bell pepper, chopped
2 tablespoons onion, chopped
1 6-ounce can tomato paste
2 cups corn, or 1 15-ounce can corn
½ cup water
1 teaspoon salt
Dash pepper

Prepare the macaroni-and-cheese dinner as directed. In a skillet, brown the meat, celery, green pepper, and onion until tender. Stir in the tomato paste, corn, water, salt, and pepper. Add the macaroni-and-cheese dinner and mix. Stir well. Pour into a greased casserole dish. Bake at 350° for 15 to 20 minutes.

Makes about 4 servings.

Barry Berrier
The Lost and Found

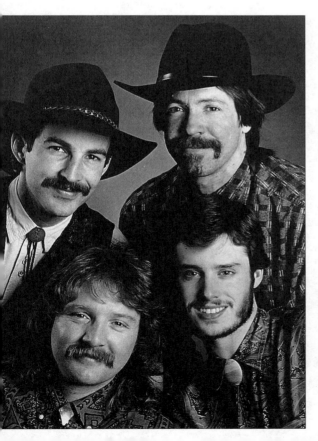

Front Range is: (*clockwise from top left*) Bob Amos, lead vocals and guitar; Ron Lynam, banjo and vocals; Bob Dick, bass and vocals; and Mike Lantz, mandolin and vocals. Though they were already well known in their home state of Colorado, Front Range first gained national recognition in the early 1990s. Their sound combines elements of traditional and contemporary bluegrass, and their original material often has a unique Western flavor.

RIO GRANDE WARRIOR'S CHICKEN CASSEROLE

1 pound chicken pieces
½ cup chopped onions
½ cup chopped green bell peppers
¼ cup margarine
1 10¾-ounce can cream of chicken soup
1 10¾-ounce can cream of mushroom soup
1 15-ounce can tomatoes and chilies
1 5-ounce can evaporated milk
1 bag tortilla chips (nacho flavored)
1 pound cheddar cheese, grated

Boil and debone the chicken. In a large skillet, brown the pepper and onion in the margarine. Add both cans of soup, the can of tomatoes and chilies, and the milk to the skillet and stir together. Place ½ of the chips in the bottom of a greased casserole dish. Pour the soup mixture on top of the chips. Place the chicken on top of the soup mixture. Sprinkle cheese on top of the chicken. Place the remaining chips on top of the cheese. Bake at 350° for 25 minutes.
Makes 4 to 6 servings.

David Davis
The Warrior River Boys

TALL TALES BLACK BEAN VEGGIE BURRITOS

Balsamic vinegar
1 green or red bell pepper, seeded and
    chopped
1 onion, chopped
1 to 4 garlic cloves, minced
1 jalapeño pepper, finely chopped (optional)
1 teaspoon each (or to taste) cumin powder,
    thyme, and cayenne pepper
2 15-ounce cans black beans, drained
1 15-ounce can corn kernels (vacuum-
    packed type), drained
1 6-ounce can tomato paste
1 to 2 tablespoons soy sauce
12 flour tortillas
Grated cheese of choice (optional)
Salsa (optional)

In a large skillet, sauté the peppers, onion, and garlic in balsamic vinegar with the spices until soft and the onion is clear. Add the beans, corn, tomato paste, and soy sauce. Stir mixture and cook until warm. (The mixture should be thick, not liquid.)

Spoon the mixture into the flour tortillas and top with salsa and/or cheese if desired. Roll up the tortillas and bake at 350° in a greased casserole dish for 10 to 15 minutes.

This dish freezes well. Cover with a damp paper towel when reheating in microwave to keep tortillas from getting tough.
Makes 12 servings.

Pat and Randall Hylton

FIRE ON THE MOUNTAIN CHICKEN SPAGHETTI

This is my mother's best recipe.

2 fryer chickens, cooked, deboned, and cut
    into bite-sized pieces (to make 4 to 5
    cups chicken)
1 pound spaghetti
3 large onions, cut into chunks
2 cups celery, cut into chunks
2 cups green bell pepper, cut into chunks
2 cups American cheese, grated
2 cups sharp cheddar cheese, grated
1½ teaspoon cumin seed, or 1 teaspoon
    cumin powder
Salt and pepper to taste
1 tablespoon Worcestershire sauce
1½ tablespoons chili powder
1 20-ounce can whole tomatoes
1 6-ounce can tomato paste
2 4½-ounce cans mushrooms
Ripe olives (optional)

Boil the chickens (fryers) in plenty of water and retain the broth (you'll need about 3 quarts of broth to cook the spaghetti). I cook the chickens the day before, so I can skim off the fat. Use some of the chicken fat to sauté the onions, celery, and peppers. Cover and cook until tender. Boil the spaghetti in the chicken broth. When the spaghetti has had a chance to absorb as much of the stock as it can, pour off the excess stock.

MOM'S TOUGH EGG NOODLES

1 cup flour
$^1/_2$ teaspoon salt
1 teaspoon baking powder
1 egg
$^1/_2$ to $^1/_3$ cup milk
2 quarts chicken or beef broth

Mix together thoroughly the flour, salt, and baking powder. Add the egg and enough milk so that the mixture is stiff enough to roll out; roll the dough $^1/_8$-inch to $^1/_4$-inch thick. Cut into $^1/_2$-inch strips. Boil the noodles in the chicken or beef broth for 15 to 20 minutes. Do not prepare the mixture in advance—only just before cooking. This recipe is a favorite memory of my childhood.

Makes about 4 servings.

Mac Wiseman

David Holt may have the best description of who he is: "A one-man celebration of stories and songs." Along with playing eight or ten different instruments (who can count them all?), David is a singer, dancer, and accomplished storyteller. There are few people doing more to preserve and demonstrate traditional musical folkways than David. And sometimes that means using the power of communications satellites, as he did with his top-rated *Fire on the Mountain* series on The Nashville Network during the early '80s.

Immediately mix the cheese, spices, tomatoes, and tomato paste into the hot spaghetti; then add the vegetables, mushrooms, and chicken. You may also add ripe olives if desired.

Put the pot containing the spaghetti mixture in a pan of hot water and place it in the oven. Do not cover, but stir once in a while. Serve when you are ready. It is better if made the day before, refrigerated, and reheated because the flavors are mixed.

Makes 10 servings.

David Holt

Mac Wiseman has been performing bluegrass for about fifty years now. He was made a member of the IBMA Hall of Honor in 1993.

THATSA PASTA WITH CAULIFLOWER SAUCE

We love this recipe and use it often when we are home. Cauliflower is a vegetable that keeps a while in the refrigerator, and everything else is usually in our pantry, so for people like us who live in the boondocks, it's a good, easy way to have fresh vegetables without having to go to the store every day. It's also a great leftover.

4 to 8 cloves garlic, minced
2 to 3 tablespoons olive oil
1 to 2 tablespoons basil or oregano, or both
1 teaspoon salt
Pinch pepper, freshly ground, if available
1 head cauliflower, cut into bite-sized pieces
1 tablespoon water
8 ounces tomato sauce (If we have time, we make it fresh with roma tomatoes, if not we use canned.)
1 pound pasta of your choice (We usually use something long like spaghetti or linguine, but any kind will do.)
Grated cheese (optional)

In a large skillet or saucepan, sauté the minced garlic in the olive oil with basil, salt, and pepper. Add the cauliflower and sauté 3 to 5 minutes. Then add a tablespoon or so of water and cover. Let steam for 3 to 5 minutes, until almost tender. Add the tomato sauce and simmer while the pasta cooks. Cook the pasta according to the directions on the package (you can toss the pasta with a little olive oil if you like). Serve the sauce over hot pasta with or without cheese (Parmesan, Romano, or even cheddar is good).

Makes 8 servings.

Robin and Linda Williams

SEEGER'S SPICY SESAME NOODLES

I got this from my sister Penny and have found it to be a great one for potlucks.

1 pound linguine
3 tablespoons toasted sesame oil

Singers/songwriters Robin and Linda Williams have been making beautiful music together for a long time. Their powerful songs have been recorded by many other bands as well. Robin and Linda have always straddled the line between bluegrass and folk, but their current Fine Group, which includes Kevin Maul on resonator guitar and Jim Watson on bass, may be their most bluegrass-flavored lineup yet. Robin and Linda record for Sugar Hill Records.

1½ tablespoons fresh ginger root, grated or minced
2 tablespoons honey or sugar
³/₈ cup tahini
³/₈ cup tamari (dark soy sauce)
3 tablespoons wine vinegar
¼ teaspoon crushed red pepper, or 1 tablespoon chile pepper oil

Optional, sprinkled on top:

2 to 3 scallions, cut in ½- to 1-inch pieces

Cook the linguine and drain in a colander or strainer. Rinse with cold water and drain well. Put the noodles in a bowl, toss with the sesame oil, and allow to cool. With a wire whisk, combine remaining ingredients in small bowl and pour over cold noodles. Toss until well-coated. I like it best after the ingredients have all been together at least a few hours. If desired, sprinkle scallions on top before serving.

Makes about 6 to 8 servings.

Mike Seeger

Mike Seeger has produced many highly acclaimed recordings, and he continues to perform his own brand of folk/bluegrass/old-time music around the world. He is currently touring with the regrouped New Lost City Ramblers.

UNION STATION SPAGHETTI SAUCE

2 slices bacon
1½ pounds ground beef
2 medium onions, chopped
1 green bell pepper, chopped
2 16-ounce cans tomato sauce
1 7-ounce can mushrooms, with liquid
1 20-ounce can Hunt's tomatoes
2 6-ounce cans tomato paste
1 tablespoon Worcestershire sauce
½ cup sliced stuffed olives
½ teaspoon oregano
Garlic salt and celery salt (optional)
Red pepper to taste
Salt and pepper to taste
½ teaspoon sweet basil
Chili powder to taste

In a skillet, fry the bacon slices real brown and chop them. Add the beef, onion, and green pepper, and continue cooking until the red just leaves your beef.

Open the cans into a pot, then pour in the beef mixture. Add Worcestershire sauce, olives, and spices, then cook at a simmer for about 3 hours.

Makes sauce for 6 to 8 servings.

Barry Bales
Alison Krauss and Union Station

ACHIES SPAGHETTI

Vegetable oil
2 medium onions, chopped
½ green bell pepper, chopped
1 small clove garlic, chopped
½ pound lean ground beef
1 15-ounce can tomatoes
¼ teaspoon spaghetti seasoning
1 6-ounce can tomato paste
1 7-ounce can mushrooms
4 ounces thin spaghetti
6 ounces sharp cheese, grated
2 ounces pimiento-stuffed olives, sliced

Sauté the onions, pepper, and garlic in a small amount of vegetable oil. Add the ground beef and stir until brown. Add the tomatoes, spaghetti seasoning, tomato paste, and mushrooms. Mix well and season with salt and pepper. Simmer on low heat while preparing spaghetti. Cook spaghetti in salted boiling water; drain but don't rinse. In a greased 2-quart casserole dish, layer the spaghetti, sauce, cheese, and olives; repeat for 3 layers. Bake at 350° for about 45 minutes, or until it bubbles.

Makes 2 servings.

Hairl Hensley
Host of The Orange Possum Special
WSM Radio (650 AM)

PASTA ENSEMBLE WITH GREEN SAUCE

A lot of my friends are "casual" vegetarians and/or not voracious meat-eaters, so I have developed quite a few mouth-filling concoctions to whet that prudent appetite. Generally, I shun oil and grease; but occasionally one needs to add a bit of that stuff 'cause there isn't any substitute!

8 ounces fat-free cream cheese
½ stick butter
¼ cup virgin olive oil
½ cup grated Parmesan cheese
2 tablespoons dried basil, or ½ cup fresh
 basil, chopped
2 tablespoons dried parsley, or ½ cup fresh
 parsley, chopped
2 cloves fresh garlic, pressed or finely
 chopped
¼ teaspoon freshly ground black pepper
Red pepper (cayenne) to taste
12 to 16 ounces thin pasta
Fresh parsley and Parmesan or Asiago
 cheese for garnish
Salt and pepper to taste

Soften the cream cheese in a large bowl along with the butter, olive oil, and grated Parmesan. Stir in the basil and parsley. Add the fresh garlic, black pepper, and some red pepper to taste, and mix well. Boil thin pasta to al dente. Drain the pasta but reserve ¾ cup of boiling water to add to sauce. Mix the sauce again and pour over the hot pasta. Garnish with fresh parsley and freshly grated Parmesan or Asiago. Salt and pepper to taste.
Makes about 6 servings.

Paul Martin Zonn
Nashville Mandolin Ensemble

OK, SON, GARLICKY PASTA WITH WHITE BEANS AND SPINACH

2 cups water
1 10-ounce bag fresh spinach
2 teaspoons olive oil
4 large cloves garlic, peeled and minced
Pinch of crushed red pepper flakes
2 14½-ounce cans Italian stewed tomatoes,
 undrained, or equivalent fresh tomatoes,
 chopped
1 teaspoon dried basil, crushed
1 teaspoon dried oregano, crushed
¼ teaspoon salt
¼ teaspoon freshly ground black pepper
1 15-ounce can white beans, drained, rinsed,
 and drained again
3 pounds tiny spiral pasta

2 tablespoons fresh Parmesan or Romano
 cheese, grated

Put 2 cups water in a large pan and bring to a boil. Add the spinach and cook for 3 minutes, stirring occasionally. Drain and rinse in cold water. Squeeze out the excess moisture and chop coarsely. In a large, non-stick skillet, heat the olive oil over medium heat. When it is hot, add the garlic and red pepper flakes; sauté for 1 minute. Add the undrained tomatoes, basil, oregano, salt, and pepper. Simmer for 5 minutes. Add the beans and simmer for 5 minutes more. Stir in the cooked spinach and keep warm.

Next, cook the pasta and drain. Add the pasta to the sauce and stir to coat. Stir in the Parmesan or Romano cheese, adjust the seasonings, and serve. Additional grated cheese may be sprinkled on top when served.
Makes about 10 servings.

Wayne Rice
Host of The Bluegrass Special
KSON Radio

Bluegrass deejay Wayne Rice has been on the air for over twenty years with his Sunday evening show, *The Bluegrass Special,* on San Diego's KSON Radio. In 1995, Rice was named IBMA Broadcast Personality of the Year. He is also the author of *Bluegrass Bios: Profiles of the Stars of Bluegrass Music.*

MOM'S LASAGNA

This is a family get-together favorite. It can feed an army. It has also been known to feed an entire bluegrass band. Ask Sammy Shelor or Ronnie Simpkins for a reference!

1 pound lasagna noodles, cooked and drained
32 ounces ricotta cheese
2 pounds ground meat, cooked and drained (I use 1 pound hamburger and 1 pound sliced Italian sausage.)
20 ounces mozzarella cheese, sliced or shredded
8 cups spaghetti sauce
Grated Parmesan cheese for top

Put a little oil on the pan—I like to use a glass lasagna dish.

Layer as follows:

Sauce on the bottom, then (in this order): lasagna noodles, ricotta, meat, mozzarella, sauce, lasagna noodles, ricotta, meat, mozzarella, sauce, and Parmesan cheese on top. Bake at 350° for 45 minutes to 1 hour.

It's better the second day—the cat likes it too!
Makes about 8 servings.

Claire Lynch

JUG BAND PESTO SAUCE

2 cups fresh basil leaves
2 cloves garlic
2 tablespoons pine nuts
4 tablespoons grated Parmesan cheese
4 tablespoons grated Romano cheese
½ to ¾ cup olive oil

Place all the ingredients in a food processor and purée until the consistency is smooth. The sauce can be stored in a refrigerator for a few weeks. You can add extra olive oil to cover the top of the sauce.

Makes enough for about 1 pound of pasta.

Jill Klein
The Nashville Jug Band

THE LITTLE KID'S QUICK MEXICAN PIZZA

In the New South, guitarist Greg Luck calls himself "The Kid," so I started calling myself "The Little Kid." I guess when you travel a lot you just run out of important things to do with your time—other than to think up stupid things.

½ pound ground beef chuck
1½ teaspoons chili powder
½ teaspoon cumin powder
1 cup salsa
4 10-inch flour tortillas
2 cups Monterey Jack cheese, grated
Toppings: green or red bell peppers, onions, mushrooms, chopped, or other toppings, as desired

Cook the meat in a skillet. Drain. Stir in the seasonings. Spread ¼ cup of the salsa and ½ cup of the meat mixture on each tortilla. Top each tortilla with ½ cup of the cheese and the desired toppings. Place the tortillas on a baking sheet and bake in a preheated 400° oven for 8 to 10 minutes, or until crisp and lightly browned.

Makes 4 pizzas.

Phil Leadbettter
J.D. Crowe and the New South

HOMEMADE KENTUCKY SWEETHEART PIZZA

1 tablespoon dry yeast
1 cup warm/hot water
3 tablespoons oil
3 cups flour
Meat toppings (your choice)
13 ounces tomato sauce
Other toppings (black olives, pineapple, mushrooms, etc.)
Salt and pepper to taste
Kraft American cheese slices, or cheese of your choice

Make the dough three hours before mealtime, if possible; if not, mix it and let it stand while cooking the meat toppings.

Dough: Dissolve 1 tablespoon yeast in 1 cup warm/hot water. Then add the oil. Mix in the flour. Knead the dough on a floured surface for 5 minutes, cover, and let rise in a greased bowl for 1 hour.

Cook the meat toppings 45 minutes before you intend to eat. (My family's favorite is beef.) While meat toppings are cooking, knead the dough on a floured surface for 2 minutes, then roll out the dough to the size of your pizza pan and your desired thickness. Grease a pan or spray with non-stick coating. Put the dough on the pan and spread the desired amount of tomato sauce over it (usually 13 ounces of sauce for a 16-inch pizza). Distribute the sauce evenly over the dough with your fingers. Add all desired meat toppings, then any other toppings. (My favorite toppings are black olives, pineapple, mushrooms, and beef.) Add salt and pepper to taste. Bake at 425° for approximately 10 minutes. When the crust starts to brown lightly, remove the pizza and cover with cheese. (I use Kraft American cheese slices. You can top with the cheese of your choice.) Bake for another 5 minutes, or just until the cheese is melted. Cut and serve.

Makes 1 16-inch pizza.

Rhonda Vincent

PIZZA BY THE YARD

When you're too far away in the mountains for pizza delivery, this is good to make for "pickin' sessions" or NASCAR parties. Serve with suds.

1 loaf French bread
1 6-ounce can tomato paste
^{1}/4 cup finely chopped onions
^{1}/3 cup grated Parmesan cheese
1 2^1/4-ounce can chopped ripe olives
^{3}/4 teaspoon salt
1 teaspoon oregano
^{1}/8 teaspoon pepper
1 pound ground round, browned
Homegrown tomatoes
1 8-ounce package American cheese slices

Cut the French bread in half lengthwise (horizontally). Combine the next 8 ingredients and spread the mixture on the bread halves. Bake at 400° for 20 minutes. Remove the bread from oven and top with thin slices of homegrown tomatoes. Lay the American cheese slices, cut in strips and crisscrossed, on the tomatoes. Bake for 5 minutes more.

Makes about 4 servings.

Jon Randall

FIESTA BREAD SUPREME

1 pound ground beef

Rhonda Vincent grew up in the Missouri Ozarks playing bluegrass with her family's band, the Sally Mountain Show. She began playing the mandolin at age five and has since mastered the fiddle, bass, banjo, guitar, and resonator guitar. Her fiddle playing and singing have probably won her the most recognition (including seven Best Female Vocalist awards from SPBGMA). She frequently performs on the Grand Ole Opry and has a budding career as a country music recording artist.

1 pound pork sausage
2 large onions, chopped
1 medium green bell pepper, diced
2 cloves garlic, minced
3 packages Sazon Goya, or 3 teaspoons
    Accent (Sazon may be found in the
    international section at the grocery.)
2 teaspoons salt
2 teaspoons pepper
8 ounces tomato sauce
2 large potatoes, cooked and diced
3 frozen bread dough loaves
Mozzarella cheese, sliced
Melted butter
Garlic powder

In a large pot, brown the beef and pork, then drain off the fat. Add the onion, green pepper, and garlic. Cook until tender. Add the Sazon Goya and simmer for 15 minutes. Add the salt, pepper, tomato sauce, and potatoes. Cook for 5 minutes more. Cool the mixture until lukewarm.

Follow the package directions for thawing the bread dough. Spread 1 loaf of the dough to 12 by 14 inches. Spoon 1/3 of the meat filling down the center of the loaf and cover with slices of mozzarella cheese. Bring the dough up and over the filling. Tuck the ends, seal, and place seam side down on a greased baking sheet. Repeat with the remaining filling and loaves.

Place the loaves in a cold oven over a pan of hot water. Let rise for 15 minutes. Remove the water and loaves from the oven. Preheat oven to 375° and bake loaves for 25 minutes. Remove and brush the loaves with butter. Dust with garlic powder and bake 5 minutes more.

Makes 3 loaves.

Lillie Suttles for
5 for the Gospel

LOUISIANA PICKERS SHRIMP PIQUANT SAUCE

1 cup white onion, chopped
2 cloves garlic, chopped
½ cup cooking oil
½ cup chopped celery
1 28-ounce can tomatoes
1 15-ounce can tomato sauce

1 teaspoon salt
¼ teaspoon black pepper
¼ teaspoon red pepper
2 pounds cleaned shrimp
1 slice lemon
¼ cup green onions, finely chopped
¼ cup parsley, finely chopped

Cook the onion and garlic in the oil until lightly browned. Lower heat, cover, and cook until tender. Stir in the celery, tomatoes, tomato sauce, salt, and peppers. Cook uncovered for 30 minutes, stirring continuously. Add the shrimp and lemon slice and cook until shrimp is tender. Just before serving, add the chopped green onions and parsley. Serve over hot rice.

Makes 6 servings.

Marie Cox
The Cox Family

CLINCH MOUNTAIN SPAGHETTI SAUCE

Serve with a little glass of wine.

1½ pounds lean ground beef
Salt and pepper to taste
1 medium onion, chopped
1 medium green bell pepper, chopped
1 4-ounce jar whole mushrooms
1 large (28-ounce) jar Prego pasta sauce,
    variety of your choice (I often use sauce
    with ground beef since I like lots of meat
    in the sauce.)

Sprinkle the ground beef with salt and pepper if desired and brown in a skillet over medium-high heat until almost cooked through. Drain the meat and return to heat. Add the onion, green pepper, and mushrooms; then sauté for another 5 minutes, or until onion is soft. Add the Prego sauce and stir well. Continue to simmer for about 15 minutes, stirring occasionally. Serve with or without pasta. "Take a fork to it, and eat all you can."

Makes about 6 servings.

Ralph Stanley

The Stanley Brothers

Ralph (left) and Carter Stanley in a publicity photograph from around 1950.
Courtesy of Dave Freeman

Bluegrass pioneers Ralph and Carter Stanley began performing traditional mountain music as teenagers in the hills of southwest Virginia. In 1946, at ages nineteen and twenty-one respectively, Ralph and Carter formed a professional band and began to tour and record as the Stanley Brothers and the Clinch Mountain Boys. With a unique style based on Carter's warm stage personality and blossoming talent for songwriting, along with Ralph's unique, hard-edged banjo style and their experience of singing in the emotionally expressive Primitive Baptist Church, the brothers soon found success.

Over their twenty years together, the Stanley Brothers were acclaimed for many aspects of their music, including their distinctive, tradition-based sound; the intensity of feeling expressed in their music; and their contribution of an immense volume of new material, while at the same time preserving many of the ballads and hymns of their ancestors. Well-known songs written by or strongly associated with the Stanley Brothers include "How Mountain Girls Can Love," "The White Dove," "Rank Stranger," "Clinch Mountain Backstep," "Could You Love Me One More Time," "Daybreak in Dixie," "Nobody's Love Is Like Mine," and many more.

In 1966, Carter Stanley passed away, leaving Ralph to continue the Stanley legacy alone. It was not easy, yet continue he did. Through the years, Ralph unearthed a series of great young lead singers from the Appalachian hills to fill Carter's vacant shoes. Several of these singers, such as Larry Sparks and Charlie Sizemore, have gone on to lead successful groups of their own. Two of the best, Keith Whitley and Roy Lee Centers, like Carter, met with tragedy before their time. Probably the most exciting Ralph Stanley group ever was the legendary band of the early 1970s, which included Jack Cooke, Curly Ray Cline, Roy Lee Centers, and teenagers Keith Whitley and Ricky Skaggs. Recordings from this band are available in a four-CD boxed set released in 1995 by Rebel Records. In 1994, Ralph's sixteen-year-old son, Ralph Stanley II, became a full-time Clinch Mountain Boy, playing guitar and singing several songs with his dad each set. He soon progressed to the lead singing

slot, and much to Ralph's delight, his voice sounds remarkably like a young Carter Stanley.

The Stanley Brothers were inducted into the IBMA Hall of Honor in 1992. In 1993, Ralph's highly acclaimed *Saturday Night/Sunday Morning* recording was named IBMA Recorded Event of the Year, in addition to being a Grammy finalist in three categories. In 1996, Ralph celebrated his fiftieth anniversary in music, and he continues to tour and record prolifically. Ralph is a member of the Virginia Country Music Hall of Fame, recipient of a National Heritage Award, and recipient of an honorary doctor of music degree from Lincoln Memorial University.

In 1992, Freeland Records released Ralph Stanley's *Saturday Night/Sunday Morning*, a double-length recording pairing Ralph with a guest list that reads like a who's who of country and bluegrass music. Included were Dwight Yoakam, Vince Gill, Emmylou Harris, George Jones, Patty Lovelace, Bill Monroe, Jimmy Martin, Ricky Skaggs, Alison Krauss, and more. The recording was the most significant of Ralph's career and won him praise from such publications as the *Wall Street Journal* and *Playboy*. Since that time, a number of other celebrities have stepped forward to proclaim themselves Stanley fans, including Dolly Parton, Jerry Garcia, Naomi Judd, and Bob Dylan.

Ralph Stanley is pleased to have his son, Ralph II, poised to carry the torch for Stanley-style bluegrass into the next century. Here father and son perform together in 1994. Though Ralph Stanley recently celebrated his fiftieth anniversary in music, he shows no signs of slowing down. Ralph marked the occasion with a special Clinch Mountain Boys reunion at his 1996 Memorial Weekend Festival in Coeburn, Virginia. Among the performers were Dwight Yoakam and Ricky

Skaggs. In November, 1996, Ralph was honored at a fiftieth anniversary celebration reception at the Country Music Foundation in Nashville.

Carter Stanley was one of bluegrass music's true great talents. He had a sincere, expressive singing voice and a warm, outgoing personality that made him one of bluegrass music's best emcees. (Just listen to the recordings of the Stanley Brothers's radio shows on Rebel Records. Carter will have you ready to buy a new Jim Walter home before the end of the first show!) Carter was also one of the best and most prolific songwriters of bluegrass music. Though he died in 1966 at age forty-one, his songwriting legacy will live on for many, many years through such classics as "How Mountain Girls Can Love," "The White Dove," "Could You Love Me One More Time," and "Say Won't You Be Mine."

Ralph Stanley recalls that Carter wasn't much for cooking, though bass player Jack Cooke remembers that he did enjoy eating. "He loved onions," Cooke recalls. "One of his favorite things was a cheeseburger with lots of onions on it. " When asked for a recipe associated with Carter, Ralph came up with the following: "Pig's Tail: You put the pig's tail in the pot with the rest of the meat and boil it up good. When it's done, you take it out and gnaw on it." Sounds like a pretty tough tale to swallow!

Carter Stanley
Courtesy of Gary Reid

SEXY PASTA TOMATO SAUCE

I hate Ragu.

Pasta sauce from a jar is like listening to the Muzak version of your favorite song in an elevator while on your way to the dentist. It's artificial and leaves you stressed. Yes, I take my pasta sauce seriously. Almost as seriously as my brand of guitar strings. Trust me when I tell you, if pasta sauce could be a beautiful, buxom blonde . . . then this is it, right here.

So, turn the lights down low, put on something comfortable, set your stereo softly, and get a pan. We're gonna make sweet sauce together.

You will need:

Mountain burgundy wine (the best you can afford)
¹/₈ cup real olive oil
2 cloves fresh garlic, diced
I 32-ounce can tomato sauce
I 16-ounce can diced tomatoes
I 6-ounce can tomato paste
I 16-ounce can tomato purée
I teaspoon dried basil
4 tablespoons garlic powder
I teaspoon sugar
¹/₂ teaspoon salt
¹/₄ stick real salted butter
Parsley

Now, the wine is important. Pour a glass and drink it. This will get you in the mood. Pour a glass for your partner, too. This will not only get him or her in the mood also, but it will also help him or her not notice if this recipe doesn't work out for some reason.

Step one: In a good-sized pot, pour about ¹/₈ cup of real olive oil. Don't wimp out and think using vegetable oil or corn oil will work just as well. It don't. 'Nuff said. Turn the heat on the stove and heat up the oil. Don't let it burn or boil, just get it good and hot. Get your garlic cloves (make sure they're diced nice and small) and put them in the hot oil.

Step two: Add the tomato sauce, diced tomatoes, tomato paste, and tomato purée to the pot. Get an electric mixer and slowly mix the contents while it heats up. Add the basil, garlic powder, sugar, and salt. Put your mixer away, get a wooden spoon, and stir.

Slowly, with your left hand, put your arm around your partner and sway in unison to the movement of the sauce in the pan while stirring. After a few minutes of tenderly teasing your partner, get the bottle of burgundy wine and drink a swig. That's right—from the bottle, don't even bother with a glass. This makes you look "cool" and worldly, two very important qualities you need to appreciate a good pasta sauce. Next . . .

Step three: Add 5 tablespoons or 2 swigs or 1 good-sized gulp of wine to the pot. Add the butter and several good shakes of fresh, diced parsley.

Cover and cook slowly for at least 1 hour. If you want to ruin it by adding meat or chicken, this is the time. This is great with a thin linguine or angel hair pasta. When you cook the pasta, add a slab of butter while it is still in the drainer. Serve with some homemade bread, some fresh grated cheese, a candle or two, my latest album on the stereo . . . and, oh yes! That mountain burgundy wine!

Makes 8 servings, or 2 romantic servings plus leftovers.

Michael Johnathon

Michael Johnathon considers himself to be a folk singer, "part of a long chain of musical caretakers who pass the songs and melodies of our lifetimes from one generation to another."

Another Song-Matching Quiz

Match the song titles with their songwriters.

1.	"Endless Highway"	A.	Bobby Osborne
2.	"Nashville Skyline Rag"	B.	Bill Clifton
3.	"Bluegrass Express"	C.	Gillian Welch
4.	"Tear My Stillhouse Down"	D.	Arthur Smith
5.	"Love and Wealth"	E.	Roger Rasnake
6.	"Dark as a Dungeon"	F.	Merle Travis
7.	"Walking in My Sleep"	G.	Jack Tottle
8.	"Feudin' Banjos"	H.	Bob Dylan
9.	"Hickory Hollow"	I.	Doug Dillard
10.	"It's a Long, Long Road"	J.	Carter Stanley
11.	"The Fields Have Turned Brown"	K.	Ralph Stanley
12.	"Ridin' That Midnight Train"	L.	Charlie and Ira Louvin

Answers: 1. E; 2. H; 3. A; 4. C; 5. L; 6. F; 7. B; 8. D; 9. I; 10. G; 11. J; 12. K

Festival Matching Quiz

Match the bluegrass festival to its hometown.

1.	Winterhawk Festival	A.	Escoheag, Rhode Island
2.	Bass Mountain Festival	B.	Yosemite, California
3.	Festival of the Bluegrass	C.	Conway, Missouri
4.	Withlacoochee River Jamboree	D.	Ancramdale, New York
5.	RockyGrass	E.	Columbus, Ohio
6.	Strawberry Bluegrass Festival	F.	Burlington, North Carolina
7.	Lewis Family Homecoming Festival	G.	Elizabethton, Tennessee
8.	Frontier Ranch Bluegrass Classic	H.	Lexington, Kentucky
9.	Bluegrass and Cajun Music, Dance, and Food Festival	I.	Rocky Mount, Virginia
10.	Tripple Creek Park Festival	J.	Lyons, Colorado
11.	Slagles Pasture Festival	K.	Lincolnton, Georgia
12.	Starvy Creek Festival	L.	Dunnellon, Florida

Answers: 1. D; 2. F; 3. H; 4. L; 5. J; 6. B; 7. K; 8. E; 9. A; 10. I; 11. G; 12. C

Teamwork Matching Quiz

Occasionally, well-known bluegrass artists who don't normally perform together team up to record special projects. Match the artist/group from each list who have recorded a joint release.

1. Flatt and Scruggs
2. Peter Rowan
3. Jimmy Martin
4. Mac Wiseman
5. Ricky Skaggs
6. The Seldom Scene
7. Carl Jackson
8. Tony Trischka
9. Alison Krauss
10. Nashville Bluegrass Band

A. Ralph Stanley
B. Jonathan Edwards
C. The Cox Family
D. John Starling
E. Jerry Douglas
F. Bela Fleck
G. Peter Rowan
H. Doc Watson
I. Lester Flatt
J. Tony Rice

Answers: 1. H; 2. E; 3. A; 4. I; 5. J; 6. B; 7. D; 8. F; 9. C; 10. G

VEGETABLES

OSAGE POKE SALLET GREENS

I usually fill a colander twice with greens to steam enough for a mess. Use mainly tender poke leaves, but other greens that you can add are lamb's quarter, curly dock, wild lettuce, dandelion, watercress, etc.

Steam each colanderful (with cover) until limp before cutting up and putting the greens in a covered pot or pan to wait for frying. In a large skillet, fry 3 or 4 pieces of thick bacon until crisp. Remove the bacon and break it into tiny pieces. Into the bacon grease, pour 3 tablespoons of white or balsamic vinegar and stir well. Add the broken-up bits of bacon and then the chopped greens, a little at a time, stirring to coat them. Reduce heat and cover. Simmer until served.

Makes enough for 3 to 4 servings.

Mitch Jayne
The Dillards

RICHARD'S GREENES

A Japanese-American vegetable course or side dish suitable for all seasons or holidays.

1 large bunch Swiss chard
1 tablespoon mayonnaise
1 teaspoon soy sauce
Juice of 1 lemon
Dash cumin

Trim and rinse the Swiss chard in cold water. Chop the chard into roughly 2-inch pieces.

Steam the "greenes" until cooked. Drain the "greenes" thoroughly (lots of water here).

Combine the remaining ingredients in a serving bowl. Add the steamed, drained chard, then toss. It all takes about 15 minutes. Preparation: 5 minutes; Attention: 5 minutes; Finishing: 5 minutes.

Makes 2 servings.

Richard Greene
The Grass Is Greener

Fiddler Richard Greene began his career in the 1960s as one of Bill Monroe's Blue Grass Boys. He went on to perform in various cutting-edge acoustic and rock groups in the '70s and '80s, including Muleskinner and Sea Train. Richard is in great demand as a studio musician; he has recorded with Jerry Garcia, Emmylou Harris, Loggins and Messina, Rod Stewart, Bruce Springsteen, and many others. His heart belongs to bluegrass, however, and in 1993 he formed The Grass is Greener, a hot quintet whose members have at times included Bill Keith, Chris Thile, Kenny Blackwell, and Tim Emmons. Pictured here are band members (l-r) Tony Trischka, Buell Neidlinger, Richard Greene, Butch Baldassari, and David Grier.

GARDEN OF EDEN DREAMY CREAMED SPINACH

Adam's favorite.

1 stick butter or margarine
3 tablespoons onion, minced
½ to 1 teaspoon garlic, minced
2 tablespoons all-purpose flour
Dash ground nutmeg
1 cup whipping cream
1 teaspoon lemon juice
¼ to ½ teaspoon Tabasco sauce
¼ teaspoon salt
1 teaspoon or 1 cube chicken bouillon
1 tablespoon real bacon bits
3 tablespoons Parmesan cheese, grated
3 tablespoons mozzarella cheese, grated
¾ cup sour cream
2 10-ounce packages frozen chopped spinach
½ cup grated Parmesan cheese for topping

Melt the butter or margarine in a saucepan. Add the onion and garlic and sauté for 3 to 5 minutes. Add the flour and nutmeg, stirring or whisking to make a smooth sauce or roux. Do not brown.

Add the cream, stirring with a wire whisk. Cook until the mixture is almost boiling. Add the lemon juice, Tabasco, salt, chicken bouillon, and bacon bits. Once the mixture comes to a boil, stir in the cheeses, beating well. Turn off heat, then stir in the sour cream. Cook the spinach according to package directions and drain well. Add the spinach to the cheese mixture. Stir well and cook on low heat for 5 to 10 minutes. Pour into a serving dish and sprinkle with Parmesan cheese.

Makes about 6 servings.

Adam Steffey
Alison Krauss and Union Station

BASS MOUNTAIN SUNSHINE CABBAGE

1 small head cabbage, cut or shredded
½ teaspoon salt
A little water
3 tablespoons all-purpose flour
3 tablespoons butter
1 cup milk
Salt and pepper to taste
Saltine crackers, crushed
¾ cup cheese, grated

Bile that cabbage down with about ½ teaspoon of salt and a little water until the cabbage is tender. Make a white sauce by heating the flour and butter in a saucepan over medium-low heat until bubbling. Slowly stir in the milk. Continue to stir until the mixture is smooth and thick. Remove from heat and add salt and pepper to taste. Drain the cabbage and place it in a greased casserole dish. Add the white sauce. Cover with the crushed saltines and grated cheese. Bake in a 350° oven until the cheese melts.

Makes 4 servings.

Mike Wilson
The Bass Mountain Boys

Mandolinist Adam Steffey grew up in Kingsport, Tennessee, in the heart of bluegrass country. He began playing in area bands at age fifteen. In 1990, he was playing with Dusty Miller when Alison Krauss invited him, Tim Stafford, and Barry Bales to be part of her new band Union Station. In addition to his work with Alison, Adam has recorded with a number of country and bluegrass artists, including Dolly Parton, Randy Travis, Jerry Douglas, and the Cox Family.

The Bass Mountain Boys were a fixture on the North Carolina bluegrass scene for nearly twenty years. Founding member Mike Wilson stuck with the group until it disbanded in 1996. Mike and his partner, John Maness (who was an original member of the band), launched the popular Bass Mountain Bluegrass Festival soon after the group started, and the festival has grown to include two weekend events a year, in May and September. Pictured here are the Bass Mountain Boys of 1996: (l-r) Jim Mills, Mike Wilson, Mike Aldridge, Johnny Ridge, and Mike Street.

BROTHER BOYS MIXED GREENS

Buy or pick greens that have crisp, clean leaves of color.

2½ pounds kale, mustard, and turnip greens
1 cup water
½ teaspoon sugar
Small piece salt pork, or bacon grease

Discard any tough stems and yellow leaves before washing the greens. (I let mine sit in warm salt water for 15 minutes to get rid of any unwanted bugs or pests, then I rinse them through water three times.) Place the clean greens in a large pot, then add the 1 cup water and the sugar and pork. Cook until tender. Serve with a sprinkle of pepper vinegar. Be sure to have some hot, buttered corn bread handy.

Makes about 6 to 8 servings.

Ed Snodderly
The Brother Boys

EAST TENNESSEE VEGATABLE STIR-FRY

1 boil-in-bag wild rice mix
3 tablespoons cashew halves
1 10-ounce package frozen mixed vegetables
1 tablespoon oil
½ tablespoon cornstarch

The Brother Boys's sound evokes memories of some of the classic brother duos of all time—folks like Jim and Jesse, The Louvin Brothers, and even the Everly Brothers. Pictured are (l-r) Roger Rasnake, Eugene Wolf, and Ed Snodderly.

½ tablespoon garlic powder
¾ cup water
¾ teaspoon chicken bouillon
⅛ teaspoon ground ginger
1½ tablespoons soy sauce

Prepare the rice. Brown the cashews in a skillet over medium heat. Boil the vegetables tender as directed on the package. Combine all

Paul Williams (a.k.a. Paul McCoy Humphrey) is perhaps best known as a member of Jimmy Martin's band in the 1950s and 1960s. He is a highly respected mandolin player, tenor singer, and songwriter. Some of his songwriting credits include "What Was I Supposed to Do" (a recent hit for the Lynn Morris Band), along with classics cowritten with Jimmy Martin like "Mr. Engineer," "Prayer Bell of Heaven," and "Give Me the Roses Now."

the ingredients, except the rice, in a large skillet. Cook for 4 minutes. Serve over the rice.

Makes 2 to 3 servings.

Paul Williams

GREAT SMOKY MOUNTAINS GRILLED VEGGIES

1 medium potato
1 small butternut squash, peeled
1 small onion
½ bell pepper, any color or colors
1 carrot
¼ teaspoon olive oil
½ teaspoon butter
¼ teaspoon garlic salt
Salt and pepper to taste

Cut the potato and squash into ⅛- to ¼-inch rounds. Cut the onion, pepper, and carrot into small wedges, so that they may cook faster. Place the veggies on a sheet of aluminum foil. Mix the olive oil, butter, and garlic salt in a small

saucepan, then heat them until the butter is melted. Pour the liquid over the veggies. Wrap the veggies and shake lightly to mix the oil and vegetables. Place on an outdoor grill for about 15 to 20 minutes, or until done.

Makes 2 to 3 servings.

James Price
Ralph Stanley
and the Clinch Mountain Boys

STOP, LOOK AND LISTEN SWISS VEGETABLE MEDLEY

16 ounces frozen broccoli, carrots, and cauliflower combination, thawed and drained.
1 10¾-ounce can cream of mushroom soup
1 cup shredded Swiss cheese
⅓ cup sour cream
¼ teaspoon black pepper
4 ounces chopped pimiento, drained
1 2.8-ounce can Durkee's french-fried onions

Combine the vegetables, soup, ½ cup cheese, sour cream, pepper, pimiento, and ½ cup onions. Pour mixture into a greased 1-quart casserole dish. Cover and bake at 350° for 30 minutes. Top with the remaining cheese and onions. Bake uncovered 5 minutes more.

Makes 4 to 6 servings.

Steve Pye
Highstrung

WEAVER'S DREAM BROCCOLI-CHEESE CASSEROLE

10 ounces chopped broccoli (frozen or fresh)
4 ounces Cheez Whiz or Velveeta cheese, softened
1 10¾-ounce can cream of mushroom soup
Cooked rice (enough to fill the empty soup can)
½ cup milk
Salt and pepper to taste
1 2.8-ounce can Durkee's french-fried onions

Cook the broccoli until tender. Mix the cheese, soup, rice, seasonings, and milk in a small

The Rarely Herd has a true bluegrass sound that comes through loud and clear. Jeff Weaver provides a solid bass for the band, while the Stack brothers (Jim on guitar and lead vocals; Alan on fiddle and mandolin) give the group its musical backbone. That leaves Calvin Leport with all the ingredients he needs to get audiences stirred up by his superb banjo playing. One thing's for sure: bands with as much promising talent as The Rarely Herd are seldom seen indeed. Pictured are (l-r) Alan Stack, Jeff Weaver, Jim Stack, and Calvin Leport.

bowl. Gently add the broccoli to this mix. Pour into a small greased casserole dish. Bake covered at 350° for 30 to 40 minutes. Uncover and add the fried onions on top. Bake for another 10 minutes. It's ready to serve.

Makes 4 servings.

Jeff Weaver
The Rarely Herd

KING BROCCOLI CASSEROLE

2 tablespoons margarine
I large onion, chopped
I 10¾-ounce can cream of mushroom soup
¼ to ½ pound cheddar cheese, mild or
  sharp, shredded
I cup cooked rice
I stick margarine
I bunch broccoli, trimmed and sliced
  lengthwise, or 10 ounces frozen broccoli
Canned fried onions

In a large saucepan, sauté the onion in the 2

tablespoons margarine. Stir in the soup and cheese. Add the rice and margarine. In a greased casserole dish, layer the broccoli and the sauce mixture, ending with the sauce. Top with canned fried onions. Bake at 350° until bubbly (10 to 15 minutes), or microwave on medium until bubbly.

Makes about 4 to 6 servings.

Beverly and Rodney Dillard
The Dillards

CHINA GROVE BROCCOLI-RICE CASSEROLE

10 ounces frozen chopped broccoli
I medium onion, chopped
½ cup uncooked rice
¾ stick margarine
I 10¾-ounce can cream of mushroom soup
Salt and pepper to taste
Grated cheese

Cook the broccoli according to the directions

on the package but also include the onions, then drain. Cook the rice for 10 minutes according to package directions. Combine the broccoli, rice, margarine, and soup (add a little milk if mixture is too thick). Add salt and pepper to taste. Pour into a greased Pyrex dish and sprinkle the top with grated cheese. Bake at 350° for 20 to 30 minutes.

Makes about 4 servings.

Curly Seckler

Grease a deep casserole dish. In a large bowl, mix the melted butter, flour, sugar, salt, and eggs. Blend the milk and corn into the mixture. Pour the mixture into the casserole dish. Bake at 325°, stirring the mixture after 15 minutes, then baking for an additional 30 minutes (for a total baking time of 45 minutes). Serve hot.

Makes 6 to 8 servings.

Jim Armstrong
New Dominion Bluegrass

SOUTHERN MOON CORN PUDDING

This is a recipe I learned from my mother, Julia Ann Bennett.

6 tablespoons melted butter
2 tablespoons all-purpose flour
2 tablespoons sugar
I teaspoon salt
4 eggs, beaten
1¾ cups milk
2 cups fresh, frozen, or cream-style corn

AUNT HELEN'S CORN PUDDING

This makes a tasty side dish for holiday meals, and it is a sure hit at a potluck.

I stick butter
¼ cup all-purpose flour
I cup milk
2 eggs, separated
16 ounces cream-style corn
2 slices bread, broken into pieces
½ teaspoon sugar
½ teaspoon salt

North Carolina native Curly Seckler has been picking and singing for nearly sixty years with such groups as the Smoky Mountaineers, the Foggy Mountain Boys, and Jim and Jesse. Seckler led the Nashville Grass after the death of Lester Flatt in 1979.

Preheat oven to 350°. In a saucepan, melt the stick of butter. Add the flour and cook until the mixture bubbles. Pour the mixture into a casserole dish. In a separate bowl, combine the milk and the egg yolks and beat slightly. Add this to the butter mixture.

Beat the egg whites until stiff. Add the following to the butter mixture in this order: the cream-style corn, bread, sugar, salt, and beaten egg whites. Mix and bake at 350° for 30 minutes, or until golden brown.

Makes 6 to 8 servings.

Jackie and Greg Cahill
Special Consensus

MOM'S CORN CASSEROLE

1 12-ounce can cream-style corn
1 8³/₄-ounce can whole kernel corn
¹/₃ cup sugar
1 cup sour cream
¹/₄ cup butter, melted
1 package Martha White corn bread mix

In a mixing bowl, stir together all the ingredients and pour into a greased oblong baking dish. Dot with butter. Bake at 425° for 30 to 35 minutes.

Makes 6 to 8 servings.

Kathy Kuhn
The New Coon Creek Girls

FLATT'S FRIED CORN

1 cup margarine
1 teaspoon bacon grease
12 ears of corn
1 tablespoon sugar
1 cup water
Salt and pepper

Melt the margarine and bacon grease in a large skillet. Cut the corn off the cob into the skillet. Scrape each cob over the skillet after cutting the corn. Don't lose a drop. Add sugar, water, and salt and pepper to taste. Cook until the corn mixture thickens, about 20 minutes.

Makes 8 servings.

Lester Flatt and family

Lester Flatt and the Nashville Grass in 1974 consisted of (*back row, l-r*) Curly Seckler, Paul Warren, Marty Stuart, Flatt, Jack Hicks, (*front row, l-r*) Charlie Nixon, booking agent Lance LeRoy, and Kenny Ingram.
Photograph by Lanny LeRoy

FOX ON THE RUN
BAKED ONION SPECIAL

Great for festival times!

1 medium onion
½ bouillon cube (chicken or beef)
Butter or margarine
Garlic salt
Thyme

Peel the skin off a medium-sized onion. Cut a cross in the onion halfway down. Take out ½ inch in the center of the onion. Place ½ of a bouillon cube in the cavity, along with a dab of butter. Add a touch of garlic salt and, if available, a little thyme. Wrap the onion in aluminum foil and place it directly on the hot coals of a hibachi. Bake for 30 minutes, or until done. It's delicious served with a baked potato and steak.

Makes 1 serving per onion.

Charlie Waller
The Country Gentlemen

PEAS TO PLEASE

1 pound frozen early (small) peas
1 teaspoon butter
1 teaspoon olive oil
1 teaspoon dried mint leaves, finely chopped
¼ teaspoon cayenne pepper flakes
Pinch of thyme
1 generous teaspoon vermouth

Rinse the peas in warm water to refresh them, then drain and set them aside. In a saucepan, place the butter, olive oil, mint leaves, cayenne pepper, and thyme. Bring to a sizzle and stir for about 1 minute. Add the drained peas and the vermouth. Serve as soon as heated through, or cook a little longer if you like your peas mushy.

Makes 4 to 6 servings.

Paul Martin Zonn
Nashville Mandolin Ensemble

BLACK MOUNTAIN
BLACK BEANS AND RICE

2 pounds black beans
4 quarts water
2 teaspoons baking soda
1 pint dry white wine
8 medium yellow onions, peeled and chunked
3 medium green bell peppers, cored and coarsely chunked
¼ pound dark smoked bacon, solid piece
¼ pound salt pork, solid piece
2 cups olive oil
4 whole bay leaves
2 tablespoons tarragon white wine vinegar
6 cloves garlic, peeled and thinly sliced
1 tablespoon salt
Pepper
Boiled white rice (2 cups per person)
1 medium purple onion

On the day before, boil the 4 quarts of water and dribble beans in so the water does not stop boiling. Boil for 5 minutes, turn off heat, and soak. After 1 hour, stir in the 2 teaspoons of baking soda. Soak the beans overnight.

On the next day, drain and wash the beans under cold water. Using a large pot, pour in the 1 pint of wine and add enough water to cover the beans. Cook on medium heat. While cooking, sauté the yellow onions and green peppers in the olive oil. Cut the bacon and salt pork into ½-inch cubes and add to the onions and peppers. When cooked, add these ingredients to the beans. Add the bay leaves, vinegar, garlic, 1 tablespoon salt, and a few grinds of pepper. Keep simmering for several hours, adding hot water so as not to stop simmering. Simmer up to 4 or 5 hours if you like. Beans are best when cooled and reheated. Serve over rice and garnish with red or purple onion. Serve a Spanish red wine if you like.

Makes 8 to 10 servings.

Jill Klein
The Nashville Jug Band

In the studio recording 1989's **Classic Country Gents Reunion** *album are (l-r) John Duffey, Eddie Adcock, Charlie Waller, and Tom Gray.*

The Country Gentlemen

On July 4, 1957, the Country Gentlemen played their first official show. Two years later, founding members Charlie Waller and John Duffey were joined by Eddie Adcock and Tom Gray, and the classic Country Gentlemen sound was born. This foursome made electrifying music together, probably doing more to expand the boundaries of bluegrass music than any other band before them. Their driving, daring, and often revolutionary picking pushed well beyond the stylistic limits of the time.

The Country Gentlemen were the first bluegrass group to incorporate instrumental experimentation into their sound by regularly departing from a straight melody line, and the first to draw a significant amount of material from non-bluegrass sources (most notably contemporary folk and folk-rock). In so doing, they gave bluegrass a new accessibility, and with regular performances in their home base of Washington, D.C., and other urban areas, they brought bluegrass to a whole new audience. Additionally, they inspired a whole new generation of pickers and set the stage for the "newgrass" movement of the 1970s.

This "classic" Country Gentlemen group remained together for nearly a decade (except for Tom Gray's

departure in 1964). Duffey and Gray went on to form The Seldom Scene; Adcock and his wife, Martha, have remained at the forefront of the progressive bluegrass scene; and Charlie Waller has continued to lead the Country Gentlemen for over forty years. Through those years, the band has served as a training ground for many of today's stars, including Doyle Lawson, Jimmy Gaudreau, Bill Emerson, Ricky Skaggs, and Jerry Douglas. Despite many personnel changes, Waller has maintained the group's remarkably consistent sound. His mellow, resonant voice and heartfelt singing style are the focal point of the Country Gentlemen sound of the '90s, and have won him repeated honors as Male Vocalist of the Year from SPBGMA.

Over the years, the Country Gentlemen have made a significant contribution of material to the bluegrass canon. Their hits include "Legend of the Rebel Soldier," "Two Little Boys," "Bringing Mary Home," "Matterhorn," and the well-known standard, "Fox on the Run." Many of their best recordings will be available on a four-CD boxed set to be released by Rebel Records to commemorate the Country Gentlemen's fortieth anniversary. In 1996, the "Classic" Country Gentlemen were inducted into the IBMA's Hall of Honor.

TASTY BAKED ONIONS

Perfect with barbecue or any outdoor cookout fare.

12 medium onions, thinly sliced
1 4- to 6-ounce bag potato chips
1/2 pound cheddar cheese, grated
2 10³/₄-ounce cans cream of mushroom
   soup
1/2 cup milk
1/8 teaspoon cayenne pepper
1/8 teaspoon garlic powder
A few dashes green Tabasco sauce

In a 9- by 11-inch buttered casserole dish, place alternate layers of thinly sliced onions, crushed potato chips, and grated cheese. In a medium bowl, mix together the soup and milk. Add the cayenne pepper, garlic powder, and Tabasco sauce. Pour over the layers in the casserole dish. Bake covered at 350° for 1/2 hour. Remove the cover and continue to bake for about 1 hour.
   Makes 8 servings.

Jill and Jerry Douglas

MIXED MELODY RICE PILAF

1/4 cup butter
1 1/2 cups uncooked rice

3 1/4 cups chicken broth
1/2 cup celery, chopped
1/2 cup carrots, diced
1/4 cup water chestnuts, sliced
1 10³/₄-ounce can celery soup, undiluted
1/4 cup water
1/4 cup almonds, sliced (optional)

Melt the butter in a skillet. Add the rice and cook, stirring until light brown. Stir in the chicken broth and heat to boiling. Pour the mixture into a casserole dish, cover, and bake at 375° for 15 minutes. Remove the dish from the oven and add the vegetables. Add 1/4 cup water to the celery soup and stir into the mixture. Top with the sliced almonds. Bake at 375° for 30 minutes.
   Makes 6 servings.

Millie and Vassar Clements

TONY RICE

1/4 cup vegetable oil
4 cups cooked brown rice
1 tablespoon sesame seeds
3/4 cup green onions, sliced
1 cup fresh mushrooms, sliced and sautéed
2 cloves garlic, chopped
2 eggs, beaten

Heat the oil. Fry the rice until hot. Add the other ingredients and stir until the eggs are cooked. Season with soy sauce and serve steaming hot.
   Makes 4 servings.

Kathy Chiavola

Ohio native Jerry Douglas was a track star in high school before he traded his running shoes for a set of finger picks and a slide bar. He first gained national recognition in the 1970s during stints with the Country Gentlemen, J.D. Crowe and the New South, and Boone Creek. Today, he is regarded as one of the finest resonator guitar players in the world, with a repertoire spanning bluegrass, country, "new-acoustic," and pop. He is in great demand as a studio musician. Chances are if you hear a resonator guitar on a country recording or a movie soundtrack, it's "Flux." Jerry is also a skilled producer; he has supervised projects by Del McCoury, the Nashville Bluegrass Band, the Brother Boys, Tim O'Brien, and others. In 1995, he produced and performed on the award-winning *Great Dobro Sessions* on Sugar Hill Records.

A former member of the Doug Dillard Band, Kathy Chiavola now leads the always-entertaining, Nashville-based Kathy Chiavola Band. She is much in demand as a session singer for Nashville's top recording artists, but be sure to catch her live show. With a master's degree in voice from Oberlin Conservatory of Music, Kathy is a threat to make a crowd-pleasing "diva" into "Cripple Creek" at just about any moment.

Tony Rice

Tony Rice has the sort of musical range you'd expect from someone who was born in North Carolina and spent much of his life living in California and Florida.

Esteemed by fellow musicians for his extraordinary flat-pick guitar playing and compelling vocals, Rice names Clarence White and the Kentucky Colonels as the leading musical influences of his formative years.

Rice joined the Bluegrass Alliance in 1971. After a term in that band, he joined his mandolin-playing brother Larry in J.D. Crowe's band, which eventually became the New South. During Rice's tenure with the New South, band members included Jerry Douglas on resonator guitar, Ricky Skaggs on fiddle and mandolin, and Bobby Slone on bass.

Rice then joined the all-instrumental David Grisman Quintet, which gained a reputation for producing a delicious rainbow of sounds from a wide range of influences, including bluegrass.

In 1979, Rice decided to follow his rainbow in a different direction and began pursuing a solo career. In 1980, Rice teamed with longtime friend Ricky Skaggs to record the classic *Skaggs and Rice* duet album, a tribute to their old-timey roots. During the 1980s, he also spearheaded the formation of the Bluegrass Album Band with Doyle Lawson, Bobby Hicks, J.D. Crowe, and Todd Phillips. The group has produced a series of well-received albums and won an IBMA award for Instrumental Group of the Year in 1990. Rice himself has won multiple Guitar Player of the Year awards from the IBMA.

With his most recent band, the Tony Rice Unit, Rice continued to push the frontiers of bluegrass with what he calls "spacegrass." In recent years, Rice has also become a respected producer and is in great demand as a studio musician. However, no matter what direction he takes, there's no doubt about one thing: Tony Rice can flat pick!

WHAT'S HOPPIN' JOHN

A New Year's tradition to bring good luck to anyone who eats it on the first day of the year.

**2 cups dried black-eyed peas or cowpeas,
  soaked overnight and drained**
Water
**1 piece salt pork (fatback), slashed in several
  places**
1 hot red pepper, chopped
1 medium onion, chopped
Salt and black pepper to taste
1 cup uncooked rice
4 tablespoons drippings, preferably bacon

Place the peas in a large pot and cover with water. Add the salt pork, red pepper, onion, and the salt and black pepper and bring to a boil. Add more water as needed. Reduce heat and simmer until tender.

Remove the peas and reserve enough liquid in the pot (about 3 cups) to cook the rice. Add the rice and the drippings to the pot. Bring back to a boil, cover, reduce heat, and let the pot simmer until the rice is cooked (about 30 minutes). Return the peas to the pot. Stir together and cook a few more minutes. Turn into a large dish and serve.

We like ours served with corn bread.

Makes about 6 servings.

Wilma Lee Cooper

NEW YEAR'S DAY BLACK-EYED PEAS

2 cups dried black-eyed peas
Water
1 onion, chopped
1 slice ham (approximately 1 cup cubed)
1 14- or 16-ounce can stewed tomatoes
1 8¾-ounce can whole kernel corn, drained
Salt and pepper to taste

Rinse the peas thoroughly. Soak overnight in a covered 4-quart saucepan, using enough water to cover the peas by 2 or 3 inches. Boil the peas for 15 to 20 minutes, then reduce heat. Add the ham and let simmer for ½ hour. Add onion and tomatoes and simmer for another ½ hour. (The

Stoney Cooper was one of the finest hill country musicians to come out of West Virginia. Early in his career, he fiddled with the Green Valley Boys, but after joining up with the Leary Family, he discovered his true love in Wilma Lee. The Coopers and their Clinch Mountain Clan became stars and were members of the Wheeling Jamboree before they landed on the Grand Ole Opry.

peas should be tender by now, but dried peas sometimes take longer.) Just before serving, add the can of corn and add salt and pepper to taste (approximately ½ teaspoon of each).

Note: If you're lucky enough to have fresh peas, you should probably lightly brown the ham and onion together in a frying pan before you start the peas boiling, then add the ham and onions to the pot as you reduce the heat. Add the tomatoes and simmer for approximately ½ hour, then add the corn and serve. Always be ready to add more water if needed, and judge the actual cooking time by the tenderness of the peas.

Makes 6 servings.

Lynn Morris

BILL MONROE'S JERUSALEM RIDGE FRIED POTATOES

This was his favorite food.

Bill didn't use a frying pan with the lid that fits on it. Instead, use a flat lid and an iron skillet. "My mother did it like this," Bill said.

Peel the potatoes and then slice them about ⅛-inch thin, so that the pan is about ¾ full of taters. Put about ½ cup of lard and about a ½ cup of water in the pan. Put the lid on and let it cook over medium heat till tender. Stir from the bottom every little bit. When the potatoes get brown, take the lid off and finish frying; salt to taste and add pepper.

Makes about 4 to 6 servings.

Bill Monroe
From close friend Hazel Smith

Bill Monroe and the Blue Grass Boys play on WSM Radio in the late 1940s. Pictured are (l-r) Bill Monroe, Chubby Wise, Birch Monroe, Lester Flatt, and Earl Scruggs.
Photograph courtesy of Dave Freeman

Bill Monroe

He was "The Father of Bluegrass," and it's as simple as that. For Bill Monroe, making beautiful music became a way of earning a living over sixty-five years ago, when, in 1930, he and his brothers, Charlie and Birch, formed the Monroe Brothers for a radio show.

Born in Rosine, Kentucky, in 1911, Bill learned his art from his fiddling mother and his uncle Pendleton Vandiver. As the youngest of eight kids, he was handed a mandolin since the others already manned the guitars and fiddles. He made out all right.

In 1938, Monroe started up the Blue Grass Boys. The band's name and sound became a new brand of music, with the fiddle, mandolin, and banjo carrying the lead. Monroe and his group became Grand Ole Opry members in 1939. They were so popular that Opry chief George D. Hay told Monroe, "If you ever leave, it'll be because you fired yourself!" After that, he had a passel of hits such as "Blue Moon of Kentucky," "Uncle Pen," "Footprints in the Snow," "Kentucky Waltz," "Mule Skinner Blues," "Christmas Time's A-Comin'," and "Molly and Tenbrooks."

His band, the Blue Grass Boys, churned out an impressive list of bluegrass greats, including Jimmy Martin, Vassar Clements, Stringbean, Don Reno, Mac Wiseman, Peter Rowan, Del McCoury, and Byron Berline, among others. The Blue Grass Boys lineup that many consider to be the "original bluegrass band" included the legendary artists Lester Flatt, Earl Scruggs, Robert "Chubby" Wise, and Howard Watts ("Cedric Rainwater"). This version of the Blue Grass Boys made its debut on the Opry in December of 1945

and made its first recordings in September of 1946, changing the face of Monroe's music forever.

As Bill Monroe's career progressed, he earned all of bluegrass's top honors. He became a member of the Country Music Hall of Fame (1970), the IBMA Hall of Honor (1991), was awarded the first Grammy given for bluegrass music (1989), and was honored with a Lifetime Achievement Award from the National Academy of Recording Arts and Sciences.

About his sound, he once said, "It's got a hard drive to it. It's Scotch bagpipes and ol' time fiddlin'. It's Methodist and Holiness and Baptist. It's blues and jazz and it has a high lonesome sound. It's plain music that tells a good story. It's played from my heart to your heart, and it will touch you. Bluegrass is a music that matters. It's not a music you play, get it over with, and forget it."

Two of bluegrass music's leaders summed up Bill Monroe's life and legacy. "He put his whole life in the music," said bluegrass banjo legend Earl Scruggs. "I've heard him say so many, many times that he created that sound. I think he wants to be remembered as that. He created 'Bill Monroe' for sure. Nobody will ever take his place."

Ralph Stanley, the new elder statesman of bluegrass, said, "He knew how to sing a song; he knew what to put in it to make the people feel it. He was a wonderful mandolin player. He loved his music and he kept it clean. He worked on it all the time, and he always wanted it to be the best."

BOOTLEG JOHN'S
FRIED POTATOES

5 medium potatoes, washed and diced
2 tablespoons cooking oil
½ cup all-purpose flour
I teaspoon garlic powder
Salt and pepper to taste
½ cup onion, chopped

In a large skillet, preheat the oil on medium heat. Add the potatoes. Mix the flour, garlic powder, salt, and pepper together and sprinkle over potatoes. Fry for 20 minutes. Add the onion and cook until onion is translucent.

Makes 4 to 6 servings.

Don Rigsby
The Lonesome River Band

REALLY GOOD MASHED
POTATOES FOR VENISON

A bunch of small potatoes
¼ stick butter
I teaspoon parsley, chopped
½ teaspoon garlic salt
I teaspoon dried basil leaves
½ cup milk

Cut small white potatoes into quarters, leaving on the skin. Boil the potatoes until tender and then drain. With a fork, mash in the butter, parsley, garlic salt, basil, and milk. (The potato masher can be used, but it isn't necessary.)

Makes a bunch.

Mitch Jayne
The Dillards

CREWE
CURRIED POTATOES

2 tablespoons butter or margarine
I large onion, thinly sliced
I cup celery, thinly sliced
I 10¾-ounce can cream of chicken soup (or cream of celery or cream of mushroom, if desired)
½ teaspoon curry powder
3 large baking potatoes, sliced ¼- to ½-inch thick

Melt the butter in a large skillet; sauté the onion and celery until tender. Add the soup to the skillet and blend well. Add the curry powder and blend well. Spray the bottom of a deep casserole or baking dish with a vegetable coating. Layer some of the potato slices to cover the bottom of the dish. Cover the potatoes with a layer of soup mixture. Continue to layer the potatoes and soup mixture to fill the dish. Dot butter over the top. Cover and bake at 350° for 40 to 45 minutes.

Makes 4 to 6 servings.

Emma and Jody Rainwater

IN THE SWEET POTATO
CASSEROLE BY AND BY

3 cups cooked sweet potatoes, mashed
2 eggs, beaten
½ cup milk
I cup sugar
¾ stick margarine, melted
I teaspoon vanilla extract
I cup flaked coconut
½ teaspoon salt
I tablespoon ground cinnamon

Mix all ingredients together and pour into a greased 9- by 12-inch Pyrex baking dish. Set aside.

Topping:

²/3 stick margarine, melted
I cup brown sugar
¹/3 cup all-purpose flour
¹/3 cup pecans, chopped

Mix the topping ingredients and crumble over the sweet potato mixture. Bake the casserole for 40 minutes at 350°.

Makes about 8 servings.

Helen (Mrs. Carl) Story

ENDLESS HIGHWAY SHREDDED POTATOES AU GRATIN

6 medium potatoes
2 cups cheddar cheese, grated
½ cup yellow onion, diced
Salt and pepper to taste
6 tablespoons butter, melted
2 cups sour cream

Boil the potatoes whole in their skins until they're fork-tender. Drain the potatoes and cool them down in the refrigerator. Peel the potatoes and shred them on a cheese grater into a mixing bowl. Stir in the grated cheese, onions, plenty of pepper, salt to taste, and 4 tablespoons of the melted butter. Fold in the sour cream. Pour the mixture into a greased casserole dish and dot with the remaining 2 tablespoons butter. Bake uncovered in a 375° oven for 20 to 25 minutes.
Makes 6 servings.

Roger Rasnake
The Brother Boys

MARSHALL'S TEXAS RANCH-STYLE BEANS

This recipe goes very well with Bramble and Rose Catbird Corn Bread. (See pages 62-63.)

Water
1 pound dried pinto beans
1 slice ham, cubed (approximately 1 to 2 cups)
1 yellow or white onion, chopped
Salt and pepper to taste
1 teaspoon sugar (optional)

Wash and rinse the beans. Put the beans in a 4-quart pan with a lid and soak them overnight in the water—allowing about 2 to 3 inches of water to cover the beans.

The next day, trim the fat from the ham (or sliced bacon or ham hock—whichever you like best) and then cut it into small cubes. Bring the beans to a boil and add the ham. Bring to a boil a second time. Add more water as necessary and watch to make sure the beans don't boil dry. Cover and reduce the heat to a low boil and let the beans simmer for about 1 hour. Dried beans can be temperamental, and some must cook much longer than an hour before they begin to soften up. Once the beans begin to get tender, add the chopped onion. Cook for another 30 minutes to 1½ hours, depending on the beans. Add salt and pepper to taste; add a teaspoon of sugar if you like. This recipe can cook on very low heat for several hours if you like. It just gets thicker and tastier.
Makes about 6 servings.

Lynn Morris

HOT RIZE RANCH BEANS

O'Boy!
What little I know about cooking, I learned from one of three sources: my wife, Kit Swaggert; cookbook and newspaper recipes; and trial and error. This recipe started with Steve Ramsey, and then Kit adapted it after some trial and error.

2 cups dry pinto beans
4 cups water
1 large onion, diced
5 to 6 cloves garlic, diced
1 jalapeño pepper, chopped with veins and seeds included (optional)
2 tablespoons chili powder
1 teaspoon ground coriander
2 tablespoons peanut oil (optional)
Salt to taste

Soak the beans overnight if you can. If you do, pour off the water before cooking. Some say this reduces the gas-producing power of the beans. Depending on how spicy you like your Mexican food, you can use more or less jalapeños and chili powder. You can also discard the seeds and veins of the jalapeño for a milder taste.

Bring the water and beans to a boil with all the other ingredients except the salt. We like to cook the beans slowly in a crockpot, but be warned: it takes all day (7 or 8 hours) for the beans to cook this way. You can cook them faster, in about 4 hours, on the stovetop at a low boil. It may be necessary to add more water to keep the beans covered. You'll know they're done when you can blow on them and the skins break apart. Add salt to taste. Then mash the beans a little to thicken the liquid, leaving most of the beans whole. Serve in small bowls on the side with some of the liquid.

Makes 6 servings.

Tim O'Brien

DOUG'S GREAT WHITE BEANS

1 pound dried navy or great northern beans
4 strips of swine (bacon)
1 teaspoon salt
2 cups chopped ham of hog

Remove all of the rotten beans, rocks, dirt, and foreign types of beans. Wash each bean in-dividually with a toothbrush until there's not a speck of dirt left. Boil the beans once in pure water for 2 minutes. Meanwhile, fry the 4 strips of swine until almost crisp. Take the beans off the heat, drain, and rinse with hot water, so as to put the beans into shock and cause the skins to come off. Put the beans back in clean hot water on low heat. Render the grease and add the fried swine to the beans. Add 1 teaspoon of salt, or salt to taste, and the chopped ham. Cook on low heat for about 2 hours. The beans should not be overcooked, as the soup will have the consistency of library paste. The broth should be fairly clear, while the beans should be firm and not cooked to death. If you don't like white beans, try 'em. Remember, eatin' speaks louder than words. Bone appetite.

Makes 6 to 8 servings.

Douglas Dillard

If you're counting influential banjo players on one hand, you might start with Earl Scruggs on your thumb, but Douglas Flint Dillard would be your index finger. Few banjo players have influenced generations of pickers as much as Doug has. From his days with the Dillards, to the Dillard and Clark Expedition with Gene Clark, and on to his current band, Doug Dillard has always been on the cutting edge of music. (You'll also see—and even more often hear—Doug in movies like *Popeye* with Robin Williams.)

The Doug Dillard Band has had many configurations over the years, but the one thing you can always figure on is that they will put on a great show. With Doug Dillard working his magic on banjo and Ginger Boatwright's passionate vocals and guitar picking, there's showmanship enough for several bands. (You can also fill a hefty catalog with the memorable songs the two have written.)

Following the example of its leader, the Doug Dillard Band always has fun. Seen here with Doug and Ginger in 1996 is Barney Fife impersonator David Browning. The photograph was taken during a performance at the annual Mayberry Days festival in Mount Airy, North Carolina. (The backdrop was quilted by Ginger from Mayberry T-shirts donated by fans.) Among the talented musicians who have performed regularly with the band through the years are Kathy Chiavola, Roger Rasnake, David Grier, Jonathan Yudkin, Laurie Harmon, and Jim Langford.

Photograph by Bart Boatwright

BOLA PINTA PINTO BEANS

Wash and pick through a pound of pinto beans. Remove any non-bean material (small rocks, sticks, etc.). Save these items; they are cooked separately. Cover the beans with water in a large pot. Leave overnight. Put on a Joe and Al CD.

The next morning, drain and rinse the beans. Don't ask why—just do it. Cover the beans again with fresh water. Add a square of salt pork (or a bouillon cube for less fat) and cook until tender. Add water as necessary and salt to taste. Eat with corn bread. If you're in a hurry, leave out the overnight soak and rinse, but remember, we warned you!

Makes about 6 servings.

Joe Carr and Alan Munde

BLUEGRASS BREAKDOWN BEANS

1 small onion, chopped
1 small green bell pepper, chopped
Margarine
3 slices bacon
2 15-ounce cans pork-and-beans
2 tablespoons molasses
1 tablespoon brown sugar

In a large skillet, cook the onion and green pepper with a little margarine. Add the bacon and cook slightly—not crisp. Pour off the grease. Add the pork and beans and stir. Add the molasses and brown sugar. Cover and simmer on low, stirring from time to time for about 20 minutes, or until you just can't wait any more.

Makes 4 to 6 servings.

Randall Franks

BIG MON'S BARBECUED PORK-AND-BEANS

I dedicate my recipe to my longtime friend Stormy, my faithful dog I have had since she was a pup.

1 small onion, chopped
1 16-ounce can pork-and-beans
2 tablespoons light brown sugar
1/3 cup honey barbecue sauce

Sauté the onion in a 10-inch skillet sprayed with non-stick cooking spray. Add the pork and beans, brown sugar, and barbecue sauce; mix well. Simmer for 15 minutes.

Makes 2 to 3 servings.

Bill Monroe
Recipe courtesy of
Animaland Cookbook Vol. II:
Pet Project of the Stars
and Dixie Hall

Gathering around the WSM microphone around 1948 are (l-r) **Bill Monroe, Earl Scruggs, Birch Monroe, and Lester Flatt.**
Photograph courtesy of Dave Freeman

Pictured are (l-r) Don Reno,
Red Smiley, Mack Magaha,
and John Palmer.
Courtesy of Dave Freeman

Reno and Smiley

Banjoist Don Reno first gained national attention when he joined Bill Monroe's Blue Grass Boys in 1948, following the departure of Earl Scruggs. After a year with Monroe, Reno met guitar player Red Smiley. This pair worked together in several bands before forming their own group, Don Reno, Red Smiley, and the Tennessee Cutups, in 1951.

By all accounts, the Reno and Smiley band of the late 1950s and early 1960s was one of the most musically exciting and entertaining groups in bluegrass. Don Reno developed a distinctive banjo style that incorporated elements of jazz, swing, and country, and he was renowned for his phenomenal skill in negotiating the banjo neck. Additionally, he was an excellent flat-picking guitarist at a time when the guitar was just beginning to be used as a lead instrument in bluegrass. Don was also a skilled and prolific composer; a large volume of the band's material, both vocal and instrumental, consisted of Reno originals. These include "I Know You're Married, But I Love You Still," "I'm Using My Bible For a Roadmap," "I'm the Talk of the Town," and "Dixie Breakdown."

Smiley's rhythm guitar style was dynamic and tasteful, frequently punctuated with his signature runs on the lower strings. His smooth, rich baritone voice blended well with Reno's clear tenor, contributing greatly to the appeal and accessibility of the Reno and Smiley sound. The group had a vast repertoire, which included breakneck instrumental numbers, love songs, ballads, gospel quartets, and even covers of the popular country songs of the day. Their popularity was further enhanced by a daily morning television show on WDBJ in Roanoke, Virginia. A videotape from these TV performances was released by Pinecastle Records in 1996.

More than any other group of their time, Reno and Smiley made entertainment an important part of their performances. Both men had warm and outgoing stage personas, but it was Reno, with his flamboyant showmanship and effusive personality, who dominated. In addition, Reno masterminded the group's elaborate comedy routines, with the band dressed in costumes and playing characters such as Chicken Hot Rod and Mutt Highpockets.

With each partner suffering from health problems, Don Reno and Red Smiley parted ways in 1964 and went on to lead their own groups for a time. They reunited in 1970 and worked together until Red's death in January of 1972. Don continued to lead the Tennessee Cutups along with his new partner, Bill Harrell, until Harrell left to form his own group in 1977. Reno then fronted the Tennessee Cutups alone until he passed away in 1984. During those last years, the band included his two youngest sons, Dale on mandolin and Don Wayne on banjo. Years before, older son Ronnie had been a regular on the Reno and Smiley show, back when he was so small he had to stand on a chair to reach the microphone. Soon after Don's death, Ronnie, Dale, and Don Wayne united to form the Reno Brothers, and they continue to record and tour together today.

As a lasting tribute to the popularity of Reno and Smiley, they were inducted into the IBMA Hall of Honor in 1992.

DALE'S HAMMED-UP ACOUSTIC CELEBRATION BEANS

1 1-pound bag pinto beans
2 large slices country ham

Fill a large crockpot ¾ full with water. Wash your beans and remove all small pebbles. Cut the fat from the ham and then cut the ham into 1-inch squares. Add the beans and ham to the crockpot, cover, and turn heat to high. It takes a while to cook this so it's best to start them early in the morning. No salt will be needed because the ham has plenty. Periodically, check the beans and stir, or add a little water if needed. When this is cooking, the smell is enough to die for. The ham is as tender as a mother's love. Enjoy and leave the gas in 'em. That's the fun part.

Makes about 6 servings.

Dale Reno
The Reno Brothers

LEATHER BRITCHES BEANS

Now, these really *are* string beans!

Wash and drain a batch of firm green beans. Remove the ends and the strings. With a large darning needle and heavy white thread, run a thread through the pod near the middle of each bean, pushing the pods along the thread so that they are about ¼-inch apart. Hang up the strings of beans in a warm, well-ventilated place to dry. They will shrivel and turn greenish gray.

To cook the beans in the winter, as the pioneers did, cover them with water and soak overnight. Drain and renew the water, then parboil the beans slowly for 30 minutes. Drain again. Cook slowly with ham hock or salt pork until tender. Serve with corn bread.

Servings depend on how much stringing up you do.

Ramona Church Taylor
The New Coon Creek Girls

LONNIE'S SUMMER SQUASH

4 slices good bacon
2 to 3 cups yellow summer squash, sliced thin to medium
1 good-sized onion, chopped
¼ teaspoon marjoram
¼ teaspoon thyme
Salt and pepper to taste
1 tablespoon sugar
¹/₃ cup milk

In a 12-inch skillet, fry the bacon until crisp. Pour off the fat and break the bacon into bits. Add the squash, onion, marjoram, thyme, salt, and pepper. Sauté for a few minutes until the vegetables begin to soften. Add the sugar and milk. Let the milk boil for an instant, then stir again. Cover and turn off the heat. Serve soon.

Makes 5 to 6 servings.

Paul Martin Zonn
Nashville Mandolin Ensemble

CAROLINA MEMORIES LOW-FAT SQUASH-TOMATO CASSEROLE

3 cups squash (yellow or zucchini), chopped
1 medium onion, chopped
1 egg, beaten
1 cup fresh mushrooms, sliced
1 teaspoon fat-free butter or margarine
1 15-ounce can stewed tomatoes
½ cup fat-free sour cream
Garlic to taste
Mrs. Dash Table Blend to taste
Crazy Salt to taste
1 cup toasted bread crumbs (sprinkled with garlic powder and spices, but not butter)
4 slices reduced-fat American cheese

Boil or steam the squash and onion until slightly tender, then drain. Add the next 8 ingredients to the vegetables. Lightly coat a 9- by 13-inch pan with non-stick spray. Add the mixture to the pan. Top with bread crumbs. Bake at 400° for 15 minutes. Top with the cheese and bake for an additional 5 minutes.

Makes about 8 servings.

Ric-O-Chet

SOUTHERN
SQUASH SOUFFLÉ

1½ pounds yellow squash, boiled, drained,
    and mashed
1 tablespoon minced onion flakes
1 teaspoon sugar
3 eggs, beaten
½ cup mayonnaise
2 tablespoons margarine, melted
1 cup cheddar cheese, grated

Mix all the ingredients. Pour into a greased
casserole dish and bake for 35 to 45 minutes at
350°. When a table knife inserted into the
middle of the soufflé comes out clean, the soufflé
is done.

Makes 6 to 8 servings.

Glenn Tolbert

WEDDING BELLS SUMMER
SQUASH CASSEROLE

I learned this recipe from my wife, Becky.

6 cups yellow summer squash, sliced
¼ cup chopped onion
1 teaspoon salt
1 10¾-ounce can cream of chicken soup
1 cup dairy sour cream
1 cup carrot, shredded
1 8-ounce bag Pepperidge Farm herb-
    seasoned stuffing mix
½ cup melted margarine

In a saucepan, cook the squash and onion in
boiling salted water for about 10 minutes, then
drain. In a large bowl, mix the soup, sour cream,
and carrot. Fold the drained squash and onion
into the mixture. Combine the stuffing with the
melted margarine. Spread ½ of the stuffing mixture into the bottom of an 8- by 12- by 2-inch
pan, spoon in the vegetable mixture, and then
sprinkle the remainder of the stuffing mixture
on top. Bake in a 350° oven for 30 minutes. Serve
hot.

Makes about 8 servings.

Jim Armstrong
New Dominion Bluegrass

HARVEST TIME
SQUASH CASSEROLE

2 cups squash, sliced, cooked, and drained
2 large onions, chopped fine
2 large carrots, grated (optional)
1 10¾-ounce can cream of chicken soup
1 8-ounce package Pepperidge Farm
    cornmeal stuffing mix
½ stick margarine
1 cup sour cream
1 cup cheese, grated

Mix together the first 7 ingredients. Place in
a greased casserole dish and bake at 350° for 30
to 40 minutes. Sprinkle the grated cheese on top
during the last 5 minutes of baking. This amount
is too much for a small family at one meal; if
desired, it can be placed in 2 dishes, with 1 dish
frozen for later.

Makes 6 to 8 servings.

Dempsey Young
The Lost and Found

Dempsey Young is an
award-winning
mandolin player, who
played rock music and
"newgrass" before
helping form The Lost
and Found. Dempsey
is known for his
distinctive mandolin
style, and for
incorporating fun
surprises from other
musical genres into his
playing.

DAN'S FAVORITE SUMMER
SQUASH CASSEROLE

2 pounds summer squash, sliced
¼ cup onion, chopped
3 tablespoons butter or bacon drippings
1 10¾-ounce can cream of chicken soup
1 cup sour cream
1 cup carrots, shredded
½ cup cheese, grated
½ cup melted butter

8 ounces Pepperidge Farm herb-seasoned
    stuffing mix

Sauté the squash and onions in the 3 tablespoons of butter or bacon drippings for 5 minutes. In a separate bowl, combine the soup, sour
cream, carrots, and cheese. Add soup mixture
to the squash.

In a separate bowl, combine the stuffing mix
and the ½ cup melted butter. Put ½ of the stuffing mix in the bottom of a 9- by 13-inch baking
pan. Spoon the vegetable mixture on top.
Sprinkle on the remaining stuffing. Bake at 350°
for 25 to 30 minutes.

Makes 8 servings.

Elise and Dan Tyminski
Alison Krauss and Union Station

GROUNDSPEED EGG AND VEGETABLE CASSEROLE

2 tablespoons butter
2 tablespoons all-purpose flour
1²/₃ cups undiluted evaporated milk
¹/₃ cup water
1 teaspoon salt
¹/₈ teaspoon white pepper
2 teaspoons instant minced onion
1 teaspoon Worcestershire sauce
1 tablespoon prepared mustard
3 pounds fresh asparagus, cooked and
    drained, or 3 15-ounce cans asparagus
4 hard-boiled eggs, sliced
1 cup low-fat American cheese, shredded

Melt the butter in a saucepan and stir in the
flour. Gradually stir in the evaporated milk and

Though he grew up in the hills of Vermont, not Virginia,
Dan Tyminski was exposed to lots of traditional sounds
at many of the bluegrass festivals held in New England
during the 1970s. Dan began singing before he started
school, and with encouragement from his musician
brother, he took up the guitar and mandolin at age six.
Prior to joining Alison Krauss and Union Station in
1994, Dan performed with The Lonesome River Band
and several Vermont groups. Today, he has become
known as one of the most talented singers in bluegrass.

water. Cook over medium heat, stirring until the
mixture comes to a boil and thickens. Add the
salt, pepper, onion, Worcestershire sauce, and
mustard. Arrange ½ the asparagus in the bottom of a greased 12- by 7½- by 2-inch baking
dish. Top the asparagus with ½ the egg slices,
then pour ½ the sauce over the eggs. Sprinkle ½
the cheese over the top, then repeat the layers.
Cover the dish with foil. Bake at 350° for 20 to
30 minutes until the sauce is bubbly.

Makes 8 servings.

Louise and Earl Scruggs

Got Time to Breathe, Got Time to Eat—
Flatt and Scruggs and company take time to
grab a bite to eat while on the road through
Mississippi in 1961. Seated at the counter are
(l-r) Paul Warren, Lester Flatt, Curly Seckler,
and Earl Scruggs. The waitress's name is not
known, but it might be Juanita.
Photograph by Les Leverett

PILOT MOUNTAIN FRUIT CASSEROLE

1 stick butter
1 cup self-rising flour
1 cup sugar
1 cup milk
1 egg
1 teaspoon vanilla extract
2 to 3 cups fruit pieces
¼ cup sugar

Preheat a large casserole dish with the butter in it. In another dish, mix well the next 5 ingredients, then pour them over the butter. (Do not stir at any time after pouring the mixture over the butter.) Put the fruit on top of the batter in the casserole dish (most of the fruit will sink). Sprinkle the ¼ cup sugar on top and bake for 30 minutes in a 325° to 350° oven.
Makes about 8 servings.

Cindy and Jim Vipperman

CATTLETTSBURG BAKED PINEAPPLE

2 15¼-ounce cans chunk pineapple, drained
½ cup all-purpose flour
¾ cup sugar
1 stick margarine, melted
1 sleeve Ritz crackers

Mix the first 4 ingredients in a greased baking dish. Crush the crackers and sprinkle evenly over the top. Bake at 350° for 30 to 40 minutes.
Makes 6 to 8 servings.

Willia and Melvin Goins

NEW FRONTIER PINEAPPLE CASSEROLE

This casserole has been a favorite in our family for years. It's great with ham, pork, or cold cuts. It is my favorite thing to make for potluck dinners because it's easy and always one of the first dishes to disappear! OK, so it's not so great on the cholesterol chart, but as a very wise person once said, "Everything in moderation . . . including moderation."

¾ stick margarine
1 cup sugar
4 eggs
5 slices white bread, broken fine
1 20-ounce can unsweetened crushed pineapple, with juice

Cream the margarine and sugar. Add the remaining ingredients and mix well. Place in a greased medium casserole dish and bake uncovered in a 350° oven for 1 hour.
Makes about 6 servings.

Bob Amos
Front Range

TURKEY GOBBLE STUFFING

8 cups dried out bread, cut into cubes
¹/₃ cup butter
¹/₂ cup onion, chopped
2 cups celery, diced
2 teaspoons salt
1 teaspoon pepper
2 teaspoons dried sage
¾ cup hot water

Mix and toss all the ingredients together. Stuff inside a turkey, or bake in a greased casserole dish at 375° for 30 to 35 minutes.
Makes about 8 servings.

Cindy and Jim Vipperman

PURE HOMEMADE DRESSING

1 loaf of bread (between 22 and 30 slices)
2 teaspoons salt
2 teaspoons dried sage
1 teaspoon poultry seasoning
3 small or 2 medium onions, chopped
1½ cups celery, chopped (optional)
1 stick butter
2 cups salted turkey broth (chicken or beef bouillon will work also)

Break the bread into small pieces in a large bowl. Mix the salt, sage, and poultry seasoning with the bread. Sauté the onions and celery in butter until tender. Add the broth to the onions and celery, then stir. After the broth has warmed, pour the broth mixture over the bread and mix all together lightly.

Fork the mixture into a greased casserole dish. Cover with foil and bake at 350° for 45 minutes.

Remove the foil cover and bake for 10 to 15 minutes more. Then it's ready to eat.

Makes 8 to 10 servings.

Jeff Weaver
The Rarely Herd

How 'Bout Those Nicks Quiz

Match the bluegrass artist to his nickname.

1. Jerry Douglas
2. Pete Kirby
3. Bill Monroe
4. Pete Wernick
5. Ralph Stanley
6. Gary Brewer
7. Curly Ray Cline
8. David Akeman
9. Larry Sparks

A. Doctor Banjo
B. The Old Kentucky Fox Hunter
C. Stretch
D. The Elvis of Bluegrass
E. The Father of Bluegrass
F. Stringbean
G. Flux
H. The First Doctor of Bluegrass
I. Brother Oswald

Answers: 1.G; 2.I; 3.E; 4.A; 5.H; 6.C; 7.B; 8.F; 9.D

Artists And Their Songs Matching Quiz

Match the bluegrass group or artist with their trademark song.

1. Flatt and Scruggs
2. New Grass Revival
3. Doyle Lawson and Quicksilver
4. Hot Rize
5. Reno and Smiley
6. The Lonesome River Band
7. Alison Krauss and Union Station
8. Doc Watson
9. The Johnson Mountain Boys
10. Peter Rowan
11. The Seldom Scene
12. The Dillards

A. "Too Late to Cry"
B. "Walk the Way the Wind Blows"
C. "There is a Time"
D. "Tennessee Stud"
E. "Free Mexican Airforce"
F. "On the Sea of Life"
G. "Rider"
H. "Don't Let Your Sweet Love Die"
I. "Reach"
J. "Hobo Blues"
K. "Foggy Mountain Breakdown"
L. "Let the Whole World Talk"

Answers: 1. K; 2. I; 3. F; 4. B; 5. H; 6. J; 7. A; 8. D; 9. L; 10. E; 11. G; 12. C

JAMS, JELLIES, RELISHES, AND SAUCES

ZONN'S TENNESSEE SALSA

This is always a party favorite.

1 bunch green onions
1 medium red onion
2 to 3 cloves garlic
1 cup fresh parsley
1 red bell pepper
1 green bell pepper
1 yellow bell pepper
1 or 2 fresh jalapeño peppers
2 15-ounce cans diced tomatoes (or peel
    and dice 1½ pounds fresh roma
    tomatoes)
2 15-ounce cans black-eyed peas, drained
2 15½-ounce cans hominy, drained
1 to 2 15-ounce cans black beans, drained
¼ cup olive oil
¼ cup vinegar (wine or balsamic or
    raspberry; each will give a slightly
    different tang)
1 tablespoon dried Italian herbs
1 teaspoon ground cumin
Chili powder to taste (optional)
Salt to taste (optional)
1 10-ounce can of Ro-tel tomatoes with
    green chilies, for extra heat (optional)

Slice the green onions; dice the red onion; chop or press the garlic; finely chop the parsley; slice and dice the red, green, and yellow peppers; and chop the jalapeños. Put all of these ingredients in a large mixing bowl with the diced tomatoes. Add the black-eyed peas, hominy, and black beans. Add the olive oil, vinegar, Italian herbs, cumin, and the optional ingredients. The flavor develops as the salsa sits for a while. Drain and serve with crackers or chips, or serve as a salad in a lettuce cup. Enjoy!

Makes about 12 cups.

Paul Martin Zonn
Nashville Mandolin Ensemble

Paul Martin Zonn is one of the only bluegrass clarinetists in the world. He plays with the Nashville Mandolin Ensemble, whose members include (*seated in front, l-r*) Fred Carpenter, Charlie Derrington, John Hedgecoth, (*standing, l-r*) Zonn, Gene Bush, Rob Haines (*front*), Richard Kriehn (*rear*), Walter Carter, David Spicher, Aubrey Haynie, and Butch Baldassari.

RAYBON SALSA

2 15-ounce cans stewed chopped tomatoes
1 medium onion, chopped
1 teaspoon chopped cilantro
5 slices jalapeño pepper, diced
1½ tablespoons green chilies, chopped
Salt to taste

Mix together all the ingredients and refrigerate. Makes about 4 cups.

Marty Raybon
Shenandoah

AW, HOT AIN'T THE WORD FOR IT PEPPER RELISH

32 ounces ketchup
1 cup vinegar
1 cup sugar
1 cup vegetable oil
1 clove garlic, finely chopped
2 quarts peppers (cayenne, jalapeño, and
    yellow hot Hungarian), finely chopped
2 quarts onion, finely chopped

Bring the ketchup, vinegar, sugar, oil, and garlic to a boil. Remove from heat. Add the peppers and onions. Be sure to use equal parts peppers and onions. Return the mixture to the burner until evenly heated, and then can in sterilized pint jars.
Makes about 10 pints.

Jan Harvey, David Harvey,
and Jill Snider
Wild and Blue

The sound of the popular country music group Shenandoah has strong echoes of lead singer Marty Raybon's roots in bluegrass and bluegrass gospel music. The Shenandoah vocalist began his career as a teenager playing guitar and singing with his father and two brothers in the family bluegrass ensemble, American Bluegrass Express. For five consecutive years, the group won Florida's statewide bluegrass band competition. Singing along with Raybon and Shenandoah on their hit "Somewhere in the Vicinity of the Heart" was Alison Krauss.

TEXAS HOT SAUCE

2 32-ounce cans whole tomatoes
6 to 10 fresh green onions, finely chopped
4 fresh jalapeño peppers, finely chopped
1 large garlic clove, finely chopped
Salt to taste

Put tomatoes in a food processor or blender and blend just until frothy. Add the remaining ingredients and refrigerate overnight.
Makes about 8 cups.

Debra Sinclair
WhiteHouse Harmony

CRANBERRY ORANGE RELISH

This is an old Mennonite recipe.

4 cups cranberries
2 oranges
3 apples
2 cups sugar

Wash cranberries, apples, and oranges. Core the apples and remove the seeds, but leave on the peel. Quarter the oranges and remove the seeds, but again, leave on the peel. Grind the cranberries, apples, and oranges with a food grinder or chopper. Stir in the sugar. Let stand

The Lewis Family has been performing for nearly half a century and has earned the title "The First Family of Bluegrass Gospel Music." Three generations of the family make up the current band, which features Little Roy Lewis on banjo. Pictured here are (*l-r, front row*) Lewis Phillips and Travis; (*l-r, middle row*) Janis Lewis Phillips, Miggie, and Polly Lewis Copsey; (*l-r, back row*) Little Roy, Roy "Pop," and Wallace.

in a refrigerator for at least 12 hours before serving. Relish will keep for days.

Makes about 8 cups.

Janis Lewis Phillips
The Lewis Family

OZARK ZUCCHINI RELISH

10 cups ground zucchini (about 2 big
    zucchinis)
8 medium onions
4 medium green bell peppers
4 teaspoons salt
4 cups sugar
2 cups white vinegar
2 teaspoons celery seed
2 teaspoons turmeric
2 teaspoons mustard seed
½ teaspoon black pepper
½ teaspoon green food coloring

Combine the zucchini, onions, peppers, and salt. Let stand for 30 minutes, then drain well. Add the remaining ingredients and boil for 3 to 5 minutes. While hot, pack into sterilized jars.

Makes 6 or 7 pints.

Sandy and Dean Webb
The Dillards

The Dillards of 1977 were (*clockwise from far left*) Dean Webb on mandolin, Paul York on percussion, Rodney Dillard on guitar and lead vocals, Billy Ray Lathum on banjo, and Jeff Gilkinson on bass. They're seen here in a publicity shot for "An Evening of Bluegrass," a television special for PBS.

Bluegrass Festivals

Merle Watson's son, Richard, continues the long line of fine pickers in the Watson family. He often performs with grandpa Doc, and he surely favors his dad, both in appearance and in his rock-solid fingerpicking. Here, Richard and Doc perform on the Cabin Stage at the annual Merle Watson Memorial Festival (a.k.a. MerleFest) in Wilkesboro, North Carolina.

Bluegrass music was beginning its third decade when the first weekend-long bluegrass festival was staged in 1965. Prior to that, bluegrass had been incorporated into folk festivals such as Newport (Rhode Island), Chicago, and Mariposa (Ontario). Bluegrass artists were also booked at country music parks like New River Ranch in Maryland and Sunset Park in Pennsylvania, but rarely would more than one bluegrass band perform at these shows on the same day.

On July 4, 1961, Bill Clifton staged the first day-long bluegrass event at Oak Leaf Park in Luray, Virginia. The lineup included Bill Monroe, the Stanley Brothers, Jim and Jesse, Mac Wiseman, the Country Gentlemen, and Bill Clifton. Twenty-two hundred people attended this event. Present in the audience that day was promoter Carlton Haney, who managed a number of bluegrass and country music artists during the 1950s and 1960s (including Bill Monroe, Reno and Smiley, Conway Twitty, and others). Based upon ideas he encountered at Clifton's event, as well as at other venues like the Newport Folk Festival, country music parks, and at

fiddlers conventions (contests) such as the one in Union Grove, North Carolina, Haney decided to stage a three-day bluegrass festival.

In 1965, the "First Annual Roanoke Blue Grass Festival" was held on September 3, 4, and 5 in Fincastle, Virginia, about twelve miles north of Roanoke. Tickets were six dollars for the weekend or $2.50 per day, and included camping. The performers were Bill Monroe, Jimmy Martin, the Stanley Brothers, Mac Wiseman, the Osborne Brothers, Doc Watson, Clyde Moody, Don Reno and the Tennessee Cutups, and Red Smiley and the Bluegrass Cutups. In addition to concert-type performances, the schedule included workshops, talent contests, and a Sunday morning gospel show. The Sunday afternoon finale, billed as "The Story of Bluegrass," was a series of performances by Bill Monroe narrated by Haney. Monroe was joined by former Blue Grass Boys (in chronological order of their tenure in the band) as they recreated the songs they recorded together and discussed Monroe's music and its impact.

Haney's festival became an annual event (it moved to

Though he never played an instrument, Bill Vernon was involved with bluegrass music in just about every other way possible. He grew up in New York and went to college in Boston, but he flunked out because he was too busy listening to his beloved bluegrass. He even worked on Wall Street for a time, but chucked it all to move to southern Virginia to be at the geographic center of the music he loved. Bill had an encyclopedic knowledge of bluegrass history, which he readily shared through his writing for various publications (including Muleskinner News and Bluegrass Unlimited), his liner notes for various recordings, and his work as a radio disc jockey on various stations in the Roanoke area. He also frequently served as an emcee for bluegrass festivals and other events. He is pictured here at the Berkshire Mountains Festival in New York in 1982. Bill passed away suddenly in late 1996. His warm heart, wonderful wit, selfless devotion to the music, and colorful stories are sorely missed by all who knew him.

Watermelon Park in Berryville, Virginia, in 1967), and soon other festivals were springing up in Virginia and neighboring states. Several bluegrass artists, including Bill Monroe and Ralph Stanley, started festivals of their own, which they continued to host each year. By the mid-1970s, growth had mushroomed, and by the '90s, there were over five hundred bluegrass festivals in this country and around the world.

Through the years, the style of festivals has varied somewhat as the music has evolved. Today's festivals cover a broad spectrum—from those that present only straight-ahead bluegrass to those which incorporate many other forms of acoustic music, including old-time, folk, blues, Irish, and Cajun. But many of the basic elements conceived by Carlton Haney still survive. The concept of presenting a large variety of entertainment for one ticket, the inclusion of workshops and contests to encourage audience participation, and performances that not only entertain but also educate the audience about the history of the music continue as important elements of festivals today.

As the number of festivals has grown, so has the audience base. Bluegrass music has become a bridge across many cultural boundaries, as young and old, blue collar and white collar, conservative and counterculture, and many different nationalities all are brought together by this common passion. Many bluegrass lovers spend their summer vacations driving in recreational vehicles or campers from one festival to another for weeks at a time. In addition, since bluegrass music encourages audience participation, many fans attend festivals not to watch the stage shows but to play music with other "parking lot pickers." Enduring long-distance friendships often are formed from these encounters.

For a comprehensive listing of bluegrass and acoustic music festivals, see the January issue of *Bluegrass Unlimited* magazine.

The Ryman Auditorium inside ...

... and out.

The Grand Ole Opry

The day that WSM Radio in Nashville went on the air in 1925, the station hired announcer George D. Hay. He immediately began to develop programming along the lines of the National Barn Dance, a show he had done with WLS Radio in Chicago.

In 1928, and almost by accident, the "Solemn Old Judge," as Hay became known, coined the moniker "Grand Ole Opry" for his show, putting the WSM hoedown on the path towards becoming a national treasure. By 1939, WSM was heard nationwide thanks to a clear-channel, fifty-thousand-watt signal. By coincidence, Bill Monroe and his Blue Grass Boys were inventing bluegrass music at the same time the Grand Ole Opry was earning a national following, and the two entities climbed the ladder of success together.

Although the bluegrass sound was finding popularity in other areas, it was Nashville and the fertility of WSM and the Grand Ole Opry that gave Bill Monroe the proper ground for planting his distinctive bluegrass seeds. He went on to become one of the Opry's "Four Pillars," along with Roy Acuff, Hank Snow, and Ernest Tubb.

A milestone year for bluegrass music's connection to the Grand Ole Opry was 1955, when Flatt and Scruggs officially joined the Opry (they had been doing an early morning radio show for WSM and Martha White Flour since 1953). The dynamic duo and their Foggy Mountain Boys were among the Opry's most popular acts until Lester Flatt and Earl Scruggs decided to pursue separate musical paths in 1969. Their rendition of the "Martha White Theme" can still be heard as a highlight of Grand Ole Opry broadcasts each week.

The bluegrass torch continues to burn strong at the Grand Ole Opry. Regular performances by Opry members such as Jim and Jesse, the Osborne Brothers, Ricky Skaggs, and Alison Krauss keep the relationship between bluegrass and the Opry as solid as ever. The depth of that relationship was symbolized in the moving memorial service for the late Bill Monroe held in the Opry's old home, the Ryman Auditorium. Without question, there's a bond between bluegrass and the Grand Ole Opry that will last as long as the music itself.

ARMSTRONG DILL PICKLES

This is a recipe I learned from my mother, Ida B. Armstrong. These pickles have won first prize at the Kentucky State Fair.

35 to 40 pickling cucumbers, each about 4 inches long and 1 inch in diameter; or larger cucumbers split into slices.
Boiling water for scalding cucumbers
4 large-mouth, 1-quart canning jars with lids
4 small garlic cloves
4 small red chile peppers
4 sprigs fresh dill
2 quarts water
1 quart vinegar
1 cup salt

Brush and wash the cukes. Scald the cukes by placing them in boiling water for about 1 minute. Remove the cukes from water and place in jars along with 1 small garlic clove, 1 small red chile pepper, and sprig of fresh dill (if fresh dill is not available, 1 tablespoon dill seed and ½ tablespoon dried dill weed may be substituted). Bring 2 quarts water, 1 quart vinegar, and cup of salt to a boil. Pour the hot water mixture over cukes and tighten the jar lids. Turn the jars upside down and let stand until the next day, then turn upright. Pickles need to sit for about 1 week before eating.
Makes 4 quarts.

Jim Armstrong
New Dominion Bluegrass

PAM PERRY'S PICKER'S PICKLES

4 quarts medium cucumbers, thinly sliced
6 medium onions, finely chopped
3 cloves garlic, minced or finely chopped
1 or 2 green bell peppers, cut into narrow strips
1 red bell pepper, cut into narrow strips
¹/₃ cup salt
Cracked ice
3 cups distilled vinegar
5 cups sugar
1½ teaspoons turmeric

1½ teaspoon celery seed
2 tablespoons mustard seed

Combine the cucumbers, onions, garlic, peppers, and salt. Cover the mixture with cracked ice and mix thoroughly. Let stand for 3 hours. Drain the cucumber mixture. Combine the remaining ingredients and pour them over the cucumbers. Heat the cucumber mixture to boiling. Pour the mixture into sterilized jars and seal.
Makes 8 pints.

Pam Perry
The New Coon Creek Girls

BACK HOME TO YOU HOMEMADE MAYONNAISE

1 egg
½ teaspoon salt, optional
½ teaspoon dry mustard
1 tablespoon tarragon vinegar
1 tablespoon lemon juice
1 cup salad oil

Put the first 5 ingredients and ¼ cup salad oil into a blender. Cover and blend. Remove the top from the blender and, with the blender running, slowly drizzle the remaining oil into the mixture. As the mayonnaise thickens, use a rubber spatula to gently push the oil to the center. If the taste isn't to your liking, omit the salt, or use 2 tablespoons vinegar and omit the lemon juice. This recipe may be varied in numerous ways. For different tastes, change the designer vinegar used. *Bon appétit!*
Makes 1 heaping cupful.

Ginger Boatwright

SOOEY SAUCE FOR COLD HAM

This is a very old recipe from the kitchen of my great-great-grand aunt, Mrs. James Knox Polk.

4 tablespoons butter
4 tablespoons ketchup

4 tablespoons sherry
2 tablespoons Worcestershire sauce

In a saucepan, brown the butter and mix it with the other ingredients. Simmer on low heat while stirring gently. On a hot platter, slice the ham very thinly and pour the sauce over it.
Makes enough to sauce 2 to 4 servings.

Buell Neidlinger
The Grass Is Greener

HAY HOLLER HONEY JELLY

Especially good for kids—it's not messy.

3 cups honey
I cup water
½ bottle fruit pectin

Mix the honey and water in a large kettle. Bring to a boil over high heat and add the pectin at once. Stir constantly. Bring to a full, rolling boil and immediately remove from heat. Skim and pour quickly into clean, hot, sterilized jelly glasses. Seal with paraffin at once.
Makes 6 6-ounce glasses.

Willia and Melvin Goins

THE OLD RAMBLER'S BLACKBERRY JAM

I grow blackberries in my garden in Louisville. I learned this recipe from my family but have added a few little extras myself.

3 cups fresh, "tame" blackberries
5½ cups sugar
½ teaspoon lemon juice
I¾ cups spring water
I box Sure-Jell fruit pectin

Use ripe fruit (not under- or overripe). Wash the berries and place them in a medium bowl with a little water and the sugar. Let the berries sit at room temperature until the sugar is completely dissolved. Place the berries in a food processor set on "chop," or use a potato masher to crush. (Remember: It is a jam, so leave plenty of

Gary Brewer is one of the outstanding third generation singers and guitarists who is carrying on the bluegrass tradition in the 1990s. Some of the last recordings made by Bill Monroe were on Gary's *Guitar* album, released in 1995 on Copper Creek Records.
Photograph by Hank Widick; courtesy of Copper Creek Records

fruit pieces.) Transfer the fruit to a medium pan. Add the lemon juice, 1¾ cups spring water, and fruit pectin. Bring mixture to a boil for 1 minute while stirring continuously. Set the mixture aside for 5 minutes, then pour into your choice of container(s) and seal. Let jam sit at room temperature for 24 hours. For immediate use, place the mixture in the refrigerator until the jam stiffens.
Makes 7 cups.

Gary Brewer

BLUEGRASS JAM

4½ cups slightly crushed blueberries
7 cups sugar
2 tablespoons lemon juice
6 ounces liquid pectin

Combine the blueberries, sugar, and lemon juice in a large Dutch oven. Bring to a rolling boil. Boil for 1 minute, stirring constantly. Remove from heat and immediately stir in the pectin. Stir and alternately skim off the foam with a metal spoon for 5 minutes. Quickly pour the mixture into hot sterilized jars, leaving a ¼-inch

As one of the original members of the famed band New Grass Revival, **Curtis Burch** has left his mark as an innovative bluegrass stylist on resonator guitar and guitar. He left the band in 1981 after a decade with the group, but he has stayed close to his bluegrass roots in Kentucky, where he currently is a member of Barren County Revival.

headspace. Cover at once with metal lids and screw on the bands. Process in a bath of boiling water for 10 minutes.

Makes 9 half pints.

Curtis Burch

ANN LYNCH'S STRAWBERRY JAM

Granny Phillips has always had a strawberry patch, and come the month of May in Alabama, we make great use of fresh strawberries by using this quick recipe for jam. You can also easily put up strawberries in the freezer and grab some for making jam anytime.

1 cup strawberries
1 cup sugar

Combine the berries and sugar in a saucepan. Boil and stir for 10 to 12 minutes.

Makes 1 full cup.

Claire Lynch

COUNTRY CROCKPOT APPLE BUTTER

6 to 8 pounds apples
1 cup vinegar
8 cups sugar
4 teaspoons cinnamon

Peel and core the apples. Cook with only enough water to soften apples. Press the apples through a sieve, then combine all the ingredients. Cook until the butter is the desired color (about 4 hours in the crockpot).

Makes about 8 pints.

Molly O'Day

HOT TYME PEPPER JELLY

Watch out for IIIrd-degree burns!

3 large green bell peppers
6 hot peppers (red, long, and thin)

Molly O'Day left a legacy as one of the greatest female country/bluegrass/gospel singers ever. Mac Wiseman has called her "the female Hank Williams."

1½ cups cider vinegar
6½ cups sugar
1 6-ounce bottle Certo pectin
Green food coloring

Remove the seeds, core, and cut up the green peppers. Cut up the hot peppers, retaining the seeds. Put some of each pepper type in a blender with ¼ cup vinegar and blend until smooth. Place in a large kettle or stew pot. Repeat until all the peppers are blended. Add the remaining vinegar and the sugar to the pot, and stir well. Bring to a rolling boil and cook for 5 minutes, stirring occasionally. Remove from the heat. Add the Certo pectin and 2 or 3 drops of food coloring. Cool and skim. Place the mixture in sterilized jars and seal. Wax if desired. Serve with meat or over cream cheese with crackers.

Makes 6 to 8 6-ounce jars

Russell Moore
IIIrd Tyme Out

SWEET PERRY PEAR HONEY

1 quart pears, peeled, cored, and finely
   chopped
4 cups sugar
20 ounces crushed pineapple
1 ounce water (optional)
1 box fruit pectin (optional)

Cook the pears until they're soft and clear. Add the sugar followed by the crushed pineapple. Cook until thick. If the pears are dry, add 1 ounce of water. Add the fruit pectin if desired. Can in sterilized jars.

Makes about 4 pints.

Pam Perry
The New Coon Creek Girls

Food ForThought Matching Quiz

Bluegrass musicians love to eat, and bluegrass is full of songs with references to food. Match the song to the artist with whom it is associated.

1. "Leftover Biscuits"
2. "Shuckin' the Corn"
3. "Sugar Coated Love"
4. "Singing All Day, Dinner on the Ground"
5. "Honey in the Rock"
6. "One Loaf of Bread"
7. "Burning the Breakfast"
8. "Dixie Fried"
9. "Canadian Bacon"
10. "Banana Boat Song"

A. Eddie Adcock Band
B. The Lewis Family
C. Front Range
D. Flatt and Scruggs
E. Blue Highway
F. The Country Gentlemen
G. Bill Monroe
H. The Lost and Found
I. Jimmy Martin
J. Dave Evans

Answers: 1. H; 2. D; 3. G; 4. I; 5. B;
6. J; 7. C; 8. A; 9. E; 10. F

DESSERTS

Cakes

MAYBERRY CAKE

No eggs, no milk.

1½ cups all-purpose flour
½ teaspoon salt
1 cup sugar
3 tablespoons cocoa
1 teaspoon baking soda
1 tablespoon vanilla extract
1 tablespoon vinegar
5 tablespoons margarine, melted, or oil
½ cup semi-sweet chocolate bits
1 cup cold water

Preheat oven to 350°. Using a fork, combine the flour, salt, sugar, cocoa, and baking soda in an 8-inch square pan. Stir in the vanilla, vinegar, margarine (or oil), and the chocolate bits. Pour the water over all. Stir well. Bake until a cake-tester inserted in the center comes out clean (30 to 35 minutes). Cool on a rack.
Makes 9 servings.

Pat and Randall Hylton

ACOUSTIC TRAVELER CHOCOLATE POTATO CAKE

2 squares baking chocolate
½ cup butter
1½ cups sugar

Acclaimed songwriter Randall Hylton has written a slew of bluegrass and bluegrass gospel hits, including "Gonna Be Moving," "Hallelujah Turnpike," and "The Likes of You." His songs have been recorded by the likes of the Lewis Family, the Country Gentlemen, Doyle Lawson, and Larry Sparks. Randall has recorded a number of albums himself, including *The Singer and the Songster* with Charlie Waller.

3 eggs, separated
2 cups all-purpose flour
2 teaspoons baking powder
1 teaspoon ground cinnamon
1 teaspoon ground cloves
½ teaspoon ground nutmeg
1 teaspoon ground allspice
½ cup milk
1 cup hot mashed potatoes
1 cup nuts, chopped
½ cup raisins
Flour
½ cup peanut butter or chocolate chips
   (optional, but good)

Preheat oven to 350°. Melt the chocolate squares and butter quickly in a large microwave-safe bowl in the microwave. Cream the sugar into the chocolate. Beat the egg yolks well and add. Mix 2 cups flour, spices, and baking powder with a sifter and add to the creamed sugar mixture, along with the milk. Add the potatoes and mix well. Dredge the nuts and raisins in flour and fold in with well-beaten egg whites. Add the chips if desired. Mix well and pour into two 9-inch greased and floured cake pans. Bake for 30 minutes. Frosting is optional.

Makes 10 to 12 servings.

*Gerie Anthony McEuen,
mom of John McEuen*

Banjo wizard John McEuen, one of the founders of the Nitty Gritty Dirt Band, has been making music for over thirty years. He is one of the instigators begind the historic *Will the Circle Be Unbroken* album of 1971. Lately, John has been scoring television films and documentaries, while continuing to be an acoustic ace.

BEYOND THE CITY
CARAMEL POUND CAKE

Most of you know that during World War II things were rationed. But growing up on the farm gave us the opportunity to enjoy some of the things you can't buy in the store.

The highlight of the day was when the school bus stopped, and we made our way to an old pie safe where there were leftover biscuits, cake, corn bread, and raisin cookies. Today, one of our favorite recipes is a caramel pound cake that Willard's mother handed down. This cake was found in the old pie safe on several occasions. It's simple to make, but delicious, and I'd like to share it with everyone.

1 stick margarine
¼ cup Crisco shortening
2 cups sugar
6 eggs
¾ cup milk
2½ cups self-rising flour*
½ teaspoon vanilla extract

Preheat oven to 325°. Mix the margarine, Crisco, and sugar until the mixture is fluffy. Add the eggs one at a time, mixing well. Add the milk, flour, and vanilla, and mix well. Pour into a greased and floured 9- by 5-inch loaf pan, or tube pan. Bake for 1 hour, or until done (depending on the oven). Let the cake cool before icing.

* You may substitute all-purpose flour, but remember to use salt and baking powder.

Icing:

2½ cups dark or medium brown sugar
1½ cups milk
1 stick butter
8 tablespoons white sugar
2 teaspoons vanilla extract

Mix all the ingredients and heat in an iron skillet or pot until the mixture comes to a boil. Test a drop in water: it should form a sugar ball. After the icing cools, pour over the cool cake.

Makes 10 to 12 servings.

*Marie Cox
The Cox Family*

CLEAR CUT COCONUT POUND CAKE

1 cup oil
2 cups sugar
5 eggs
2 cups self-rising flour
½ cup milk
1 teaspoon vanilla extract
1 teaspoon coconut extract
1½ cups Angel Flake coconut

Preheat oven to 350°. Combine all the ingredients in the order listed, mixing well after each addition. Pour the batter into a greased and floured tube pan and bake for 40 to 45 minutes.

Glaze:

1 stick margarine
½ cup water
1 cup sugar
1 teaspoon vanilla extract
1 teaspoon coconut extract

Combine all the ingredients in a saucepan, bring to a boil, and pour over the warm cake in the pan. Let the cake sit for 30 minutes before serving.

Makes 10 to 12 servings.

Tim Stafford
Blue Highway

The Cox Family hails from Cotton Valley, Louisiana, and is led by father Willard Cox. The family has performed together for more than two decades. They rose to national fame after beginning an association with Alison Krauss in the early 1990s. Sisters Suzanne and Evelyn have received repeated nominations as IBMA Female Vocalist of the Year, and brother Sidney is an accomplished songwriter. Pictured here are (l-r) Suzanne, Lynn, Willard, Evelyn, and Sidney.

Blue Highway burst on the bluegrass scene in 1995, garnering three IBMA Awards in '96: Emerging Artist of the Year; Album of the Year for their debut recording, *It's a Long, Long Road;* and Dobro Player of the Year award to Rob Ickes. The Blue Highway members write much of their own material, and some of them even do their own cooking! Band members are (l-r) Wayne Taylor, Rob Ickes, Jason Burleson, Shawn Lane, and Tim Stafford.

CAROLINA CREAM CHEESE POUND CAKE

3 sticks butter
8 ounces cream cheese, softened
3 cups sugar
6 eggs
3 cups all-purpose flour
2 teaspoons vanilla extract

Preheat oven to 300°. Cream the butter and cream cheese. Add the sugar, beating well. Add the eggs one at a time, beating well after adding each one. Add the flour and vanilla. Pour into a greased and floured tube pan. Bake for 1½ hours.
Makes 10 to 12 servings.

Emma and Jody Rainwater

GRANDMA HOLLBROOK'S APPLE POUND CAKE

1½ cups salad oil
3 whole eggs
3 cups self-rising flour
1½ teaspoons vanilla flavoring
3 cups diced apples
2 cups sugar
¾ cup flaked coconut
1 cup chopped pecans
1 cup raisins

Preheat oven to 350°. Mix the oil and eggs. Add the flour and vanilla. Add the remaining ingredients, mix well, and pour into a greased tube pan. Bake for 1 hour and 20 minutes.

Granny Vallie's Butter Cream Icing

1 16-ounce box powdered sugar
1 stick margarine, softened
1 teaspoon vanilla flavoring
2 to 3 tablespoons milk

Mix all ingredients well with an electric mixer. Spread over cooled cake.
Makes 10 to 12 servings.

Ramona Church Taylor
The New Coon Creek Girls

As they man the lookout post at Thomas Point Beach, Maine, the New Coon Creek Girls are head and shoulders above the crowd. Pictured are (l-r) banjo player Ramona Church Taylor, mandolin player Kathy Kuhn, guitar player Dale Ann Bradley, and bass player Vicki Simmons.

New Coon Creek Girls

The formation of the New Coon Creek Girls in 1979 was inspired by the original Coon Creek Girls. The original group formed in 1937 and was a fixture on the Renfro Valley Barn Dance until the band dissolved in the early 1950s.

HAPPY SACK FRESH APPLE CAKE

2 cups sugar
1¼ cups cooking oil
3 eggs
3 cups all-purpose flour
½ teaspoon salt
1 teaspoon baking soda
¼ teaspoon ground cinnamon
¼ teaspoon ground nutmeg
¼ teaspoon ground cloves
1 teaspoon vanilla extract
1 cup pecans, broken
3 cups fresh apples, diced (Granny Smith recommended)

Preheat oven to 350°. Beat together the sugar, oil, and eggs until they're very light-colored (approximately 10 minutes). Sift together the flour, salt, baking soda, and spices; add this to the egg mixture. Then add the vanilla, pecans, and apples. Mix well. Bake the cake in a greased tube pan for 1 hour.

Glaze:

½ stick butter
1 cup brown sugar
½ cup evaporated milk

Combine all the ingredients and bring to a boil, stirring when the mixture thickens. Continue stirring until the mixture is creamy. Spread on the cooled cake.
Makes 10 to 12 servings.

Emmylou Harris

FANCY GAP APPLE CAKE

2 cups sugar
1¼ cups cooking oil
2 eggs
3 cups all-purpose flour
1 teaspoon salt
1 teaspoon soda
3 cups fresh apples, diced
2 teaspoons vanilla extract
1 cup black walnuts, chopped

Emmylou Harris has achieved critical and commercial success in a variety of musical fields, but her deep bluegrass roots are evident on acclaimed albums such as *Roses in the Snow* (1980) and the Nash Rambler's *At the Ryman* (1991). She's seen here kicking up some "hillbilly dust" on the Ryman Auditorium stage with Bill Monroe during the recording of *At the Ryman*.

Preheat oven to 325°. Cream the sugar, oil, and eggs. Combine the flour, salt, and soda, then fold into the sugar mixture. Add the apples, vanilla, and walnuts. Bake in a greased 10- by 13-inch pan for 45 minutes.

Frosting:

1 cup brown sugar
¼ cup margarine
3 tablespoons milk

Mix and boil all the ingredients in a saucepan for 3 minutes, then pour over hot cake.
Makes 12 servings.

Barry Berrier
The Lost and Found

VIRGINIA APPLESAUCE CAKE

3 eggs
2 cups sugar
I cup real butter
1½ cups applesauce
I teaspoon vanilla extract
2 cups all-purpose flour
I teaspoon baking soda
¼ teaspoon salt
I teaspoon ground cinnamon
2 cups chopped pecans
2 cups raisins

Preheat oven to 300°. Blend the eggs, sugar, butter, applesauce, and vanilla in a large bowl. In another bowl, mix flour, baking soda, salt, and cinnamon. Set aside ½ cup of flour mixture; add the remaining flour mixture to the batter. With the ½ cup of flour mixture, lightly coat the pecans and raisins (this can be done by placing the flour mixture, pecans, and raisins in a plastic zipper-type bag and shaking well), then fold this mixture into the batter, gradually stirring by hand.

Pour the batter into a well-greased and floured tube pan. Bake for 2½ hours.

Makes 10 to 12 servings.

Emma and Jody Rainwater

David Davis and the Warrior River Boys have bluegrass roots that extend back to the days before the music was even called "bluegrass." (Cleo Davis, David's uncle, was hired by Bill Monroe in 1938.) David (*pictured here*) leads the band on mandolin, Marty Hays handles the bass, Tom Ewing is the guitarist and lead singer, Randy Lindley plays banjo, and Bill Sage makes sparks fly for the band on the fiddle.

WARRIOR RIVER FRESH APPLE CAKE

1¾ cups sugar
I cup oil
3 eggs
2 cups self-rising flour
I teaspoon ground cinnamon
2 apples, chopped thin
I cup chopped nuts (optional)

Preheat oven to 350°. Stir up the sugar, oil, and eggs. Sift the flour and cinnamon into the mixture. Beat well. Add the apples and beat well. Add the nuts, if desired, and beat well. Pour the batter into either a greased 13- by 9- by 3-inch pan or 2 greased loaf pans. Bake for 45 minutes, or until done.

Glaze:

I stick margarine
I teaspoon baking soda
I teaspoon vanilla extract
I tablespoon white syrup
½ cup buttermilk
I cup sugar

Combine the ingredients in a saucepan. Cook 15 minutes on medium heat. Pour over hot cake. This cake can be frozen.

Makes 12 servings.

David Davis
The Warrior River Boys

GRANDMA ISON'S DRIED APPLE STACK CAKE

1½ cups shortening, softened
2 cups brown sugar
2 eggs
½ cup molasses
4½ cups sifted all-purpose flour
2 teaspoons baking soda
½ teaspoon salt
1 teaspoon ground cloves
2 teaspoons ground cinnamon
2 teaspoons ground ginger
¼ cup buttermilk

Preheat oven to 350°. Mix together the first 4 ingredients. Sift together the flour, baking soda, salt, cloves, cinnamon, and ginger, then mix thoroughly into the sugar mixture. Stir in the buttermilk. Roll out the dough and cut into skillet-sized circles. In an iron skillet, bake each circle for about 12 minutes, or until slightly brown.

Apple mixture:

2 cups dried apples
Ground cloves to taste
Sugar to taste
Ground cinnamon to taste
Ground allspice to taste
Water as needed

Cook the dried apples in the spice mixture in a saucepan, adding just enough water to cover the apples. Spread the mixture between the cake layers and let stand for 2 days before serving.
Makes 10 servings.

Wayne Lewis

BETTER THAN APPLE PYE CAKE

3 or 4 apples
1¾ cups sugar
3 eggs
1 cup oil
1 teaspoon vanilla extract
2 cups all-purpose flour
1 teaspoon salt
1 teaspoon baking soda
2 teaspoons ground cinnamon
1 cup chopped nuts (optional)
Powdered sugar

Peel, core, and chop the apples. Set aside. Preheat oven to 350°. Grease a 9- by 13-inch pan, or spray pan with non-stick spray. Blend together the sugar, eggs, oil, and vanilla. Sift together the flour, salt, baking soda, and cinnamon, then add to the first mixture a little at a time. The batter will be stiff. Fold in the apples and chopped nuts. Pour into the prepared pan and bake for 40 to 45 minutes. Dust with powdered sugar while still warm.
Makes 12 servings.

Steve Pye
Highstrung

Wayne Lewis of the Wayne Lewis Band is best known for handling lead vocals for Bill Monroe's Blue Grass Boys from the mid–1970s to mid–1980s. He's seen here with Mr. Monroe (left) and Butch Robins (center).

From the early '70s through the early '90s, banjoist Hubert Davis and his Season Travelers were a Nashville institution at Davis's Bluegrass Inn. The bluegrass club was located on Broadway for nearly twenty years. Growing up with Earl Scruggs near Shelby, North Carolina, Davis originally played the banjo left-handed, but eventually learned to pick right-handed. He always concluded his shows with: "That's every Wednesday, Thursday, Friday, and Saturday night every week that rolls around right here at the Bluegrass Inn. If you like our music, tell your friends about us. If you don't, keep your mouth shut and everything's going to be all right. You better do it." Hubert Davis's favorite meal was buttermilk and corn bread made with Martha White cornmeal. Pictured here are (l-r) Hubert Davis, Gene Bush, and Rubye Davis taping a live album in the early 1980s at the Wind in the Willows club in Nashville. Legendary WSM announcer Grant Turner is watching at the front of the stage.

SEASON TRAVELER FRUIT COCKTAIL CAKE

1¾ cups sugar
2 cups all-purpose flour
2 eggs
2 teaspoons baking soda
1 16-ounce can fruit cocktail

Preheat oven to 350°. Combine all the ingredients and bake in a greased 9- by 13-inch pan for 30 minutes.

Topping:

1¾ cups evaporated milk
1½ sticks butter
1½ cups sugar
1½ teaspoons vanilla extract
1 3½-ounce can flaked coconut
¾ cup chopped nuts

Cook the milk, butter, and sugar over medium heat in a saucepan for 2 to 3 minutes, or until thick. Remove from heat. Add the vanilla, coconut, and nuts. Mix well and pour over cake.
Makes 12 servings.

Hubert Davis

PEACH PICKED SKILLET CAKE

Fruit mixture:

¼ cup butter
¾ cup brown sugar
1 cup pecan meats (optional)
1 15-ounce can sliced or halved peaches

Melt the butter in a 9-inch iron skillet. Remove from the fire. Sprinkle brown sugar and nut meats over bottom. Arrange the fruit on the sugar.

Batter:

2 eggs
1 cup sugar
½ cup rich milk
1 tablespoon oil
1 teaspoon vanilla extract
1 cup cake flour
1 teaspoon baking powder

Preheat oven to 350°. Beat the eggs until light.

Add the sugar gradually while beating constantly. Heat the milk to the boiling point. Add the oil to the milk, and then beat the milk mixture into the egg mixture. Add the vanilla. Add the flour and baking powder to the egg mixture. Beat until blended. Pour over the fruit.

Bake for 35 minutes. Turn out on a plate while warm. Serve upside down.

Makes 8 servings.

Randall Franks
The Peachtree Pickers

HEART AND SOUL HOMEMADE POUND CAKE

1 pound butter
3 cups sugar
9 eggs
4 cups all-purpose flour, sifted
1 teaspoon baking powder
½ teaspoon salt
1 cup milk
1 teaspoon vanilla extract

Preheat oven to 350°. Cream the butter and sugar together until thick and fluffy. Add the eggs one at a time, beating well after each egg. Sift the flour, baking powder, and salt together. Add the flour mixture to the egg mixture, alternating with the milk. Mix well and stir in the vanilla. Pour into 2 small tube pans that have been greased and floured. Bake for about 45 minutes, or until tested done. Let cool 10 minutes in pan.

Makes 12 to 15 servings.

Ruby Ann Gillis for
The Gillis Brothers

SISTER'S OOOEY GOOEY CAKE

2 eggs
1 stick butter, melted
1 box yellow cake mix
¾ cup pecans, chopped

Preheat oven to 350°. Whip the eggs and butter together. Add the cake mix and pecans. Mix well and put the batter into a greased and floured 9- by 13-inch pan.

Randall Franks has had a varied career, earning a reputation as a country-folk artist, humorist, and Appalachian-style singer and fiddler. He even portrayed Officer Randy Goode on television's *In the Heat of the Night.* He has been playing bluegrass since he was a boy and was one of Bill Monroe's Blue Grass Boys in the mid-1980s. Pictured right, he's wearing a costume that belonged to musician Cotton Carrier, the host of the WSB Barn Dance in Atlanta in the 1940s and 1950s.

Photograph by Ned Burris

This 1981 photograph of the Peachtree Pickers, a Georgia-based bluegrass children's band, was used on the cover of the band's first album, titled *Ivory Halls.* Band members at the time were (l-r) Wes Freeman, Mark Nelson, Jeff Blaylock, and Randall Franks. The group made five albums in its eight-year history.

Photograph courtesy of the Randall Franks Collection

Topping:

1 stick butter, softened
8 ounces cream cheese, softened
2 eggs
1 16-ounce box confectioners' sugar

Cream the butter and cream cheese. Add the eggs. Pour in the confectioners' sugar. Mix until smooth and creamy. Pour over the cake batter. Bake for 45 minutes. Cut into squares.

Makes 12 servings

Wayne Lewis

For nearly thirty years and through a dozen albums, the Born Again Bluegrass Band has been bringing all-gospel bluegrass music to countless church groups and festivals. The group members include: (l-r, top) Lanny Cram and Jerry Kinkade; (l-r, bottom) founders Steve Hatfield and LeRoy Mack McNees.

SAD CAKE

I don't know why it's called a Sad Cake. I'm always more than happy to eat some. That's just the name it had on it when the recipe was passed to me.

1 16-ounce box brown sugar
1²/₃ cups Bisquick
4 eggs
¹/₂ cup cooking oil
1 teaspoon vanilla extract
1 cup pecans, chopped
1 3¹/₂-ounce can Angel Flake coconut (original)

Preheat oven to 350°. Grease and flour a 9- by 13-inch pan. In a bowl, mix the brown sugar, Bisquick, eggs, cooking oil, vanilla, chopped pecans, and coconut. Pour into the pan and bake for 35 minutes.
Makes 12 servings.

Bobby Hicks

HEAVENLY CHOCOLATE CHERRY CAKE

1 package fudge cake mix
2 eggs, beaten
1 teaspoon almond extract
1 21-ounce can cherry fruit filling

Frosting:

1 cup sugar
5 tablespoons butter or margarine
¹/₃ cup milk
1 6-ounce package (1 cup) semi-sweet chocolate chips

Preheat oven to 350°. Using a non-stick vegetable spray, coat a 10- by 15-inch jelly roll pan or a 9- by 13-inch pan. In a large bowl, combine the cake mix, eggs, almond extract, and the cherry filling. Stir by hand until well mixed. Pour into the prepared pan. Bake the jelly roll pan 20 to 30 minutes or the 9- by 13-inch pan 25 to 30 minutes, or bake until a toothpick comes out clean. While the cake cools, prepare frosting. In a small saucepan, combine the sugar, butter, and milk. Boil, stirring constantly, for 1 minute. Remove from heat and stir in the chocolate chips. When the chips are melted and smooth, pour the frosting over the partially cooled cake. Cut into bars when completely cooled.
Makes 12 to 15 servings.

Pattie and Jerry Kinkade
Born Again Bluegrass Band

GEORGE'S GERMAN CHOCOLATE CAKE

1 box German chocolate cake mix

Bake according to package directions, in 2 layers. Allow layers to cool and then split each layer in half (for 1 four-layer cake).

Frosting:

1 cup evaporated milk
1 cup sugar
3 egg yolks
1 stick butter or margarine

(Note: To make the cake even better, double the above ingredients.)

Combine the ingredients in a heavy saucepan. Cook over low heat, stirring constantly, until mixture thickens. Remove from heat and add:

1 teaspoon vanilla extract
14 ounces flaked coconut
1 cup pecans, finely chopped
1 9-ounce box golden raisins

Spread frosting between layers and on top and sides of cake.

Makes 10 to 12 servings.

Sue and George Shuffler

OLD TYME CHOCOLATE CAKE

1 cup margarine or butter, melted
4 eggs
1 cup milk
2 cups sugar
3 cups self-rising flour
1 teaspoon vanilla flavoring

Preheat oven to 350°. Beat together the margarine, eggs, and milk. Then beat in the sugar, followed by the flour. Add the vanilla flavoring and bake in 2 greased and floured cake pans (9-inch size) until done (about 30 minutes).

Filling:

1 cup sugar
¼ cup cocoa
½ cup milk

In a saucepan, boil all 3 ingredients until the mixture begins to thicken. Make small holes in the layers of cake and pour filling over each layer.

Four-Minute Icing:

3 cups sugar
½ cup cocoa
¾ cup milk
½ cup butter
1 teaspoon vanilla flavoring

Combine the first 3 ingredients and bring to a boil. Boil for 4 minutes and remove from heat. Add the butter and vanilla flavoring. Let cool 10 to 15 minutes, stirring occasionally. Spread over the cooled cake.

Makes 10 to 12 servings.

Ray Deaton
IIIrd Tyme Out

MISSISSIPPI MUDDY WATERS CAKE

2 sticks margarine
2 cups sugar
1½ cups all-purpose flour
1 teaspoon baking powder
1 cup flaked coconut
½ cup cocoa
4 eggs (add one at a time)
Pinch of salt
1 cup chopped nuts
1 13-ounce jar marshmallow cream

Preheat oven to 350°. Combine the first 9 ingredients and bake in a greased 9- by 5-inch loaf pan for 40 minutes. Remove the cake from the pan and pour the marshmallow cream over the cake (use just ½ jar if the cake is still hot).

Icing:

1 16-ounce box powdered sugar
½ cup cocoa
5 tablespoons evaporated milk
1 stick margarine, melted

Mix all the ingredients and spread over the top of the cake. Allow the cake to set for a while before serving.

Makes 8 to 10 servings.

Barry Berrier
The Lost and Found

at a time to the mixture. Stir in the sour cream. Add the white chocolate chips. Bake in a large, greased loaf pan for 1 hour at 350°. Cool in the pan for 1 hour. The recipe says to let stand 2 hours before cutting—IMPOSSIBLE! The cake will fall in the middle. Wait at least 3 hours before cutting. Enjoy!

Note: You can use chocolate cake mix, chocolate instant pudding, and chocolate chips if you like chocolate, or substitute any flavor cake mix, instant pudding, and chips.

Makes 8 to 10 servings.

Vince Gill

SWEETIE'S FUDGE CAKE

²/₃ cup butter
1³/₄ cups sugar
2¹/₂ tablespoons cocoa
2 eggs
1 teaspoon vanilla extract
2¹/₂ cups self-rising flour
1¹/₄ cups ice cold water

Preheat oven to 325°. Mix well the ingredients in the order given and put batter in a greased and floured 9- by 13-inch pan. Bake for 25 to 30 minutes. Put your favorite icing on it.

Makes 12 servings.

Sabrina and Mike Snider

HIGH LONESOME WHITE CHOCOLATE CAKE

1 box Duncan Hines Super Moist Butter-Flavored cake mix (you can use yellow or white)
1 6-ounce box instant vanilla pudding (not sugar-free)
¹/₃ cup sugar
²/₃ cup cooking oil
¹/₂ cup water
4 eggs
¹/₂ pint sour cream
1 6-ounce package white chocolate chips

Preheat oven to 350°. Combine the first 5 ingredients and stir really well. Add the eggs one

Country music artist Vince Gill began his career in the Bluegrass Alliance out of Louisville, Kentucky. He was also a member of Sundance and Pure Prairie League before going solo. Ripples of bluegrass continue to run throughout Vince's music, even as he has become a superstar of country music. With his superb tenor voice and world-class musicianship, Vince maintains a deep kinship with the "High Lonesome Sound."

BEATRICE RINZLER'S CHOCOLATE CAKE

This was Ralph's very favorite chocolate cake.

3 squares bitter chocolate
I teaspoon baking soda
I cup boiling water
2½ cups sifted cake flour
2 teaspoons baking powder
I teaspoon salt
¼ pound butter
2 cups white sugar
2 eggs, separated
I cup sour cream
I teaspoon vanilla extract

Preheat oven to 350°. Melt the chocolate in a double boiler. Dissolve the baking soda in the boiling water and add to the chocolate. Stir and allow to cool. Sift together the flour, baking powder, and salt. Cream the butter and sugar. Add the egg yolks one at a time to butter mixture, beating well after each addition. Add the sour cream and vanilla. Add the dry ingredients and blend well. Blend in the chocolate mixture. With dry, clean beater, beat the egg whites until stiff. Fold the egg whites into the batter. Pour batter into a greased 8- by 12-inch pan. Bake for 40 minutes.
Makes 10 to 12 servings.

Kate (Mrs. Ralph) Rinzler

GRANDMA RUTH'S CHOCOLATE MAYONNAISE CAKE WITH BITTERSWEET CHOCOLATE GLAZE

Cake:

1½ cups real mayonnaise
1½ cups sugar
1⅓ cups cocoa
1½ teaspoons vanilla extract
Pinch of salt
3 cups all-purpose flour
1½ cups water
2¼ teaspoons baking powder
1½ teaspoons baking soda

Preheat oven to 350°. Combine the mayonnaise, sugar, cocoa, vanilla, and salt. Mix thoroughly. Alternately add flour and water, beating until smooth. Add the baking powder and baking soda. Mix well. Pour the batter into a greased and floured 9-inch square pan. Bake for approximately 30 minutes, or until a toothpick inserted into the center comes out clean.

Bittersweet Chocolate Glaze:

6 tablespoons heavy cream
6 tablespoons dark corn syrup
8 ounces bittersweet chocolate, broken into small pieces

Bring the cream and corn syrup to a simmer in a heavy pan, then reduce heat to low. Add the chocolate and whisk until melted and smooth. Remove from heat and let stand until lukewarm. The glaze needs to be thick but still pourable. Pour over cake for a delicious dessert.
Makes 9 servings.

Gene Johnson
Diamond Rio

Country music group Diamond Rio's sound is decidedly influenced by bluegrass. They all play their own instruments, and several members cut their musical teeth in bluegrass, including mandolinist Gene Johnson and Dana Williams, a nephew of the Osborne Brothers. Pictured are (l-r) Gene Johnson, Jimmy Olander, Marty Roe, Dana Williams, Dan Truman, and Brian Prout.

SNOW WHITE CAKE

2 cups all-purpose flour
2 teaspoons baking powder
½ teaspoon salt
4 egg whites
1½ cups sugar, divided
¾ cup shortening, margarine, or butter
1 cup milk
1½ teaspoons vanilla extract

Preheat oven to 350°. Mix together the flour, baking powder, and salt, and then set aside. Beat the egg whites until foamy. Gradually add ½ cup of sugar, beating until soft peaks form; set aside.

Beat the shortening and the remaining 1 cup sugar until light and fluffy. Beat in the flour mixture alternately with the milk until well blended and smooth. Mix in the vanilla. With an electric mixer on low speed, fold in the egg whites (or fold in by hand). Pour into a greased and floured 9- by 13-inch pan. Bake for 35 to 40 minutes. Cool 10 minutes and remove from pan.

Makes about 12 servings.

Brenda Griffith for
5 for the Gospel

BETWEEN THE ROWS
CHERRY SNOWBALL CAKE

8 ounces cream cheese, softened
2 cups powdered sugar
1 12-ounce carton non-dairy whipped
    topping
1 angel food cake
Cherry, strawberry, or blueberry pie filling
    (I use cherry.)

Combine the cream cheese, sugar, and whipped topping, then mix. Cut the cake into small pieces and place ½ the cake pieces in the bottom of a cake pan. Top with the cream cheese mixture. Add more angel food cake pieces on top of the cream cheese mixture. Top with your choice of pie filling.

Makes 10 to 12 servings.

Shawn Lane
Blue Highway

BLUEGRASS GOSPEL
BLACK JAM CAKE

⅓ cup butter
1¼ cups white sugar
3 egg yolks, beaten
2 cups cake flour
½ teaspoon ground allspice
½ teaspoon ground cinnamon
½ teaspoon ground cloves
¼ teaspoon black pepper
½ cup buttermilk
1 teaspoon baking soda
½ cup blackberry jam
½ cup or 4 ounces of dates, chopped
½ cup nuts, chopped
2 egg whites, beaten

Preheat oven to 350°. Cream together the butter, sugar, and egg yolks. Sift the flour and spices together 3 times, and then mix into the butter mixture. Add the buttermilk and soda. Add the jam, dates, and nuts. Fold in egg whites last. Save 1 cup of dough for the icing. Bake in 2 greased and floured 9-inch cake pans until done (approximately 45 minutes).

Dough Icing:

1 cup dough from cake
1 cup brown sugar
1 cup sweet milk
½ cup dates, chopped
½ cup nuts, chopped
½ cup raisins, chopped
Hunk of butter the size of an egg

Combine the ingredients and cook in a double boiler until thick. Spread on the cake.

Makes 10 to 12 servings.

Helen (Mrs. Carl) Story

ACROSS THE MILES
JAPANESE FRUIT CAKE

1 cup butter
2 cups sugar
4 eggs
3½ cups self-rising flour

Carl Story, hailing from Lenoir, North Carolina, is one of the true pioneers of bluegrass. He formed his Ramblin' Mountaineers in 1934, and further showed his mettle as a fiddle player for Bill Monroe's Blue Grass Boys prior to World War II. After the war, Carl gave up the fiddle for the guitar. He really hit his stride as a leading performer of bluegrass gospel music, which earned him the nickname the "Father of Bluegrass Gospel Music." He recorded over five dozen albums, a few of which are shown here.

1 cup milk
1 cup raisins
1 cup blackberry jam
1 cup nuts, chopped
1 cup fig preserves
1 cup candied cherries

Preheat oven to 350°. Cream the butter and sugar, add the eggs, then add the flour and milk. Add the raisins, blackberry jam, nuts, fig preserves, and cherries. Pour the batter into two 9-inch pans that have been greased and floured. Bake until done (about 40 minutes).

Topping:

2 cups sugar
1 cup water
1 cup orange juice
1 cup flaked coconut

Cook the sugar and water in a saucepan over medium heat until it spins a thread, then remove from heat. Add the orange juice and coconut. Pour the topping over the cooled cake as you stack it.

Makes 12 to 14 servings.

Ray Deaton
IIIrd Tyme Out

NO CURB SERVICE CAKE

2 cups all-purpose flour
1 15¼-ounce can crushed pineapple (juice and all)
2 cups sugar
2 eggs, slightly beaten
½ teaspoon salt
½ teaspoon baking soda
1 teaspoon vanilla extract

Preheat oven to 350°. Mix all the ingredients and pour the batter into an ungreased 9- by

13-inch baking pan. Bake for approximately 25 to 30 minutes, or until golden brown on top.

Icing:

1 stick butter or margarine
1 cup sugar
2/3 cup Carnation cream
1 7-ounce can flaked coconut

Combine all the ingredients and boil in a saucepan for 5 minutes. Pour on the cake while hot.
Makes 12 servings.

Willia and Melvin Goins

D-28 COCONUT CAKE

1 white or chocolate cake mix (prepared as instructed on box)
1 14-ounce can sweetened condensed milk
1 12-ounce package flaked coconut
1 12-ounce carton non-dairy whipped topping

Prepare the cake mix as instructed on the box. Bake as directed in a greased and floured 9- by 13-inch pan. While the cake is still warm, pierce with toothpicks and pour the entire can of sweetened condensed milk over the cake. Allow to cool, then cover the cake with the whipped topping and a layer of coconut.
Makes 12 servings.

Greta and James Alan Shelton
Ralph Stanley and the
Clinch Mountain Boys

The Goins Brothers, Ray (*left*) and Melvin, began their careers as members of the Lonesome Pine Fiddlers in the 1950s, and Melvin worked for a time with Ralph Stanley following Carter Stanley's death. For the last twenty-five years, the Goins Brothers have fronted their own group, which features solid, traditional bluegrass. In addition, Melvin is one of the most colorful storytellers and oral historians in bluegrass.

VIRGINIA BOYS
STRAWBERRY SHORTCAKE

It's Jess right.

3 cups sifted all-purpose flour
4½ teaspoons baking powder

James Alan Shelton poses with legend George Shuffler in 1996. For two hot cross-pickers, they look pretty pleased.

2 tablespoons sugar (if desired)
1½ teaspoons salt
¾ cup shortening
1 cup milk
**2 quarts fresh strawberries, hulled, cut in
  quarters, and sweetened**
Butter
Half-and-half
Whipped cream

Sift the dry ingredients together and cut in the shortening. Add the milk and mix to a soft dough. Knead lightly for 20 seconds. Divide the dough in half. Pat ½ into a greased 9-inch layer pan. Spread a thin coating of shortening over the dough in the pan and cover with the rest of the dough, patting to fit pan. Bake at 425° for 30 minutes. Separate the layers. Spread the bottom layer with butter and cover with ½ of the berries. Place the upper layer on top of the berries and cover it with the remaining berries. Pour a little milk (preferably half-and-half) over the shortcake and serve topped with whipped cream.
  Makes 10 to 12 servings.

Jesse McReynolds
Jim and Jesse
* and the Virginia Boys*

Jim and Jesse McReynolds

Southwest Virginia natives Jim and Jesse McReynolds have been performing together for over fifty-five years. The blend of Jim's clear, polished, tenor voice and Jesse's way of playing the mandolin, known as "cross-picking" or "McReynolds-style," makes their sound unmistakable.

The pair gained national attention in 1952 when they recorded an album for Capitol Records in Nashville's old Tulane Hotel. Since that time, Jim and Jesse and their band, the Virginia Boys, have recorded more than fifty albums. They are known for such tunes as "Diesel on My Tail," "Are You Missing Me," "Sweet Little Miss Blue Eyes," "Better Times a Coming," "Cotton Mill Man," and "Drifting and Dreaming of You."

During the 1960s, the McReynolds successfully incorporated songs from the burgeoning rock 'n' roll genre into their repertoire, including Chuck Berry's "Johnny B. Goode," "Sweet Little Sixteen," "Memphis," and "Roll Over Beethoven." They also drew extensively from the material of the Louvin Brothers for many of their gorgeous duet harmonies.

During the early part of their career, Jim and Jesse had radio and TV shows, sponsored by Martha White Foods, on the air across the South. The duo joined the Grand Ole Opry in 1964 and were inducted into the International Bluegrass Music Association's Hall of Honor in 1993.

TRADITIONAL AMERICAN STRAWBERRY SHORTCAKE (DESSERT WITH A CAPITAL D)

Being known worldwide for my gastronomical prowess, I'm all the time looking for great new dishes. Strange thing, though. The ones I like best are still the ones I've always liked best. I first experienced this dessert along the shores of the Hudson River near Beacon, New York. It was at a concert for the environment put on by the folks that built the great *Clearwater Sloop*, organized and spirited by Pete Seeger, famed songwriter, folk singer, environmental wood-chopper, and Strawberry Shortcake King.

So, treat this recipe for what it is—a folk song you can chew. What I mean is, go ahead and play with the recipe instructions to fit your own pallet and imagination. Like a good folk song, strawberry shortcake is really hard to screw up. Two quarts of strawberries should do about 6 people. Like Pete says, the worst thing you can do is shortchange your guests on the shortcake, so make sure you have enough to start with.

Step 1: Slice (not mash, crush, or squish) 1 quart strawberries. Place the strawberries into a bowl. Add ¼ cup sugar on top.

Step 2: Hull (not slice, mash, crush, or squish) the other 1 quart strawberries. If the berries are nice and sweet, there's no need for sugar. Let ye ol' tongue decide.

Step 3: Make your shortcake. Use your own recipe or knead:

2½ cups all-purpose flour
½ pound butter
3 teaspoons baking powder
1 tablespoon sugar
A smidge of salt (you can define smidge as you see fit)

When you are about 25 minutes from serving your dessert, go to the next step:

Step 4: In 30 seconds, add enough milk to the kneaded flour to make it thick and sticky. Spread the mix into your cupcake-style baking tin. Ask your mother how hot the stove should be 'cause I don't have the faintest idea. Bake until golden brown.

Step 5: While the shortcakes are baking, add ¼ teaspoon of vanilla extract and ¼ cup of sugar to 2 quarts of cold whipping cream. Whip and chill.

Now, go back and finish dinner. When you're ready (or the shortcake is finished baking, whichever comes first), do the following: Quickly. Faster than a speeding bullet.

Step 6: Remove your perfectly baked, golden brown shortcakes from the oven, slit the shortcakes in half horizontally, put a pat of butter inside, and add some of the sliced berries. Put the top half of the shortbread on, add whipped cream, and toss a handful of hulled strawberries on top.

Serve on a nice small dish with a silver spoon. Sit at your kitchen table with a cold glass of milk. Fasten your seatbelts, look both ways . . . and dig in!

Makes 6 servings.

Michael Johnathon

SMOKY MOUNTAIN FLUFFY BANANA CAKE

1 cup butter
1½ cups sugar
3 eggs
3 cups all-purpose flour
¾ teaspoon baking powder
1 teaspoon baking soda
2 large or 3 small bananas, mashed
½ cup buttermilk

Preheat oven to 375°. Cream the butter and sugar, add the eggs, and beat well. Sift together the flour, baking powder, and soda. Add the flour mixture to the butter mixture alternately with the bananas and buttermilk. Pour the batter into three 9-inch cake pans lined with wax paper. Bake for about 25 minutes, or until brown.

Frosting:

2 cups sugar
¾ cup water
4 egg whites
1 teaspoon banana flavoring

In a saucepan, boil the sugar and water until

Guitar player Charlie Collins was a longtime member of Roy Acuff's Smoky Mountain Boys. He has performed on the Grand Ole Opry for more than a quarter of a century, and he is also a regular in shows for Opryland USA.

it forms a soft ball when a small amount is dropped in ice water. Have the egg whites beaten (but not dry). Slowly add the sugar syrup to the egg whites and beat well until it will stand in peaks. Add the flavoring. Spread frosting between and over the cooled cake layers.

Makes 10 to 12 servings.

Charlie Collins

UNPLUCKED BANANA CAKE

1 cup butter, softened
3 cups sugar
2 cups mashed bananas
1 8-ounce can crushed pineapple with juice
4 eggs, beaten
3¾ cups all-purpose flour
2 teaspoons baking soda
1 teaspoon ground cinnamon
1 cup buttermilk
1 teaspoon vanilla extract

Preheat oven to 350°. Cream the butter. Gradually add the sugar, beating well. Add the bananas and pineapple and mix until smooth. Stir in the eggs. In a large bowl, combine the flour with the baking soda and cinnamon. Add

the banana mixture to the flour mixture, alternating with buttermilk. Stir in the vanilla. Pour the batter into a greased 9- by 13-inch cake pan and bake for 35 to 40 minutes.

Cream Cheese Frosting:

8 ounces cream cheese, softened
½ cup butter, softened
1 16-ounce package powdered sugar
1 teaspoon vanilla extract

Cream together the cream cheese and butter. Blend in the powdered sugar. Add the vanilla. Mix until creamy. Spread on the cooled cake.

Makes 12 servings.

Kris Ballinger
The Cluster Pluckers

OLD-TIME MADE FROM SCRATCH BANANA CAKE

⅔ cup shortening
2½ cups cake flour, sifted
1⅔ cups sugar
1¼ teaspoons baking powder
1 teaspoon baking soda

1 teaspoon salt
1¼ cups mashed ripe bananas
⅔ cup buttermilk
2 eggs
⅔ cup chopped walnuts (optional)

Preheat oven to 350°. Place the shortening in a mixing bowl and stir in the cake flour, sugar, baking powder, baking soda, and salt. Add the bananas and ⅓ cup of the buttermilk. Beat until moistened, or about 2 minutes at medium speed on an electric mixer. Add the other ⅓ cup buttermilk and the 2 eggs. Beat 2 minutes longer. If desired, fold in the chopped walnuts. Bake in 2 greased and lightly floured 9- by 11½-inch pans at 350° (about 35 minutes). Cool 10 minutes, remove from pans, and cool thoroughly. Topping is optional. My favorite topping is caramel icing.

Caramel icing:

1 stick margarine
4 tablespoons canned cream
1 cup brown sugar
8 ounces powdered sugar
½ teaspoon vanilla extract

Bring the first 3 ingredients to a boil and cook until sugar is dissolved. Put the powdered sugar in a small mixing bowl, add the hot mixture, and beat. Add the vanilla and mix. If the icing is too thin to spread, add a little more powdered sugar. If it's too thick, add a little more cream. Spread icing on the cake.

Optional: Sprinkle the cake with coconut if desired. Personally, it's not my choice. This was one of my mother's favorite recipes.

Makes 12 servings.

Clarence "Tater" Tate

FARMER'S DAUGHTER CARAMEL CAKE

1 stick margarine
1½ cups sugar
2 eggs
2 cups all-purpose flour, sifted
1 cup buttermilk
1 teaspoon baking soda

Fiddler Tater Tate, a native Virginian, began playing guitar at age four. Later, inspired by Bill Monroe, he took up the mandolin. In 1948, when Flatt and Scruggs came to nearby Bristol, he began learning the fiddle by listening to them on the radio. Tater has performed in bands over the years with some of bluegrass's best. Among his musical partners have been the Sauceman Brothers, the Bailey Brothers, Bill Monroe, Hylo Brown, the Osborne Brothers, Bonnie Lou and Buster, Carl Story, Red Smiley, the Shenandoah Cutups, Lester Flatt and the Nashville Grass, Wilma Lee Cooper, and finally, with Bill Monroe again from 1984 to 1996. Tate, now semiretired, has recorded four instrumental albums over the years.

Photograph by Les Leverett

1 tablespoon vinegar
2 teaspoons vanilla extract

Preheat oven to 350°. Cream the margarine and sugar until light and fluffy. Add the eggs one at a time. Add the sifted flour alternately with the buttermilk; blend well. Stir the baking soda into the vinegar, then add to the batter. Mix in the vanilla. Bake in 3 greased and floured 8-inch cake pans for 25 minutes.

Frosting:

1 stick margarine
1 16-ounce box light brown sugar

½ cup evaporated milk
½ teaspoon baking powder

Melt the margarine in a saucepan. Add the sugar and stir to blend well. Add the milk and cook to soft ball stage. Remove from heat and let stand 5 minutes. Add the baking powder. Beat until smooth and creamy. Spread on the cooled cake layers.

Makes 10 servings.

Barry Berrier
The Lost and Found

SUNSHINE IN THE SHADOWS COCONUT CREAM CAKE

¼ cup margarine
½ cup vegetable oil
2 cups sugar
6 eggs
1 cup evaporated milk
2½ cups self-rising flour
2 teaspoons vanilla extract

Preheat oven to 400°. Cream well the margarine, oil, and sugar. Add the eggs one at a time, beating well after each one. Alternately add the milk and flour, then beat at low speed. Add the vanilla and beat well. Pour into 3 greased and floured 8-inch pans. Bake for about 20 to 25 minutes. When cool, cut each layer in half horizontally to make 6 layers.

Icing:

1½ sticks butter
2½ cups sugar
1 12-ounce can evaporated milk
1 teaspoon vanilla extract
1 14-ounce bag fine-flake coconut

Melt the butter in a skillet over low heat. Gradually add the sugar and stir until it is dissolved in the butter. Slowly stir in milk, mixing well. Add vanilla, then gradually increase temperature until mixture comes to a slow boil, stirring constantly. Add coconut and stir until mixture begins to thicken and reaches the soft ball stage (test by dropping a small amount into a saucer of cold water). With a toothpick, poke holes in each cake layer, then spread icing over each layer as you stack the cake.

Makes 10 servings.

Bobbie Jean Gillis for
The Gillis Brothers

The Gillis Brothers, John (left) and Larry, created quite a stir when they hit the bluegrass circuit in the late 1980s. With a sound that is as close to the Stanley Brothers as any recent group has come, the Gillis Brothers are preserving a powerful style while contributing their own material to the genre.

TURKEY IN THE STRAWBERRY AND PINEAPPLE CAKE

'Cept there's no turkey.

I angel food cake
I 6-ounce box instant vanilla pudding
3 cups milk
8 ounces cream cheese, softened
I 20-ounce can crushed pineapple, drained
Sliced strawberries
Non-dairy whipped topping
Coconut

Break the cake into small pieces and put in a 9- by 13-inch dish. Mix the pudding, milk, and cream cheese, and then pour the mixture over the cake. Put the pineapple and slices of strawberries on top. Cover with non-dairy whipped topping, then top with coconut.
Makes 12 servings.

Kim and Tim White
The Beagles

Banjo player Tim White is not only the leader of the popular Troublesome Hollow band, but in 1996 he organized a second bluegrass band, the Beagles, which features Richard Bennett on guitar, Jerome Webb on mandolin, and Gary Ollis on bass. Tim also hosts *Listenin' to Bluegrass* six days a week on WGOC Radio in Blountville, Tennessee, and he is an active member of the board for the Birthplace of Country Music Alliance in Bristol.

CARROLL COUNTY WHITE GRAPE JUICE CAKE

I cup chopped pecans
I box butter recipe cake mix
I 3¼-ounce box vanilla instant pudding
4 eggs
½ cup white grape juice
½ cup oil
½ cup water

Preheat oven to 350°. Grease a tube pan and spread pecans on bottom. Mix the remaining ingredients together and pour over the pecans. Bake for 50 minutes, or until done.

Glaze:

¼ cup white grape juice
½ cup butter or margarine
½ cup sugar

Combine the ingredients in a saucepan, bring to a boil, and pour over the hot cake (still in pan). Reserve a small amount of glaze. Remove the cake from the pan while still hot and pour the remaining glaze over top of the cake.
Makes 10 to 12 servings.

Willard Gayheart
Skeeter and the Skidmarks

Banjo player Edwin Lacy's roaring banjo sets the pace for Skeeter and the Skidmarks, who get plenty of traction from Willard Gayheart on guitar, Scott Freeman on mandolin and fiddle, and Sandy Grover on bass.

Jim Watson was an original member of the Red Clay Ramblers; he now plays bass and sings with Robin and Linda Williams. He also performs with several local bands around his hometown of Chapel Hill, North Carolina. When he's not playing music, Jim likes to work out, ride his bicycle, read *The Old-Time Herald* magazine, or watch *The Andy Griffith Show.*

DUKE LACROSS'S CHEESECAKE

Crust:

1½ cups graham cracker crumbs
2 teaspoons sugar
1 teaspoon ground cinnamon
¼ cup melted butter

Mix all the ingredients. Press into a 9-inch springform pan and bake at 350° for 8 minutes.

Filling:

24 ounces cream cheese, softened
½ cup sugar
1¼ teaspoons vanilla extract
3 large eggs

Beat all the ingredients together until smooth. Pour over the crust. Bake at 375° for 25 to 30 minutes. Cool for 15 minutes.

Topping:

2 cups sour cream
½ teaspoon vanilla extract
¼ cup sugar

Mix all topping ingredients together, pour over the cake, and bake at 475° for 10 to 15 minutes. Makes 10 to 12 servings.

Jim Watson
Robin and Linda Williams
and Their Fine Group

OLD-FASHIONED TEA CAKES

1 cup sugar
1 large egg
1 cup shortening
Self-rising flour

Preheat oven to 325°. Combine the first 3 ingredients and add enough flour to make a dough you can handle well. Form the dough into small balls. With well-greased hands, place the balls on a cookie sheet and pat until thin. Bake until brown around the edges.

Makes about 50 tea cakes.

Sabrina and Mike Snider

National banjo champ Mike Snider is a comedian, picker, and singer who appears often on The Nashville Network. Practically his whole hometown of Gleason, Tennessee, came to the Grand Ole Opry for his debut.

Pies and Pastries

DAISY A DAY DRIED APPLE AND RAISIN PIE

Being raised on a farm, we always dried apples and beans.

Hot apple juice or water
3 cups dried apple slices
½ cup raisins
3 tablespoons lemon juice
¼ cup flour
½ cup sugar
I teaspoon ground cinnamon
½ teaspoon ground nutmeg
3 tablespoons butter
Pastry for 2-crust pie

Pour hot juice or water over the apple slices and raisins in a bowl—using enough liquid to cover them. Let stand for 1 hour. Prepare the dough by lining a 9-inch round pie pan with bottom pie crust. Drain the apples and raisins and toss with the lemon juice. Combine the flour, sugar, cinnamon, and nutmeg. Sprinkle the flour mixture over the fruit, tossing to coat. Heap the fruit into the pie crust and dot with butter. Roll out top crust, cut slits, and cover the pie. Trim the dough, fold the top crust under the bottom crust, and flute. Bake at 425° for 15 minutes. Reduce heat to 375° and bake 25 minutes.
Makes 8 servings.

Wilma Lee Cooper

FINE AS A FIDDLE FRUIT-GRAHAM PIE

2 cups graham cracker crumbs
⅓ cup lemon juice
I 14-ounce can sweetened condensed milk
I 20-ounce can crushed pineapple, drained
I 16-ounce can fruit cocktail, drained
I cup chopped pecans
Non-dairy whipped topping (optional)

Line a 9-inch pie pan with graham cracker

Wilma Lee Cooper and husband Stoney Cooper, who played together for nearly forty years, joined the Grand Ole Opry in 1957. Since Stoney's death in 1977, Wilma Lee has kept their Clinch Mountain Clan alive and picking at the Opry and numerous bluegrass festivals.

crumbs. Mix the lemon juice with the milk, and then add the fruit and nuts. Pour into the crust. Refrigerate until set. Top with whipped topping before serving, if desired.
Makes 8 servings.

Cindy and Jim Vipperman

JIM'S HOT PICKIN' FRUIT PIE

I cup all-purpose flour
½ cup sugar
2 teaspoons baking powder
⅓ cup shortening
½ cup milk
I quart hot cooked fruit or berries

Preheat oven to 350°. Sift the dry ingredients together, cut in the shortening, and add the milk. Spread over the bottom and sides of a greased pie dish. Pour the fruit over the top. Bake until brown, about 20 to 30 minutes.
Makes 8 servings.

Jim McReynolds
Jim and Jesse
and the Virginia Boys

Jim and Jesse McReynolds, shown here in 1965, had their first band in 1947 and their first record in 1952. They have been bluegrass regulars on the Grand Ole Opry since 1964 and continue to tour the United States with their Virginia Boys.
Photograph by Les Leverett

tice pattern. Sprinkle the top of the dough with sugar (or cinnamon sugar, if desired) and dot with butter. Bake on the middle rack of the oven until light brown on top.

Makes 9 servings.

Charlie Louvin

HOOT APPLE CRUNCH

4 to 6 tart apples, peeled and sliced
$^1/_3$ cup flour
1 cup rolled oats
$^1/_2$ cup brown sugar
$^1/_2$ teaspoon salt
$^1/_2$ teaspoon ground cinnamon
$^1/_2$ cup margarine, softened

Spread the apples evenly in a greased 9-inch square pan. Mix the dry ingredients together and cream in the margarine. Crumble the mixture over the apples. Bake at 375° for 30 minutes.

Makes 9 servings.

Hoot Hester
Flat Creek Skillet Lickers

CLOSE HARMONY
SWEET POTATO COBBLER

2 large sweet potatoes
1 cup sweet milk
½ teaspoon ground nutmeg
¼ stick butter or margarine
Biscuit dough
¼ cup sugar
Butter

Cut the washed and peeled potatoes into ¼- to ½-inch cubes. Cook on high boil in a covered pot. Remove and drain when half done (save the liquid).

Preheat oven to 375°.

Combine the milk, nutmeg, and butter. Place the sweet potatoes in a greased 10-inch baking dish that is approximately 3 inches deep. Pour the milk mixture over the potatoes. If more juice is needed, add some of the liquid from the cooked potatoes.

Cut thin strips of dough about 1-inch wide. Crisscross the dough over the potatoes in a lat-

SPECIAL CONSENSUS
DRIED CRANBERRY AND
APPLE CRISP

1 cup dried cranberries
1 cinnamon stick
1 cup water
$^2/_3$ cup all-purpose flour
$^2/_3$ cup light brown sugar, firmly packed
$^1/_4$ teaspoon salt
$^3/_4$ stick unsalted butter, cut into bits
9 McIntosh apples (about 3 pounds)

Preheat oven to 400°. In a small saucepan, simmer the cranberries, the cinnamon stick, and water for 10 minutes. Drain the cranberries and remove the cinnamon stick.

In a small bowl, blend the flour, brown sugar, salt, and butter until the mixture resembles coarse meal. Toss mixture well.

Peel, core, and slice the apples. In a buttered 9- by 13-inch glass dish, toss the apples with the cranberries. Sprinkle the brown sugar mixture over the apples and cranberries. Bake for 25 minutes, or until the apples are tender and the topping is golden. This is delicious alone or spooned over vanilla ice cream.

Makes 10 to 12 servings.

Jackie and Greg Cahill
Special Consensus

LESTER FLATT'S PEACH COBBLER

It's Flatt delicious!

1 stick margarine
¾ cup Martha White self-rising flour
¾ cup sugar
¾ cup milk
2 cups canned peaches

Preheat oven to 350°. Melt margarine in a 9-by 13-inch pan in the oven. Mix the flour, sugar, and milk, then pour the mixture over the margarine. Add the peaches to the pan. Bake for 1 hour, or until brown. You bake right with Martha White.

Makes 9 servings.

Lester Flatt and family

LONESOME PINE PEACH COBBLER

1 stick butter
1 cup self-rising flour
1 cup sugar
¾ cup milk
1 21-ounce can peach pie filling

Melt the butter in a baking dish or pan. In a separate bowl, mix the flour, sugar, and milk. Pour the mixture over the melted butter, then spread the peach pie filling over the mixture as evenly as possible. DO NOT STIR. Bake at 350° for approximately 50 minutes.

Makes about 9 servings.

Willia and Melvin Goins

MEMORY OF YOUR SMILE FRUIT PIES

1 6-ounce box orange gelatin
2 bananas
1 6-ounce jar maraschino cherries, drained
½ cup shredded coconut

The 1972 edition of Lester Flatt and the Nashville Grass was composed of (l-r) Charlie Nixon, Johnny Johnson, Flatt, Paul Warren, Haskel McCormick, Marty Stuart, and Roland White.

½ cup pecans, chopped
2 graham cracker pie crusts
Non-dairy whipped topping

Mix the gelatin according to the package instructions. Allow to cool (but not set) in the refrigerator. Slice the bananas and mix with the cherries, coconuts, and pecans. Pour the mixture into the pie crusts. Pour the orange gelatin over the fruit. Let cool in the fridge until gelled. After chilled, put non-dairy whipped topping on top of the pies.
Makes 2 pies.

Bobbie Jean Gillis for
The Gillis Brothers

GEORGIA MAIL
PEACH GELATIN PIE

1 pre-made graham cracker pie crust
1 cup milk
½ cup sugar
2 tablespoons lemon juice
8 ounces cream cheese, softened
1 3-ounce package peach gelatin
1 cup sliced peaches (fresh or canned)
2 cups non-dairy whipped topping

Stir the milk, sugar, and lemon juice into a bowl with the cream cheese. Pour the mixture into the pie crust and smooth the top. Prepare the gelatin according to package directions. Place in the refrigerator to chill until it just begins to thicken. Meanwhile, arrange the peaches in a circle over the cream cheese mixture. Spoon the gelatin over the peaches evenly and place the pie in the refrigerator until the gelatin is set. Spread the whipped topping over the gelatin and serve.
Makes 8 servings.

Don Rigsby
The Lonesome River Band

SUNSHINE
LEMON SPONGE PIE

1 cup sugar
3 tablespoons all-purpose flour
Juice and grated rind of 1 lemon

2 eggs, separated
1 tablespoon butter, melted
Pinch of salt
1 cup milk

Mix the sugar, flour, lemon juice, lemon rind, slightly beaten egg yolks, butter, and salt. Stir in the milk and mix well. Beat the egg whites until stiff and fold into first mixture. Pour into a 9-inch glass pie plate. Bake at 350° for 40 minutes (or bake at 450° for 15 minutes, then turn the temperature back to 350° for 25 to 30 minutes).
Makes 8 servings.

Gloria Belle (Flickinger)

WRITTEN IN THE STARS
CHERRY PIE

1 21-ounce can cherry pie filling
⅔ to ¾ cup brown sugar
½ cup all-purpose flour
½ cup rolled oats
¾ teaspoon ground cinnamon
¾ teaspoon ground nutmeg
⅓ cup butter, softened

Preheat oven to 350°. Grease an 8- by 8- by 2-inch pan. Place the cherries in the pan. Mix together the remaining ingredients and sprinkle over the cherries. Bake for 30 minutes, or until tender and golden brown. Serve warm.
Makes 6 to 8 servings.

Rhonda Vincent

RIGHT IN KEY LIME PIE

1 (9- or 10-inch) baked pastry shell or
  graham cracker pie crust
6 egg yolks
2 14-ounce cans sweetened condensed milk
1 8-ounce bottle real lime juice from
  concentrate
Green or yellow food coloring (optional)
Whipped cream or non-dairy whipped
  topping

Preheat oven to 350°. In a large mixing bowl, beat the egg yolks with the condensed milk. Stir in the lime juice and food coloring. Pour into the prepared pastry shell and bake for 40 minutes. Cool; chill and top with whipped cream or whipped topping. Garnish as desired.

Makes 8 servings.

Millie and Vassar Clements

IN THE PINK LEMONADE PIE

1 6-ounce can frozen lemonade (pink)
24 ounces non-dairy whipped topping
1 14-ounce can sweetened condensed milk
2 graham cracker pie crusts

Mix the lemonade and whipped topping. Add the sweetened condensed milk and mix well. Pour the mixture into the graham cracker crusts. It's not at all fattening if you eat a small portion, but there's no guarantee you can stop at that.

Makes 12 to 16 servings.

Walter Bailes
The Bailes Brothers

MAMA'S CHOCOLATE PIE

1 unbaked pie crust
1 cup sugar
2 tablespoons all-purpose flour
3 tablespoons cocoa
2 eggs, separated
1 cup evaporated milk
½ stick butter, melted
1 teaspoon vanilla extract
3 tablespoons sugar
¼ teaspoon cream of tartar
½ teaspoon vanilla extract
1 tablespoon butter, melted

Preheat oven to 350°. Mix the cup of sugar with the flour and cocoa. Stir the egg yolks, add them to the milk, and gradually mix in the flour mixture. Add the melted butter and 1 teaspoon of vanilla extract. Pour the mixture into an unbaked pie crust (bought or homemade). Bake until set (around 30 minutes). Remove from

The Bailes Brothers, including Walter, Johnnie, Kyle, and Homer, performed on the Grand Ole Opry in the 1940s and recorded on such labels as Columbia, King, Homestead, Loyal, and White Dove Records. Walter, a prolific tunesmith, wrote songs for such folks as Roy Acuff, Flatt and Scruggs, the Blue Sky Boys, the Lewis Family, Molly O'Day, Bill Clifton, the Stanley Brothers, and Wilma Lee and Stoney Cooper. Pictured here are (l-r) Johnnie Bailes, Fiddlin' Arthur Smith, and Walter Bailes, circa 1943.

Photograph courtesy of Gary Reid

Walter Bailes in the 1990s.

oven. Add the 3 tablespoons of sugar and the cream of tartar to the egg whites. Beat on high until peaks form. Add the ½ teaspoon of vanilla. Spread the meringue over the pie filling. Return to oven and bake for 5 minutes. Brush melted butter on outside of the crust when pie is removed from heat.

Makes 8 servings.

Billy Smith

When they were teenagers, Billy (*left*) and Terry Smith worked on Bill Monroe's farm. Musicians all of their lives, the brothers recorded *The Grass Section* for the Red Clay label and wrote the song "Deeper Shade of Blue," which was a hit for Del McCoury. Terry plays upright bass for the Osborne Brothers. Billy and Terry recorded *A Tribute to Bill Monroe* for K-Tel records. The album features vocals by Monroe on four songs, including "Blue Moon of Kentucky." When Monroe joined them on February 21, 1996, it was to be his last recording in a studio.

FLINT HILL CHOCOLATE PIE

This is a favorite of the boys and the grand-children and is a family recipe from Louise's mother.

1 baked pie shell
1 cup sugar
3 tablespoons cocoa
2 tablespoons flour
3 eggs, separated
1½ cups milk
3 tablespoons low-fat margarine
1 teaspoon vanilla extract
½ teaspoon cream of tartar
4 tablespoons sugar

In a saucepan, mix the 1 cup of sugar, cocoa, and flour. Add beaten egg yolks, milk, and margarine. Cook on low heat, stirring constantly until very thick. Add the vanilla and pour into the baked pie shell. Then cover with a meringue made with the whites of the 3 eggs beaten with the cream of tartar and 4 tablespoons of sugar. Bake in a slow oven at 325° until the meringue is firm.

Makes 8 servings.

Louise and Earl Scruggs

Jamming at home are (*l-r*) Gary, Randy, Earl, and Steve Scruggs.

BORN TO SING CHOCOLATE PIE

3 eggs, separated
3 cups milk
1 4¹/₂-ounce box chocolate pudding/pie
    filling (not instant)
1 unbaked pie crust
¹/₈ teaspoon cream of tartar
6 tablespoons sugar

Mix the egg yolks and milk with the pudding mix. Cook the pudding according to the directions on box. Bake the pie crust.

Add the cream of tartar and sugar to the egg whites. Beat at high speed until stiff.

Put the chocolate pudding in the pie crust, gently spread the meringue over the chocolate, and bake at 350° until the meringue is brown. You have to watch it because it will brown quick. Let cool and serve.

Makes 8 servings.

Larry Stephenson

BASHFUL BROTHER OSWALD'S FAVORITE CHOCOLATE PIE

You won't be bashful about eating this.

¾ cup sugar
4¹/₂ tablespoons cornstarch
4 tablespoons cocoa

½ teaspoon salt
2 cups milk
2 egg yolks
¼ stick butter
1 teaspoon vanilla extract
1 baked pie shell

In a saucepan, combine the sugar, cornstarch, cocoa, salt, milk, and egg yolks. Cook the mixture until thick, then remove from heat and add the butter and vanilla. Pour into an 8- or 9-inch baked pie shell.

Meringue:

2 egg whites
4 tablespoons sugar

Beat the egg whites until stiff and add sugar. Beat at high speed for 2 more minutes. Spread the meringue over the pie. Bake at 350° until the meringue is lightly browned. You can use this same recipe for coconut or banana cream pie.

Makes 8 servings.

*Pete (Bashful Brother Oswald)
and Euneta Kirby*

LUCILLE'S CAROLINA CHOCOLATE PIE

1 baked pie shell
1 cup sugar

Bashful Brother Oswald, otherwise known as Pete Kirby (*standing, second from left*), joshes with his musical friends (*clockwise after Oswald*) Howdy Forrester, Pop Wilson, Jimmy Riddle, Melba Montgomery, Roy Acuff, and Shot Jackson, in 1963.

5 tablespoons all-purpose flour
5 tablespoons cocoa
Pinch salt
2 egg yolks
2 cups milk
2 tablespoons margarine
1 teaspoon vanilla flavoring
2 egg whites
Another pinch salt
½ teaspoon vanilla flavoring
¼ teaspoon sugar

Combine the 1 cup of sugar, flour, cocoa, pinch of salt, egg yolks, and milk. Cook in a saucepan over medium heat until thick. Add the margarine and 1 teaspoon vanilla flavoring, then pour mixture into baked pie shell. Combine the egg whites and pinch of salt and beat until stiff. Add the ½ teaspoon of vanilla flavoring and ¼ teaspoon of sugar to make meringue. Beat well. Spread evenly over the pie and put in the oven at 350° to brown the meringue. Watch closely. You won't want to put your fork down.

Makes 8 servings.

Gena Britt
Lou Reid and Carolina

BLUE-GRASSHOPPER PIE

1 cup sugar
½ stick margarine, melted
3 eggs
1 teaspoon vanilla extract
½ teaspoon vinegar

½ cup chopped pecans
½ cup shredded coconut
1 6-ounce bag chocolate chips
1 unbaked 9-inch pie shell

Preheat oven to 350°. Mix together the first 8 ingredients in the order given and pour into pie shell. Bake for 40 to 45 minutes.

Makes 8 servings.

Sharon White Skaggs

PICKIN' TIME PECAN PIE

1 unbaked 9-inch pie shell
½ cup butter or margarine
1 cup sugar
3 eggs, slightly beaten
¾ cup dark corn syrup
¼ teaspoon salt
1 teaspoon vanilla extract
1½ cups chopped pecans
Handful whole pecan meats

Chill the pie shell thoroughly. Set the oven temperature on 375°. Cream butter or margarine. Add the sugar gradually and continue beating until light and fluffy. Add the eggs, syrup, salt, vanilla, and chopped pecans. Pour into the pie shell and bake 40 to 45 minutes. Garnish with pecan meats. Serve with whipped cream, if desired.

Makes 8 servings.

Helen (Mrs. Carl) Story

Sharon White Skaggs has been performing with her father Buck and sister Cheryl for over twenty years, first as Buck White and the Down Home Folks, and currently as the Whites. Ricky Skaggs entered Sharon's life when he performed with the Down Home Folks in the late 1970s, and soon the two were married. Though Sharon continues to perform with the Whites, and Ricky leads his Kentucky Thunder band, they still occasionally get together on stage for some gorgeous duet harmonies. Here, Sharon and Ricky perform at Ralph Stanley's Memorial Festival in 1996.

BEST DANG PECAN PIE

Fixin's:

4 chicken eggs
I cup dark brown sugar (it dances so good)
³/4 cup light Karo syrup
¹/2 teaspoon salt, plus another ½ teaspoon
**   to throw over yer shoulder for luck**
¹/2 cup melted sweet butter
I teaspoon 'nilla X-track
2 cups shucked pecans, chopped*
I 9-inch unbaked pie crust**
¹/3 cup shucked pecan halves

1. Stoke up yer oven to 400°.

2. Whup yer eggs good in a large bowl. Add yer brown sugar, Karo, salt, melted butter, and 'nilla X-track, and mix 'em up. It don't take much to confuse 'em, so don't go crazy.

3. Pour them chopped pecans inta yer pie shell, and pour yer eggs and such on top. Take them pecan halves and put 'em 'round the edge so's they look purdy.

4. Put the pie in yer oven on the middle rack fer 10 minutes, then bring 'er down to 325° 'til it don't jiggle ('bout 45 minutes to an hour).

5. Take it out and set where the dogs can't get it. Now, here's the hard part: Wait 'til it's cool 'fore you eat on it.

* Side prefers Alabama pecans 'cause his man, Au Burns, is from Alabama. Georgia pecans will work just fine. After all, if they's good enough for Ray Charles . . .

**When Side is in a hurry, which is most of the time when it comes to food, he'll use a store-bought pie crust. When company's comin' for supper, he'll make his own crust from scratch. Do yerself a favor and give it a try.

Makes 8 helpings.

Side Burns
Run C&W

Run C&W is one of bluegrass's most unusual and funniest acts, as they take classic rock and Motown hits and turn them into bluegrass renditions. The quartet is composed of Rug Burns (Russell Smith), Crashen Burns (Bernie Leadon), Side Burns (Jim Photoglo) and Wash Burns (Dan Fogelberg).

SIDE'S BEST DANG PIE CRUST

Fixin's:

9 ounces Martha White Flower (the official
**   Tennessee State Flower)**
3 ounces frozen sweet butter, cut into
**   chunks**
3 ounces Crisco, what's been sittin' in the
**   ice box**
3 ounces ice water

Use yer best scales on them measurements. Side don't play when it comes to food.

Put yer flower, butter and Crisco in a big bowl and mash on 'em with a fork, or a biscuit masher (pastry blender), 'til it looks like cornmeal. (If you got one, a quesinart food professer will do it a whole lot quicker). Mix the ice water in 1 tablespoon at a time and cut it in with a couple of butter knives. When it look like it'll stick together, stop addin' water and gather it up in some Saran, make it into a ball, then mash it down 'til it looks kinda like a Moon Pie. Set it in the icebox for ½ hour. Roll it on a flowered table and put it in a pie plate that measures 9 inches.

Makes 1 crust.

Side Burns
Run C&W

HILTON'S PECAN PIE

½ cup butter
½ cup sugar
¾ cup white corn syrup
¼ cup maple syrup
3 eggs, beaten
1 teaspoon vanilla extract
2 cups chopped pecans
1 unbaked 9-inch pie crust

Preheat oven to 325°. Add the pecans ("pe-cahns," not "pee-cans"—that goes under your bed) to the rest of the ingredients. Fold. Pour into the unbaked pie crust. Bake for 40 to 50 minutes.

Note: A double recipe will fill 3 unbaked pie crusts. It is not necessary to double amount of pecans, but 3 cups will make it awfully tasty.

Makes 8 servings.

Ginger Boatwright

ALABAMA FRONT PORCH PECAN PIE

This is the easiest recipe, and it puts a smile on the face of every person named Larry Lynch I've ever known.

3 eggs
1 cup light corn syrup
1/8 teaspoon salt
1 teaspoon vanilla extract
1 cup sugar
2 tablespoons butter or margarine, melted
1 cup pecan halves
1 unbaked 9-inch pie crust

Preheat oven to 400°. In a bowl, beat the eggs slightly. Add the syrup, salt, vanilla, sugar, and butter. Mix well. Stir in the pecans. (Make sure the nuts get coated with the liquid mixture.) Pour the mixture into the pie shell. Bake for 15 minutes. Reduce heat to 350° and bake 30 to 35 minutes, or till the outer edge of the filling seems set. Cool completely.

Makes 8 servings.

Claire Lynch

STRING WIZARD PUMPKIN PIE

6 egg whites
1 cup sugar
3 teaspoons ground cinnamon
1½ teaspoons ground ginger
2½ teaspoons ground allspice
1 teaspoon ground nutmeg
1 29-ounce can Libby solid pack pumpkin (100% natural)
3 cups skimmed evaporated milk
2 unbaked 8- or 9-inch pie crusts (recipe below)

Preheat oven to 450°. Beat the egg whites. Add the sugar and spices and beat, then add pumpkin and beat while slowly adding milk. Pour into unbaked pie shells. Place on cookie sheets and bake for 15 minutes. Reduce heat to 350°

Claire Lynch has been writing songs and performing bluegrass and acoustic music since the mid–1970s, when she toured with the Front Porch String Band. She released her first gospel album in 1993 on Brentwood Records. In 1995, she signed with Rounder Records and released the Grammy-nominated *Moonlighter*. Claire has also appeared on recordings by Linda Ronstadt, Dolly Parton, Patty Lovelace, Kathy Mattea, Emmylou Harris, and Pam Tillis.

Photograph by Barbara Plempel

and bake 45 minutes more, or until a knife blade inserted near the center of pie comes out clean. Cool on racks. Serve with low-fat non-dairy whipped topping.

Pie Crust:

2 cups sifted all-purpose, enriched flour
5 ounces unsalted, no preservatives/no animal fat margarine (Hollywood brand)
5 to 7 tablespoons ice water

Cut the margarine into the flour until the mixture resembles cornmeal. Add enough ice water to a make a firm dough. Divide the dough in half. Roll each piece of dough on a floured board and place into pie pans sprayed with non-stick spray.
Makes 16 servings.

Gerie Anthony McEuen,
mom of John McEuen

PEERLESS DEEP DISH PEAR PIE

5 cups fresh, sliced pears
1/2 cup sugar
1 cup water
1/2 cup all-purpose flour
1/2 teaspoon baking powder
1/8 teaspoon salt
1/2 cup sugar
1 teaspoon ground cinnamon
1/2 teaspoon ground nutmeg
1/2 teaspoon ground allspice
1 stick margarine, melted
1/2 cup milk
1/2 cup raisins

Combine the pears, ½ cup of sugar, and water in a saucepan and cook over low heat until the pears are tender and the liquid is cooked down. Preheat oven to 350°. Mix together all the dry ingredients and add the melted margarine. Gradually stir in the milk, then the raisins. Spread the cooked pears into a foil-lined, 10-inch pie plate and pour the batter over the pears. Bake for 25 minutes.
Note: If canned pears are used, purchase two

15-ounce cans, omit the first amount of sugar, and use the syrup in the can instead of water.
Makes 8 servings.

Cindy and Jim Vipperman

HIGH ON A MOUNTAIN COCONUT CUSTARD PIE (NO CRUST)

4 eggs
¾ cup sugar
½ cup self-rising flour or Bisquick
2 cups milk
¼ cup butter, softened
1½ cups flaked coconut
1 teaspoon vanilla extract

Mix all of the above ingredients in a blender. Pour into a buttered or greased 9-inch pie pan and bake at 350° for 45 minutes.
Makes 8 servings.

Jean and Del McCoury

DOUG'S MAKES-ITS-OWN-CRUST COCONUT PIE

It'll duel with Del's.

4 eggs
1¾ cups sugar
½ cup self-rising flour
¼ cup melted margarine
2 cups milk
1½ cups flaked coconut
1 teaspoon vanilla extract

Combine the ingredients in order and mix well. Pour the mixture into a greased 10-inch pie pan or 2 small pans. Bake in a 350° oven for 45 minutes, or until golden brown. The middle will appear rather soft. The pie should have a delicate crust on the top, sides, and bottom. Cool before serving.
Makes 8 servings.

Douglas Dillard

The Del McCoury Band: (l-r) Ronnie McCoury, Mike Bub, Del McCoury, Jason Carter, and Rob McCoury.

The Del McCoury Band

Del McCoury is at the forefront of the traditional bluegrass resurgence of the 1990s. Del began his career as a banjo player in the Washington, D.C., area in 1956. In 1963, he was recruited by Bill Monroe, and it was as a Blue Grass Boy that Del first received national recognition for his superb lead singing and rhythm guitar playing. He formed his own group, Del McCoury and the Dixie Pals, in 1967.

Del's son Ronnie joined the band on mandolin in 1981, and Del's younger son Rob stepped into the banjo picker's slot in 1987. Together, they brought a youthful look, fresh excitement, and a new name to the Del McCoury Band. Word of this fantastic father-and-sons combination spread quickly, and soon the band became the hottest traditional bluegrass draw around.

The McCoury sound centers on Del's distinctive and powerfully expressive voice. He says, "The blues have a lot in them for a singer. I like to sing the kind of songs that have real deep feelings." Del is a fine songwriter as well, and many of his trademark songs—including "Rain and Snow," "I Feel the Blues Moving In," and "Evil Hearted Woman"—are self-penned. Ronnie McCoury supplies strong lead vocals on the skin-tight duets and trios, along with dazzling, Monroe-inspired mandolin solos. Ronnie was named the IBMA's Mandolin Player of the Year in 1995, but immediately presented his award to his mentor, Bill Monroe, who was watching from the audience. Rob McCoury is a talented musician in his own right. With his impeccable taste and timing, Rob is one of the most dynamic new interpreters of Scruggs-style banjo picking. Rounding out the Del McCoury Band are bass player Mike Bub, who also contributes smooth baritone harmony, and fiddler Jason Carter, one of the most exciting young bluegrass instrumentalists around.

In addition to making great music together, the Del McCoury Band has fun in the process. Their unabashed enthusiasm on stage is contagious and the smiles genuine, likely winning them as many fans as their electrifying music. As *Tower PULSE* magazine said, "When you're doing it right, you can put the blues in bluegrass and still feel good."

The awards keep on coming for this talented group of musicians. Del McCoury was named Top Male Vocalist for three consecutive years (1990–92) by the IBMA, and in 1994, the Del McCoury Band received IBMA awards for Entertainer of the Year and Album of the Year (for the album *A Deeper Shade of Blue*). In 1996, the IBMA again awarded Del both Male Vocalist and Entertainer of the Year honors, and Ronnie repeated as Mandolin Player of the Year.

MARGE'S CUSTARD PIE

This is my favorite dessert and is made best by my wife, Marge.

²/3 cup white sugar
¹/4 teaspoon salt
1¹/2 teaspoons cornstarch
3 eggs, slightly beaten
1 tall can evaporated milk (1²/3 cups)
1 cup boiling water
¹/4 to ¹/2 teaspoon vanilla extract
¹/4 teaspoon ground nutmeg
1 unbaked pie crust

Preheat oven to 400°. Mix the sugar, salt, and cornstarch thoroughly. Stir in the eggs, then the evaporated milk. Gradually stir in the boiling water. Blend in the vanilla and nutmeg. Pour into an unbaked 9- or 10-inch pie crust. Bake for 25 to 30 minutes, or until an inserted knife comes out clean.

Makes 8 servings.

Mac Wiseman

Mac Wiseman picks with Bill Monroe during the finale of a 1974 bluegrass concert at the Grand Ole Opry House.

Mac Wiseman

Mac Wiseman came out of Virginia's Shenandoah Valley to become one of bluegrass music's smoothest tenors. A radio deejay and newscaster before he began performing in the mid-1940s, Wiseman and his songs were "discovered" by Molly O'Day. Wiseman served for a brief time as a member of the fledgling Foggy Mountain Boys with Lester Flatt and Earl Scruggs, and then joined Bill Monroe's Blue Grass Boys in 1949. As a Blue Grass Boy, he recorded such classics as "Traveling This Lonesome Road" and "Can't You Hear Me Calling" with Monroe.

He went on to sing on radio shows across the South—from Nashville to Knoxville and from Atlanta to Shreveport—but it wasn't until 1951 that he cut his first disc on Dot Records with his own band, the Country Boys. He had a number of hits, including "Jimmy Brown, the Newsboy." This song was at the top of the charts for weeks and earned him the nickname "The Voice With a Heart."

Wiseman was one of the founding fathers of the Country Music Association and entered the IBMA Hall of Honor in 1993. He is one of the most respected men in the bluegrass field and continues to make pleasing records today.

BUSY BEE
COCONUT CUSTARD PIE

1 cup sugar
2 tablespoons all-purpose flour
2 eggs
½ stick margarine, melted
1 cup milk
1 teaspoon vanilla extract
1 6-ounce package frozen coconut, thawed
1 unbaked 9-inch pie crust

Preheat oven to 350°. Mix all the ingredients together and blend well. Pour into the unbaked pie crust and bake for 45 minutes, or until the custard is firm. This is one of Marty's favorite pies.

Makes 8 servings.

Hilda Stuart,
mom of Marty Stuart

Hillbilly rocker Marty Stuart swaps licks with his mother, Hilda Stuart.

FLAT-PICKIN' FLAN

¼ cup sugar
6 or 7 eggs
1½ cups sugar
½ teaspoon vanilla extract
2 teaspoons lemon rind (optional)
2 12-ounce cans evaporated milk

Caramelize the bottom and sides of a double boiler pan by putting the ¼ cup sugar into the pan over low heat; stir constantly until melted and straw-colored. Remove from heat. In a bowl, whisk the eggs, slowly adding the 1½ cups of sugar, vanilla, the lemon rind (optional—I personally prefer it without), and the milk. Pour into the sugar-coated double boiler pan, place over simmering water, and cover. Cook until set, about 2 hours. Periodically wipe the inside of the lid to keep it dry of condensation. Flan is done when a thin knife comes out clean when inserted. Allow to cool somewhat, then carefully remove the flan from the double boiler pan by covering with a plate, then inverting. Chill well.

Makes 6 servings.

Russ Barenberg

Pennsylvania native Russ Barenberg began performing his multidimensional brand of bluegrass in the early '70s as a member of Country Cooking with Tony Trischka and Pete Wernick. More recently, he has displayed his amazing guitar picking in trio performances with Edgar Meyer and Jerry Douglas.

FAMILY FAVORITE LEMON MERINGUE PIE

1 1/2 cups sugar
3 tablespoons cornstarch
3 tablespoons all-purpose flour
Dash salt
1 1/2 cups hot water
3 egg yolks, slightly beaten
2 tablespoons butter
1/2 teaspoon lemon peel, grated
1/3 cup fresh lemon juice
1 9-inch baked pastry shell, cooled

In a saucepan, mix the sugar, cornstarch, flour, and salt. Gradually add hot water, stirring constantly. Cook and stir over high heat until mixture comes to a boil. Reduce heat; cook and stir 5 minutes longer. Remove from heat.

Stir a small amount of the hot mixture into the egg yolks, and then slowly stir the eggs yolks into the hot mixture. Bring to a boil again and cook 4 minutes, stirring constantly. Add the butter and lemon peel. Slowly add the lemon juice, mixing well. Pour into the pastry shell. Spread meringue (see below) over filling, sealing to the edge of the pie crust. Bake at 350° for 12 to 15 minutes. Cool before cutting.

Meringue:

3 egg whites
1/2 teaspoon vanilla extract
1/4 teaspoon cream of tartar
6 tablespoons sugar

Beat the egg whites with the vanilla and cream of tartar until soft peaks form. Gradually add the sugar, beating until stiff and glossy peaks form and all the sugar is dissolved. Spread the meringue over the filling and bake as directed above.
Makes 8 servings.

Sue and George Shuffler

OREO AND SMILEY'S DESSERT

1 package Oreo cookies, crushed
1/2 stick margarine, melted
8 ounces cream cheese
1 cup powdered sugar

2 6-ounce packages instant vanilla pudding
3 1/2 cups milk
8 ounces non-dairy whipped topping

Mix the crushed Oreos and margarine in a 9- by 13-inch pan, reserving some Oreos to garnish the top of the dessert. Mix the cream cheese and powdered sugar well and spread over the Oreo crust. Mix the pudding, milk, and non-dairy whipped topping and pour over the cream cheese mixture. Sprinkle with the remaining Oreo crumbs and refrigerate.
Makes 12 servings.

Jeff and Sheri Easter

CREAM CHEESE CROW'S FEAT

It's something to crow about.

8 ounces cream cheese, softened to room temperature
1 14-ounce can sweetened condensed milk
1/3 cup lemon juice
2 cups graham cracker crumbs
1/4 cup sugar
1 stick butter or margarine, melted

Blend the cream cheese, milk, and lemon juice with fork or mixer. Blend the graham cracker crumbs, sugar, and melted butter for the crust. Press the crust into a 9- by 13-inch baking dish and bake at 350° for about 10 minutes, or until the sugar granules have melted. Cool. Place the cream cheese mixture in the dish and refrigerate for a few hours. Serve.
Makes 12 servings.

Wendy and David Crow

MADE IN THE SHADE PIE

8 ounces cream cheese, softened
1 16-ounce carton non-dairy whipped topping
Oreo cookies to taste, crushed
1 9-inch graham cracker crust

Mix the cream cheese with a hand mixer in a large mixing bowl. Mix until soft and creamy. Slowly blend in the whipped topping. Gradually mix in crumbled Oreo cookies by blending the first 2 handfuls of cookies, then folding in the rest with a spatula. Pour the mixture into the graham cracker crust. Top with whole or crushed Oreo cookies. Cover and chill for 2 hours.

Makes 8 servings.

Charlie Sizemore

Cookies and Other Desserts

TENNESSEE SUNSHINE BUTTERSCOTCH SLICES

¾ cup shortening
I teaspoon vanilla extract
I cup brown sugar, firmly packed
I egg
½ cup nuts, finely chopped (optional)
2 cups sifted all-purpose flour
½ teaspoon baking soda
½ teaspoon cream of tartar
½ teaspoon salt

Place the shortening, vanilla, brown sugar, and egg in a mixing bowl; beat until thoroughly blended. Add the nuts and mix. Sift together the flour, baking soda, cream of tartar, and salt. Divide the flour mixture into 2 portions. Add 1 portion to the first mixture and mix well, then add the remaining portion. Beat dough thoroughly. Knead the dough until smooth. Pack very firmly and shape into bars. Wrap in waxed paper. Chill in fresh-food compartment of refrigerator until firm. Cut the dough into ¹/₈-inch slices; place on greased baking sheets and bake at 400° for 6 to 8 minutes.

Makes 3 to 4 dozen.

Gloria Belle (Flickinger)

Gloria Belle Flickinger and Tennessee Sunshine (Stan Brown on banjo, G. R. Davis on bass, and Mike Long, Gloria's husband, on guitar) recorded *A Tribute to Molly O'Day* in late 1996. The album features Speedy Krise, O'Day's own resonator guitar player. Flickinger, a Pennsylvania native, began performing in 1960 on the *Cas Walker Show* in Knoxville. She plays mandolin, banjo, guitar, bass, and autoharp; over the past thirty-five years, she has harmonized with Danny Bailey, Raymond Fairchild, Jimmy Martin, and Charlie Monroe.

COUNTY LINE CORNFLAKE COOKIES

½ cup white corn syrup
½ cup sugar
¾ cup crunchy peanut butter
2 cups cornflakes

Mix the syrup and sugar in a large saucepan. Bring to a boil, then remove from heat. Add the peanut butter and mix. Add the cornflakes and mix. With a tablespoon, drop on a buttered cookie sheet. Allow to cool.

Makes about 2 dozen.

Sophie (Mrs. Carl) Tipton
and Louise Tomberlain

LETTER TO HOME OATMEAL AND PEANUT BUTTER COOKIES

2 cups sugar
4 tablespoons cocoa
½ cup milk
¼ pound margarine or butter
½ cup peanut butter
2½ cups oatmeal
I teaspoon vanilla extract

Combine the sugar, cocoa, milk, and margarine. Cook in a saucepan over medium heat for 1½ minutes after it starts to boil. Remove from the stove and add the peanut butter (crunchy, if nut pieces are desired). Stir until mixed. Pour in the oatmeal and beat well. Add the vanilla. Mix

until blended. Drop spoonfuls on waxed paper and cool.

Makes 2 to 3 dozen cookies.

Ray Deaton
IIIrd Tyme Out

BLUEGRASS INN CARAMEL BROWNIES

1 package caramel candy
$^1/_2$ cup evaporated milk
$^3/_4$ cup butter, melted
1 box German chocolate cake mix
1 cup chopped nuts
$^1/_3$ cup evaporated milk
6 ounces chocolate chips

Preheat oven to 350°. Melt caramel with ½ cup of evaporated milk in a double boiler, then set aside. Mix the butter, cake mix, nuts, and cup of evaporated milk. Spread ½ the batter in a greased 9- by 13-inch pan. Bake for 9 minutes at 350°. Sprinkle chocolate chips over the cake, pour the caramel mixture over the chips, and spread the rest of cake batter on top. Bake for 20 minutes more.

Makes 12 servings.

Hubert Davis

BACK HOME PEANUT BUTTER COOKIES

1 cup peanut butter
1 cup sugar
1 egg
½ teaspoon vanilla extract

Mix the peanut butter and sugar. Stir in the remaining ingredients. Shape into 1-inch balls and put on an ungreased cookie sheet. Press with a fork to flatten slightly. Bake in a 350° oven for 12 to 15 minutes.

Makes about 2 dozen.

Charlie Sizemore

ODE TO A MOON PIE
by Side Burns

Round
No beginning
No end

A layer of chocolate
A layer of cookie
A layer of marshmallow
A layer of cookie
A layer of chocolate

Side by side
Harmony
The Burns Brothers
Maybe . . . the world

TWO HIGHWAYS ICEBOX OATMEAL COOKIES

1 cup brown sugar
1 cup white sugar
1 cup butter

Kentucky bluegrass man Charlie Sizemore started his career at age sixteen. For nearly ten years, he sang and played with Ralph Stanley and his Clinch Mountain Boys, recording fifteen albums with the band. Since 1986, this singer and songwriter has had his own group. His 1993 album, *Back Home*, was nominated as Album of the Year by the Society for the Preservation of Bluegrass Music.

1 teaspoon salt
2 eggs, beaten
3 cups oatmeal (not instant)
1 teaspoon vanilla extract
1½ cups all-purpose flour
1 teaspoon baking soda
1 cup chopped nuts

Combine the ingredients in the order given. Form into a roll and wrap in waxed paper. Refrigerate until chilled. Slice ⅛-inch-thick pieces and place on cookie sheets. Bake at 350° until a hint of brown comes on them.

Makes about 3 to 4 dozen.

Barry Bales
Alison Krauss
and Union Station

Barry Bales has played bass with Alison Krauss and Union Station since the beginning. He grew up in Kingsport, Tennessee, began playing bluegrass at age ten, discovered the bass at sixteen, and attended East Tennessee State University. While there, he played with Tim Stafford and Adam Steffey in the band Dusty Miller. In 1990, the three joined Alison's new band, Union Station.

QUICK PICKIN' OATMEAL CHOCOLATE COOKIES

2 cups sugar
½ cup cocoa
½ cup milk
1 stick butter
2½ to 3 cups quick-cooking oats
1 teaspoon vanilla extract

Combine the sugar, cocoa, milk, and butter in a saucepan. Bring to a boil, stirring constantly for 2 to 3 minutes. Pour the mixture over the oats and add vanilla. Drop by the spoonful onto waxed paper. Allow to cool.

Makes about 2 to 3 dozen.

Ruby Ann Gillis for
The Gillis Brothers

TENNESSEE TURTLE BROWNIES

They're slow good.

Caramel ice cream topping
12 to 16 ounces chopped pecans
1 package special dark chocolate brownie mix

Use the pan size recommended on the brownie mix. Preheat oven according to package directions. Begin by drizzling the caramel topping into the greased pan. Remember: a little goes a long way. Let the pan sit for a couple of minutes to spread the caramel evenly. Sprinkle the pecans over the caramel in a thick layer. Prepare the brownie mix according to "cake-like" instructions. Pour the batter evenly over the pecans and bake, adding 6 to 8 minutes to the recommended baking time. Important: Cool, then chill the brownies for 30 minutes, cut them into squares, and invert them onto a platter in a single layer. Warm the brownies and serve with ice cream. This is a fantasy dessert, not a low-cal or low-cholesterol dessert.

Makes about 16.

Glenn Laney
Knoxville Grass

Glenn Laney led the Knoxville Grass to popularity in the late '70s and early '80s. They had a regular gig and loyal following at Buddy's Bar-B-Q in their namesake city. Pictured are (l-r) Ron Seay, Glenn Laney, Blake Reed, Gregg Hodge, and Gary Baker.

KENTUCKY DATE NUT BARS

¼ cup melted butter
1 cup sugar
3 eggs, well beaten
1 cup all-purpose flour
½ teaspoon baking powder
Dash salt
1 cup dates, pitted and chopped
1 cup pecans, chopped
Confectioners' sugar

Preheat oven to 350°. Mix the ingredients (except confectioners' sugar) in the order given and pour into 11- by 13-inch baking dish that has been well-lined with waxed paper. (The batter will be very thick.) Bake for 20 minutes at 350°, or until delicately brown. Cut into finger-shaped pieces and roll in confectioners' sugar while still warm.

Makes about 4 dozen.

Vicki Simmons
The New Coon Creek Girls

BIG DUTCH BABIES

⅓ stick butter
4 eggs
1 cup milk
1 cup all-purpose flour
Ground nutmeg

Preheat oven to 425°. Put the butter in a 3- to 4-quart baking pan and place in oven. Mix the batter while the butter melts. Put the eggs in a blender and whip at high speed for 1 minute. Continue blending and add the milk gradually, then slowly add the flour. Continue whipping for 30 seconds. (With a rotary beater, whip the eggs until light and lemon colored. Gradually beat in the milk, then the flour.) Pour the batter into the hot butter. Bake 20 to 25 minutes. Dust lightly with nutmeg and serve with lemon sauce (see below) or other toppings.

You may also add lemon wedges and powdered sugar, syrups, fresh fruit, hot fruit, canned pie fillings, etc. This also can be served with a meat topping.

Lemon Sauce:

½ cup sugar
1 tablespoon cornstarch
Pinch salt
1 cup water
2 tablespoons lemon juice
Ground nutmeg or cinnamon
2 tablespoons butter

In a saucepan, mix the sugar, cornstarch, salt, and water. Dissolve the cornstarch in the water before bringing to a boil. Boil until thick, then remove from heat and blend in the remaining ingredients.

Makes about 10 servings.

Ginger Boatwright

Making a 1996 appearance at the White House (during a trip to perform at the Smithsonian Institute), the New Coon Creek Girls seem right at home. Pictured are (l-r) Kathy Kuhn, Dale Ann Bradley, Ramona Church Taylor, and Vicki Simmons.

In the 1980s, Ginger Boatwright became rhythm guitar player, lead vocalist, and raconteur for the Doug Dillard Band, with whom she still performs when geography permits (she now lives in Alaska). Ginger is as noted for her songwriting (including such moving tunes as "If I Could Only Have Your Love," "Somebody's Missing You," and "High Ground") as she is for her performing. Ginger's soulful 1991 solo album, *Fertile Ground*, is one of the the best testimonies to why many have called her the "First Lady of Bluegrass." You can't miss when you're cooking with Ginger!

GRANNY'S SURRY COUNTY SUGAR COOKIES

½ cup shortening
¾ cup sugar
I egg
I teaspoon vanilla extract
2 teaspoons milk
1¾ cups self-rising flour

Combine all the ingredients in the order given. Roll the dough very thin and cut out cookies. Place on a baking sheet and bake at 350° for 8 to 10 minutes.
Makes 2 to 3 dozen.

Barry Berrier
The Lost and Found

AUNT NINA'S SUGAR COOKIES

¾ cup shortening
I cup sugar
¼ cup molasses
I egg
I teaspoon baking soda
2 cups all-purpose flour, sifted
½ teaspoon ground cloves
½ teaspoon ground ginger
I teaspoon ground cinnamon
½ teaspoon salt
Sugar

In a large saucepan, melt the shortening over low heat. Remove and let cool. Add the sugar, molasses, and egg to shortening; beat well. Sift together the flour, cloves, ginger, cinnamon, and salt; add to the first mixture. Mix well. Wrap the dough in waxed paper and chill thoroughly (at least 2 hours). Form into 1-inch balls and roll in sugar. Place 2 inches apart on greased cookie sheets. Bake at 370° for 8 to 10 minutes.
Makes about 3 dozen.

Chuck Duffin
WhiteHouse Harmony

Bluegrass music is a family affair for Texas-based WhiteHouse Harmony. Three generations of the White family delight audiences throughout the Southwest, the Ozarks, and beyond.

SKYLINE SWEDISH SHORTBREAD

My mother used to make these cookies when I was young. As simple as they are to make, they were always a big treat. I made them myself today for the first time to make sure they would hold culinary sway over those who devour them. Indeed, they stand the test of time.

2 cups all-purpose flour
²/₃ cup sugar
¹/₂ teaspoon double-acting baking powder
³/₄ cup soft margarine or butter
1 unbeaten egg
2 teaspoons vanilla extract
¹/₃ cup any red-colored jelly or jam

Sift together the flour, sugar, and baking powder into a mixing bowl. Blend in the margarine, egg, and vanilla to form dough. Place on a lightly floured pastry cloth or board. Divide into 4 parts and shape each into a 13-inch-long, ³/₄-inch-thick roll. Place the rolls on ungreased baking sheets—4 inches apart and 2 inches from the edge of the sheet. With a knife handle, make a ¹/₄- to ¹/₃-inch-deep depression running lengthwise down the center of each roll. Fill the depressions with jelly. Bake at 350° for 15 to 20 minutes until light golden brown. While warm, cut diagonally into bars. Cool on a wire rack.
Makes about 3 dozen.

Tony Trischka

OLD DUTCH SUGAR CAKES

Del-icious!

1¾ cups sugar
¼ to ½ cup shortening
¼ cup butter
3 eggs
1 teaspoon vanilla extract
3 cups all-purpose flour
1 teaspoon baking soda
1 cup buttermilk
Sugar for topping

Blend together the sugar, shortening, butter, eggs, and vanilla. Add the flour, baking soda, and buttermilk, mixing thoroughly. Pour into 2 baking dishes (8-inch size) that have been greased and floured. Bake at 350° for 25 minutes and then sprinkle with sugar. Cool and cut into squares.
Makes 2½ dozen.

Jean and Del McCoury

Few musicians have explored the world of the banjo as deeply as Tony Trischka. He was one of the first to play jazz on the five-string and gave Bela Fleck his first banjo lessons. All of Tony's exploration has prepared him to serve up some astounding licks with bands such as Country Cooking, Breakfast Special, Psychograss, the Big Dogs, and Skyline. And though some might say that Tony puts himself out on a limb with his adventuresome music, you can't be more traditional than following the roots of the banjo to where the instrument was born, West Africa. And Tony has done that, too. Pictured here is Psychograss: (l-r) David Grier, Todd Phillips, Darol Anger, Tony Trischka, and Mike Marshall.

Fiddle player Jim Armstrong (below) serves as lead vocalist and master of ceremonies for Virginia-based New Dominion Bluegrass pictured above. The group was formed in 1986 and records for Hay Holler Records. Other members include James Shelton on banjo, Will Snow on mandolin, Greg Elms on guitar, and Fred Staggs on bass.

KENTUCKY COLONEL BOURBON BALLS

I learned this recipe from my wife's aunt, Gladys Martin.

1 stick real butter
1 16-ounce box confectioners' sugar
4 tablespoons good Kentucky bourbon
¾ cup finely chopped pecans
1 8-ounce box baker's chocolate
1 teaspoon paraffin
30 pecan halves

Cream the butter and blend with the sugar. When smooth, add the bourbon and finely chopped pecans. Shape into balls, each about 1 inch in diameter. Place balls on waxed paper and cool in the refrigerator for 30 minutes or longer. Melt the chocolate and paraffin together. Use a toothpick to dip the cooled balls into the chocolate mixture, then place back on the waxed paper. While the chocolate is still hot, place one pecan half on the top of each ball, using the pecan to cover the toothpick hole. Place completed bourbon balls back in the refrigerator to cool. These make a great Christmas or Kentucky Derby Day gift.

Makes 30.

Jim Armstrong
New Dominion Bluegrass

THREE PEARS
WITH CHOCOLATE

A winner!

3 ripe pears
Semi-sweet chocolate chips

Halve and core the pears. Top with chocolate chips and microwave for 2 to 3 minutes on HIGH. If the pear is still too firm, heat just a little longer. Serve immediately.
Makes 3 to 6 servings.

Ginger Boatwright

COON CREEK
CARAMELIZED BANANAS
WITH RUM SAUCE

3 tablespoons unsalted sweet butter
½ cup plus 2 tablespoons packed light
**   brown sugar**
2 bananas (not too ripe), peeled and cut
**   into 1-inch pieces**
½ cup light rum

Melt the butter in a skillet over medium heat. Then add the brown sugar and stir until the mixture is thick and creamy. Add the bananas and sauté until they just turn brown, about 3 minutes. Remove from heat and pour the rum into the skillet. Ignite with a match and let the flames die out. Now it's ready to pour over ice cream, Bundt cake, or angel food cake.
Makes 3 to 4 servings.

Pam Perry
The New Coon Creek Girls

MY OLD HOME PLACE
MICROWAVE FUDGE

1 pound powdered sugar
½ cup cocoa
¼ cup milk
¼ pound butter or margarine
1 tablespoon vanilla extract
½ cup chopped nuts

Blend the powdered sugar and cocoa in a mixing bowl. Add the milk and butter. (Note: Do not mix these ingredients; merely place in the bowl.) Cook in microwave on HIGH power for 2 minutes. Remove the bowl from oven and stir just to mix ingredients. Add the vanilla and nuts, then stir until blended. Pour into a greased 8-inch square dish and put in the freezer for 20 minutes, or refrigerate for 1 hour. Cut and serve.
This fudge may be made in a conventional oven. Follow directions for microwave cooking. Preheat oven to 400° and bake for 5 minutes.
Makes about 2 dozen, if you fudge a little.

Ginger Boatwright

MARSHMALLOW
CHOCOLATE PHILLY FUDGE

2 cups sifted confectioners' sugar
1 3-ounce package cream cheese, softened
2 1-ounce squares unsweetened chocolate,
**   melted**
¼ teaspoon vanilla extract
Dash salt
1 cup miniature marshmallows
⅓ cup chopped nuts

Gradually add the sugar to the cream cheese, mixing until well blended. Stir in the chocolate, vanilla, and salt. Fold in the marshmallows and nuts. Press into a well-greased shallow pan. Chill. Cut into squares and serve.
Makes about 16 squares.

Molly O'Day

DOBRO DREAMLAND
PEANUT BUTTER FUDGE

This is Brother Oswald's favorite candy.

2 cups sugar
¾ cup milk
4 tablespoons peanut butter
1 teaspoon vanilla extract
¼ stick butter

Cook the sugar and milk until it forms a soft

ball when a small amount is dropped in cold water. Add the peanut butter, vanilla, and butter. Beat with a wire whisk. Pour the mixture onto a buttered plate or platter. Cut into squares when cool.

Makes about 12 squares.

Pete (Bashful Brother Oswald)
and Euneta Kirby

AUNT TINKIE'S BREAD PUDDING

4 cups milk, scalded
¾ cup sugar
I tablespoon butter
¼ teaspoon salt
4 eggs, slightly beaten
I teaspoon vanilla extract
6 slices bread, cubed, or 2 cups bread crumbs

Mix the first 6 ingredients and pour over the bread in a greased 2- or 3-quart casserole dish. Bake at 350° until firm and golden brown. Raisins or craisins may be added.

Makes about 6 to 8 servings.

Ginger Boatwright

GRANDMOTHER SNIDER'S PERSIMMON PUDDING

I quart all-purpose flour
I teaspoon soda
I teaspoon salt
I quart milk
2 cups persimmon pulp
2 eggs, beaten
2 cups sugar

Mix the flour, soda, and salt. Mix the flour mixture with all of the milk. Add the remaining ingredients and stir well. Pour into a greased 9- by 13-inch baking dish. Bake at 350° for approximately 1 hour, stirring every 20 minutes until creamy yet stiff. (This is not a bread-like pudding recipe.)

Makes about 10 to 12 servings.

Jan Harvey, David Harvey,
and Jill Snider
Wild and Blue

CHEERY CHERRY YUM-YUM

3 cups vanilla wafer crumbs
I stick margarine, melted
8 ounces cream cheese, softened
¾ cup sugar
I 16-ounce carton non-dairy whipped topping
I 21-ounce can cherry pie filling

Mix the crumbs and margarine and cover the bottom of a 9- by 13-inch pan with ½ the mixture. Blend the cream cheese and sugar. Add the cream cheese mixture to the whipped topping and beat until it stands in peaks. Spread ½ the whipped topping mixture on the crumbs, then spread cherry filling over top. Add the remainder of the whipped topping mix and cover with the remainder of the crumbs. Chill until serving time.

Serves 10 to 12.

Glenn Tolbert

BARREN COUNTY NO COOK BANANA PUDDING

I 6-ounce box or 2 3.4-ounce boxes instant vanilla pudding
2½ cups milk
8 ounces sour cream
8 ounces non-dairy whipped topping
5 to 6 bananas, sliced
I box vanilla wafers

Mix the instant pudding with the milk and prepare according to the directions on the box. Add the sour cream and whipped topping and beat until smooth. In a large glass bowl (4 inches deep and 9 inches wide) layer the pudding, bananas, and vanilla wafers, ending with a layer of pudding. Refrigerate overnight.

Makes 10 to 12 servings.

Curtis Burch

DARLIN' PAL OF MINE RICE PUDDING

⅓ cup uncooked rice
⅓ cup sugar

1 quart milk
1 teaspoon vanilla extract
1 tablespoon margarine or butter
Pinch of salt
1 teaspoon ground cinnamon
A few raisins (optional)

Combine the ingredients in a greased casserole dish and bake at 375°. Stir frequently, or when pudding starts to get slightly brown on top. Continue to stir occasionally until the pudding thickens to your desired tastes.

Makes about 6 servings.

Gloria Belle (Flickinger)

PINK STUFF

1 6-ounce package cherry or strawberry
   gelatin
1 12-ounce carton non-dairy whipped
   topping
1 15¼-ounce can crushed pineapple,
   drained
1 pint container cottage cheese, drained

Mix all the ingredients together, starting with the gelatin and non-dairy whipped topping. Pour the gelatin right from the box to the bowl. Add the pineapple and cottage cheese. Refrigerate and serve cold.

Makes 8 servings.

Haylie Simon, nine years old
WhiteHouse Harmony

DON'T STOP THE
GUILTLESS DESSERT

1 6-ounce box sugar-free gelatin (any flavor)
8 ounces fat-free cream cheese, softened
1 8-ounce can crushed pineapple

Prepare gelatin according to the instructions on package. While the gelatin is still hot, mix with beaten cream cheese. Stir in the pineapple and chill until firm—in a mold, if desired.

Makes 8 servings.

Jean and Del McCoury

BLACKBIRDS AND CROWS
FRESH FRUIT COMPOTE

1 banana
Several large ripe strawberries
A handful of red or white seedless grapes,
   halved
½ cup chopped fresh walnuts, or ¼ cup
   sunflower seeds
1 ripe pear or apple
¼ cup raisins
1 tablespoon orange blossom honey
Juice of ¼ to ½ lemon or lime (must be
   fresh)

Cut the fruit into bite-sized pieces. In a large serving bowl, add the fruits and nuts to the honey and juice. Mix gently and serve immediately. Eat the compote right away.

Makes 2 or 3 servings.

Roland White
The Nashville Bluegrass Band

Roland White (*center*) poses with fellow Nashville Bluegrass Band members (*from left*) Gene Libbea, Pat Enright, Alan O'Bryant, and Stuart Duncan.

Shown here in 1961's "Mayberry on Record" episode of The Andy Griffith Show are Kentucky Colonels members (l-r, after Andy Griffith) Roland White, Eric White, Clarence White, Billy Ray Lathum, and LeRoy McNees.

The Kentucky Colonels

They started out as California brothers by way of Maine. Roland, Eric, and Clarence White were the nucleus of a bluegrass group that began performing in 1956 as the Country Boys. They developed a strong following in southern California, and the group itself began to grow. Banjo player Billy Ray Lathum joined in 1957, and resonator guitarist LeRoy McNees became part of the group in 1958.

It was this configuration of the group that fans still see in reruns of two episodes of *The Andy Griffith Show*—particularly one titled "Mayberry on Record" where the band is featured playing several songs when a record producer comes to Mayberry looking for local talent. By the time of their *Andy Griffith Show* appearances, the band was performing as the Kentucky Colonels. Scott Stoneman was added on fiddle and Roger Bush eventually took over for Eric White on bass.

The young group quickly built a national reputation for its outstanding bluegrass music. When the Kentucky Colonels broke up, they were regarded as one of the most influential bluegrass bands of the '60s. Even after the group's demise, the seeds of this influence continued to grow through their inspiration to fellow musicians.

Of the places on the planet touched by bluegrass music, you'll find few not traveled by members of the Kentucky Colonels. Clarence White went on to become a key member of the Byrds before his death in an auto accident in 1973. He is still cited as a dominant influence by top musicians in bluegrass and other fields of music. Roland White has continued to be a major force in bluegrass music. He has served stints with Bill Monroe's Blue Grass Boys, Lester Flatt's Nashville Grass, Country Gazette, the New Kentucky Colonels, and the Nashville Bluegrass Band. Billy Ray Lathum has played with the Dillards and other groups. Most recently he performed with the Laurel Canyon Ramblers. LeRoy Mack has expanded his mastery of the resonator guitar with the BornAgain Bluegrass Band and a variety of successful solo projects. Roger Bush went on to be an original member of Country Gazette (along with Alan Munde, Byron Berline, and Kenny Wertz).

FULL SAIL CHOCOLATE MINT CHIP ICE CREAM

1½ cups sugar
3 pints milk
2 quarts whipping cream
2 14-ounce cans sweetened condensed milk
Green food coloring
Peppermint extract to taste
1 6-ounce bag of Nestle chocolate morsels

Combine all the ingredients in the order listed. Put the mixture in large ice cream freezer and freeze. It never fails.

Makes about 15 servings.

Robin and T. Michael Coleman
Chesapeake

HOME SWEET HOMEMADE ICE CREAM

1 14-ounce can sweetened condensed milk
½ gallon milk
1¾ cups sugar
2 eggs
2 to 3 tablespoons vanilla extract

Mix all the ingredients together very well before pouring into container for freezing.

Makes about 10 servings.

Cindy and Jim Vipperman

T. Michael Coleman got his musical start in high school, playing bass in a dance band every weekend at Moon's Dance Land in Madison, North Carolina. He went on to tour and record with Doc Watson for fifteen years, producing many of Doc's recordings during that time. When Doc reduced his touring schedule in the late 1980s, Michael spent several years in The Seldom Scene, before joining with Mike Auldridge, Moondi Klein, and Jimmy Gaudreau in the acoustic supergroup Chesapeake.

SELECTED REFERENCES

Magazines
Banjo Newsletter
P.O. Box 3418
Annapolis, Maryland 21403

Bluegrass Unlimited
Box 111
Broad Run, Virginia 20137

Bluegrass Now
P.O. Box 2020
Rolla, Missouri 65401

The Old-Time Herald
P.O. Box 51812
Durham, North Carolina 27717

Mail Order Companies
County Sales
P.O. Box 191
Floyd, Virginia 24091

Elderly Instruments
1100 North Washington
Lansing, Michigan 48901

Homespun Video (music instructional tapes)
P.O. Box 325
Woodstock, New York 12498

Roundup Records
P.O. Box 154
North Cambridge, Massachusetts 02140

The Bluegrass Calendar
Copper Creek Publications
P.O. Box 3161
Roanoke, Virginia 24015

Recommended Reading
Bluegrass: A History
by Neil V. Rosenberg
University of Illinois Press, 1985

Bluegrass: An Informal Guide
by Richard D. Smith
Chicago Review Press, 1995

Willard Gayheart of Skeeter and the Skidmarks is not only a talented musician, but his pencil sketches of country life are renowned far and wide. His artwork has been featured at several top festivals, including the Merle Watson Festival. In this work, he has beautifully captured Doc Watson, T. Michael Coleman, and the enduring presence of the late Merle Watson.

Recommended Viewing
High Lonesome: The Story of Bluegrass Music, a documentary film by Rachel Liebling. It is available on video: Shanachie-604 (1994).

Organizations
International Bluegrass Music Association
  (IBMA)
207 East 3rd Street
Owensboro, Kentucky 42303

Society for the Preservation of Bluegrass
  Music in America (SPBGMA)
P.O. Box 271
Kirksville, Missouri 63501

Online
Links to *Cybergrass, BluegrassL,* and countless other bluegrass sites can be found on the World Wide Web by typing:

http://www.banjo.com/BG-Links.html

GENERAL INDEX

Abernathy, Barry, 103
Acuff, Roy, 176, 199, 208, 210
Adams, Tom, 29, 63
Adcock, Eddie, 4, 15, 155, 180
Adcock, Martha, 4, 15, 155
Adkins, Paul, 56
Akeman, David, 24, 65, 75, 169
Akemon, Alfred, 64-65
Aldridge, Mike, 149
Alger, Pat, 32
Allen, Red, 56, 127
Amberson, Warren, 131
American Bluegrass Express, 172
Amos, Bob, 133, 168
Anderson, Eric, 38
Anger, Darol, 224
Andy Griffith Show, 79, 203, 229
Arms, Danny, 49
Armstrong, Jim, 152, 166, 177, 225
Arnold, Jimmy, 76
Arnold, Kristine, 100, 101
Auldridge, Mike, 37, 54, 85, 108, 114, 125, 230

Baez, Joan, 95
Bailes Brothers, 208
Bailes, Homer, 208
Bailes, Johnnie, 208
Bailes, Kyle, 208
Bailes, Walter, 208
Bailey Brothers, 94, 200
Bailey, Charles, 94
Bailey, Danny, 94, 219
Bailey, James, 98
Bailey, Margaret, 40
Bailey, Richard, 40
Baker, Gary, 222
Baker, Kenny, 34
Baldassari, Butch, 18, 147, 171
Bales, Barry, 58, 59, 131, 137, 148, 220-21
Ballinger, Dale, 40
Ballinger, Kris, 40, 199
Barber, Junior, 68
Barber, Mike, 68
Barenberg, Russ, 8, 32, 217
Barnes, Randy, 129
Barren County Revival, 179
Bashful Brother Oswald. *See* Kirby, Pete
Bass Mountain Boys, 107, 148, 149
Bavier, Frances "Aunt Bee," 51
Beagles, 69, 108, 202
Beatles, 49
Belle (Flickinger), Gloria, 62, 70, 77, 117, 207, 219, 227-28
Bennett, Richard, 56, 202
Benson, Wayne, 6
Bent Mountain Boys, 39
Berline, Byron, 61, 75, 76, 159, 229
Berrier, Barry, 65, 66, 107, 133, 185, 191, 192, 200-201, 223

Berry, Chuck, 197
Beverly Hillbillies, The, 71
Bibey, Alan, 129
Big Dogs, 21, 224
Blackwell, Kenny, 23, 147
Blake, Norman, 75, 76
Blatt, Joyce, 39
Blaylock, Audie, 63
Blaylock, Jeff, 189
Block, Ron, 18, 58, 59
Blue Diamond Boys, 76, 130
Blue Grass Boys, 53, 65, 71, 75, 110, 127, 132, 147, 159, 164, 176, 187, 189, 195, 215, 216, 229
Blue Highway, 20, 27, 106, 116, 131, 180, 183, 194
Blue Sky Boys, 69, 208
Bluegrass Album Band, 56, 157
Bluegrass Alliance, 157, 192
Bluegrass and Country Music Program at East Tennessee State University, 131
Bluegrass Cardinals, 19, 126, 130
Bluegrass Cutups, 174
Bluegrass Fan Fest, 11
Bluegrass Inn, 188
Bluegrass Patriots, 21
Bluegrass Special, The, 4, 138
Bluegrass Trust Fund, 11
Bluegrass Unlimited, 10-11
Boatwright, Ginger Hammond, 2-3, 38, 46, 51, 72, 83-84, 90-91, 162, 177, 213, 222, 223, 226, 227
Boatwright, Grant, 46, 121
Bonnie Lou and Buster, 200
Boone Creek, 37, 156
Born Again Bluegrass Band, 20, 24, 41, 51, 83, 124-25, 190, 229
Bornstein, Jim and Wilma, 33
Boulding, John, 57
Bowman, Becky Isaacs, 123
Bowman, John R., 123
Bowman, Ronnie, 126
Bradley, Dale Ann, 64, 65, 184, 222
Bradstreet, Rick, 21
Branham, Johnny, 42
Breakfast Special, 224
Brennan, Joan, 39
Brennan, Joyce, 39
Brennan Twins, 39
Brewer, Gary, 169, 178
Brown, Stan, 219
Bristol, Tennessee/Virginia (Birthplace of Country Music), 69, 202
Britt, Gena, 129, 210-11
Brock, Jimmy, Sr., 121
Brooks, Garth, 59
Brother Boys, 119, 149, 156, 161
Brown, Alison, 63-64
Brown, Hylo, 76, 200
Brown, Jerry, 57
Browning, David, 162
Bryson, Bill, 23, 130
Bub, Mike, 18, 32, 215
Buchanan, Jim, 76

RECIPE INDEX